7/13

SLANG

THE PEOPLE'S POETRY

MICHAEL ADAMS

OXFORD
UNIVERSITY PRESS

Oxford University Press is a department of the University of Oxford.
It furthers the University's objective of excellence in research, scholarship,
and education by publishing worldwide.

Oxford   New York
Auckland   Cape Town   Dar es Salaam   Hong Kong   Karachi
Kuala Lumpur   Madrid   Melbourne   Mexico City   Nairobi
New Delhi   Shanghai   Taipei   Toronto

With offices in
Argentina   Austria   Brazil   Chile   Czech Republic   France   Greece
Guatemala   Hungary   Italy   Japan   Poland   Portugal   Singapore
South Korea   Switzerland   Thailand   Turkey   Ukraine   Vietnam

Oxford is a registered trade mark of Oxford University Press
in the UK and certain other countries.

Published in the United States of America by
Oxford University Press
198 Madison Avenue, New York, NY 10016

© Michael Adams 2009

First issued as an Oxford University Press paperback, 2012.

Library of Congress Cataloging-in-Publication Data
Adams, Michael, 1961–
Slang : the people's poetry / Michael Adams.
     p. cm.
ISBN 978-0-19-531463-2 (hardcover); 978-0-19-991377-0 (paperback)
1. English language—Slang. 2. English language—Jargon.
3. Rhyming slang. 4. Poetry. I. Title.
PE3711.A33 2008
427'.09—dc22   2008028923

9 8 7 6 5 4 3 2 1

Printed in the United States of America
on acid-free paper

CONTENTS

Preface   *vii*

1

"WHAT IT IS?": THE ESSENTIALS OF SLANG   1
Mongo—Slang by Definition—Language of Purpose versus Language
of Being—Lowdown, or Poetry on the Down Low?—What It Is

2

FITTING IN: SOCIAL DYNAMICS OF SLANG   55
Flash Slang Cards—Boyz in the Hood Speak Slang, Soccer Moms
Don't—Youth: An Interlude—Negotiating with Slang—It's a Small
World, After All

3

STANDING OUT: AESTHETIC DIMENSIONS OF SLANG   111
How's It Goin', Protozoan?—Indiddlyfixing Is the Shiznit—
Lexifabricography and the Lexically Meaningful Infix—The Raunch
and the Hip: Two Slang Aesthetics—Slang as a Negative Capability

4

IT'S ALL IN YOUR HEAD: COGNITIVE ASPECTS OF SLANG   163
This Is Your Brain on Slang—Slang and Language Play—"My
Bad" Means Never Having to Say "I'm Sorry"—Slang as Linguistic
Spandrel—Toward a Poetics of Slang

Index   *213*

PREFACE

Reviewing my previous book, *Slayer Slang: A "Buffy the Vampire Slayer" Lexicon* (2003), in the *Journal of English Linguistics* (March 2005), Susan Tamasi wrote, "As a linguist, I have one criticism. . . . I never found an actual definition of the word *slang*, even though other linguistic terms were defined and slang was often compared to other categories, such as 'jargon' and 'standard American English.'" I thought I knew enough about slang to write that book, concerned as it was with those aspects of slang especially well illustrated in *Buffy the Vampire Slayer* and the Buffyverse. After all, even if there's lots of slang in the universe of language, the Buffyverse is a relatively small verse and more easily navigated.

Or so I thought. I soon learned that slang was both more interesting and more complex than I had realized, and that an adequate understanding of it would demand investigation far beyond the boundaries of slayer slang. Is slang merely a swath of English vocabulary, best understood in contrast with other types of words and phrases? Or is it the currency with which we negotiate our social identities? Or is it, quite impressively really, a more or less impromptu verbal art—poetry, one might say, if one were given to speaking slang, *on the fly*? Is slang something we (Homo sapiens, speakers of languages around the world) invented as a result of social interaction, or is it a type of language we can't escape, part of our biological as well as our social heritage?

Of course, if you're desperate for one, every general dictionary of English includes a definition of *slang*, and they are all informative, even if they aren't compatible with one another. After reading Tamasi's review, however, I decided that, more than a simple definition, we needed a thorough inquiry into the very nature and purposes of slang.

Slang is always with us, reinvented by each new generation, so surely, you imagine, such a treatise has already been written. Eric Partridge's *Slang: To-Day and Yesterday* (1933) tried to be that book but fell short, though it was popular for decades. Partridge devoted a whopping thirty-six pages (of 476) to what he called "general considerations," such as a definition of slang, the etymology of the word *slang*, its synonyms (namely, *jargon*, *argot*, and *cant*), and slang's range within the whole vocabulary of English; he also explored the origin of slang, reasons for its use, and attitudes that people hold toward it; in the last few pages of this meager thirty-six, he described slang's chief characteristics and claimed to touch "the essence of slang."

Slang, it turns out, is a big subject. Partridge's account of slang fundamentals is just too brief; *Slang: The People's Poetry*, in contrast, sticks with the big questions from beginning to end. At nearly one hundred pages, Partridge's history of slang remains informative (though it's been superseded in many particulars), but my book is not a history. Nostalgic accounts of the slang of yesteryear are interludes within the book's larger argument; history illustrates the general issues, and the past primarily serves the present. A historian by inclination, I have had to resist the historical tendency here, though I have given in to it on occasion. Ultimately, this book isn't about what slang was but about what makes slang slang.

Partridge, a New Zealander by birth who mingled with speakers from all over the British Commonwealth during World War I, nonetheless focused on English slang; he devoted only fifty pages to American slang, more than he offered on other "colonial" slang, but hardly enough to satisfy a primarily American audience. Though I discuss other English slang, as well as slang in other languages, I focus here on American slang, to which I listen with a native ear. When it comes to general principles, of course, any slang will do; but there's nothing wrong with a wide-ranging (and often amusing) description of contemporary American slang, while we're at it.

Anyway, *Slang To-Day and Yesterday* appeared seventy-five years ago (note that *To-Day* was plausibly a compound then, but it isn't now), so the description of slang in the book you currently hold in your hands is likely to differ significantly from Partridge's, but much else has changed in the interim, too, especially our structural, social, aesthetic, and cognitive understanding of language, and this new knowledge informs my book. Also, and this is no small thing in considering whether to write a general book about slang after Partridge had already done so, Partridge was wrong about nearly everything, from his etymology of the word *slang* (on page 2) to his etymology of *hep/hip* 'in the know', which he suggests might come from military *hep, hep, hep* (on page 442). As I explain, the etymology of *hip* is still uncertain, but even if it didn't develop from Wolof *hepi* 'open one's eyes, be aware' and enter American English from African American speech, it certainly wasn't picked up from the language of military parade. Nothing against drill sergeants, but they struggle to be hip.

So Partridge's wasn't the last word on slang, nor was it the most recent. Fine dictionaries of slang appeared in the late twentieth century and early twenty-first (the *Historical Dictionary of American Slang*, the *New Partridge Dictionary of Slang and Unconventional English*, and *Cassell's Dictionary of Slang*, particularly), each with a more or less informative introduction. But with so many slang words to account for in these books, such an introduction is little more than a sketch. The value of these dictionaries isn't mainly in their introductions, but in the immense range of slang words they have collected and in word-by-word scholarship so careful (especially in the *Historical Dictionary of American Slang*) that it saves a twenty-first-century writer about slang (this writer, in fact) from the sorts of mistakes of which Partridge, alone in the world with more slang than he could handle, was all too often a victim.

Besides the dictionaries, the really penetrating recent works of slang scholarship are an article by Bethany K. Dumas and Jonathan Lighter, "Is Slang a Term for Linguists?" (1978); Lighter's chapter on "Slang" in *Language in North America*, volume 5 of the *Cambridge History of the English Language* (2001); and Connie C. Eble's wise and elegant book, *Slang and Sociability: In-Group Language among College Students* (1996). Julie Coleman is two volumes into an impressively comprehensive and detailed *History of Cant and Slang Dictionaries* (both volumes so far published in 2004, with more to come), and there are excellent accounts of specialized slang vocabularies, such as Tom Dalzell's *The Slang of Sin* (1998) and David W. Maurer's *Language of the Underworld* (comprising articles written earlier but collected in 1981). All of these works are excellent in ways I can't match, and I couldn't have written this book if they hadn't been written first. *Slang: The People's Poetry*, however, is the only ambitious, general account of slang since Partridge, and I think it's about time.

As indebted as I am to them, my approach to slang is different from all of the works mentioned above. My range of interests is considerably wider, comprising the lexical, social, aesthetic, and general linguistic characteristics of slang, and

I have the opportunity to go into all of these areas of interest in detail, to illustrate them from everywhere in our academic, cultural, historical, poetic, and intuitive sense of slang. In four chapters (one for each area of interest) I try to pin slang down; naturally, slang resists, because resistance to authority (the authority of a professor writing a book, in this case) is a big part of what slang is all about. By the end of the book, however, slang's nature and purposes are much clearer than at the outset. I'd like to think that my subtle argument has a lot to do with this clarity, but copious examples of slang ripped from today's Web pages and plagiarized from conversations goes a long way to telling slang's story, contributing significantly to the book's interest and value, both to scholars and to other readers interested in the depths and heights to which language takes us.

In chapter 1, " 'What It Is?' The Essentials of Slang," I consider where slang fits into the English lexicon. What types of words are slang? What qualities distinguish slang from words of other types? Are slang terms necessarily synonyms for standard words? How have scholars differentiated slang from other language, and how apt are their distinctions? What usage marks words and other linguistic practices as slang, as opposed, say, to jargon (like the restaurant server's *weeded*, the stamp collector's *hammered down*, or the snowboarder's *tail grab*), argot (like the supposedly originally criminal Cockney rhyming slang that gives us *Sweeney Todd* for 'Flying Squad', the elite corps of the London Metropolitan Police), or colloquialism, which is so often on the edge of slang (like elliptical *with*, as in, "I'm going to the mall, do you want to go with?")? Unlike jargon and argot, slang is a casual language of being, not working language.

Slang is often characterized as ephemeral language, and a lot of it is. After all, ravers need ephemeral slang for ecstasy in order to keep parents, police, and the otherwise uncool confused about their illicit activities. You'd have a hard time scoring ecstasy if you kept asking for *Dennis the Menace*, *Lucky Charmz*, *Number 9*, *white robin*, or other MDMA brand names long ago replaced by new ones: the ecstasy subculture is constantly rebranding. Ephemerality isn't all a matter of concealment, however; we have lots of reasons to share our figures of speech with some people but not others, friends who won't mack our flow. We all live in our own ephemeral contexts; sometimes we invent a word on the fly during a conversation and the word is extinct by the end of that conversation—sometimes words are reusable, sometimes they're extinct. Scholars of language, both historians and linguists, are uncomfortable with ephemeral language: there isn't anything to narrate or to measure. But most people most of the time live present lives and speak language presently. The abundance of slang is evidence of our continual present.

Not all slang is here today and gone tomorrow, for various social reasons explored in chapter 1. School slang, for instance, is part of a school's tradition, and this chapter looks at examples from English public schools with centuries of tradition (as when *commoners* at Winchester sit at their *scobs* and fret over *disper*) and American universities with newer traditions and fresher slangs (Duke University, for instance, where *Cameron Crazies* tent for *bracelets*), but the value of slang is pretty much the same in either setting. Or, to take the durability of slang from a different angle: our repertoire of terms for inebriation includes unexpectedly persistent ones, like *bent* and *loaded*, intergenerational ones, like *blasted* and *polluted*, and those contrived by the most recent generation or two just to prove how much cooler they are than their parents, like *annihilated*, *fubar*, and *wrecked*. Some slang is old and some middle-aged, though most is brand spanking new until speakers have moved onto the next big thing.

Chapter 2, "Fitting In: The Social Dynamics of Slang," is about the social value of slang, how it marks groups off from one another and indicates group membership, its use among different races and genders, the extent to which it belongs to the young and eludes the old, and how we use it as social currency to negotiate our way through problems of living with others. It starts by considering how automatically we associate certain types of slang with social groups, from African Americans (a big group) to the clique that surrounds the Queen Bee in school (relatively small, but not therefore insignificant).

Because of its role in constructing our identities, slang is all about perception: how others perceive us, how we perceive others, how we perceive ourselves. As a result, our collective sense of who speaks what slang and who doesn't is partly myth, but in a region of social experience and linguistic behavior where myth counts. Are young African American men the slangiest speakers? Are adult women the least slangy? In fact, adult women are hella slangy and young African American men are, too, but not as exclusively as, for many reasons, we are prone to believe. Even though slang's strong affiliation with youth culture is beyond doubt, it isn't exclusive, as youth culture spreads into the twenties (and by some accounts into the thirties). Even oldsters who aren't hipsters still occasionally use slang, and one detects just a touch of bitterness at remembrance of lost things, youth particularly, in their occasional negative reactions to youthful speech. The natural, that is to say, biological and anthropological, relationship between adolescence and slang is explored further in chapter 4.

Finally, chapter 2 looks at the paradox of style: style is simultaneously a locus of social valuing and also a locus of self-expression. By "social valuing" I mean the complex relations among recognizing what count as markers of inclusion and exclusion from social groups, behaving like others in order to fit in (or sometimes deliberately to not fit in), and evaluating others in terms of the style they demonstrate in their everyday social interactions. Of course, "style" includes what we wear, what we do with our hair, and how we walk, as well as how we speak, but I am concerned here with stylin' speech, fluid and profoundly contextual, neither obviously rule-governed nor easily quantified. It's amazing (though we all know it when we think about it for a moment) that one simple feature of slang can influence our social relations in a particular context; just whether we say that someone should *show* versus that someone should *show up* suggests the relationship we have or hope to construct with that person. For help in explaining such subtleties, the fundamental politics of speech, I have the pleasure of returning to *Buffy the Vampire Slayer*, which got the whole ball of this book rolling.

Chapter 3, "Standing Out: Aesthetic Dimensions of Slang," is about the interrelations of slang and poetic language. Certainly slang involves a lot of metaphor (*totally baked, wicked stoned, hella wasted*, for instance), but for a good portion of the chapter I focus instead on sound, on rhyming (*How's it goin', protozoan?*) and then on "infixing." While most infixing and interposing (the phrasal equivalent) involves insertion of expressive but lexically meaningless parts into meaningful words (such as *bizatch, absofuckin'lutely, no fucking way, yee diddly haw*), a new trend is infixing and interposing with meaningful inserts (*accipurpodentally, guaranclickin'teed*, and *lexifabricography*, for instance) a practice that, in twenty-first-century America, is surely a variety of infixing but one that resembles classical (by which I mean Greek and Latin) poetics.

Although some may think that all slang is pretty much the same, I show that there are distinctive slang aesthetics, or attitudes toward slang that take it in different stylistic directions, such as Raunch (including such sexual and scatalogical gems as *bagpiping, maple bar, smile like a donut*, and *traf*) and Hip (*booze, hip, mack*, and *zooty*). Slang may not be poetry, but it's on the way to poetry. As Walt Whitman (a poet, so he should know it) suggested, slang is poetic language in everyday speech, and everyday linguistic invention is the source of poetry, from epic to sonnet to pop song lyric. Undoubtedly, though, slang is a mode of aesthetic expression, even if your particular variety of slang can't please all of the people all of the time.

Chapter 4, "Cognitive Aspects of Slang," reconsiders the status of slang. Though slang abounds with words, it isn't only words, even though we tend to think of it that way. Instead, slang is a linguistic practice grounded in language play and other structurally and anthropologically interesting aspects of language, such as indirection, which is best characterized as a spectrum from lying to poetry, with slang somewhere in the middle. Plato, some readers may recall, thought that, in most cases, poetry and lying were not only related but practically the same thing—well, all poetry is lies, but not all lies are poetry—so he didn't conceive of indirection as a spectrum. But this is the twenty-first century, and I like to think we know better.

Where does slang fit into the biological and cognitive facts of language? As language competence, slang may have a structural role, though admittedly a very minor one, honing our sense of what language can do. Slang is biologically based because all of our cognitive abilities are in the brain and slang is a product of some of those abilities, the potentials, drawn out by social interaction. Chronologically, slang is a late development, not evolutionary per se, not an adaptation in the evolutionary sense (it's not clear that language is an adaptation), but rather an offshoot of adaptation, or a spandrel in the grand architecture of language, an accidental consequence of other, necessary things, but inescapably part of language structure nonetheless.

We may want a concrete definition of slang, but obviously it isn't easy to come up with one, because slang is the area of speech in which biological, social, and aesthetic elements of human experience meet. It is liminal language, a transition between or among broader linguistic interests and motives, and it is often impossible to tell, even in context, which interests and motives it serves, though "all of them at once" isn't a bad conclusion to draw. Slang isn't on one or the other side of a line between human motives manifested in speech. Slang is on the edge.

Finally, a note about audience. Lexicographers, language historians, linguists of various stripes, and cultural critics are welcome and should find useful information and analysis throughout the book. I have written this book as much for them as for anyone else, but I have written the book for "everyone," by which I mean university-educated or other really smart people interested in slang and contemporary American culture. Specialists can take care of themselves; they will know how to insert whatever they read here into their own discourses, supply the jargon I'm not using, add references I haven't had space to include, and all of that.

Intelligent, interested nonacademic readers deserve a break. Occasionally I explain basic linguistic issues in the text and footnotes (rather than use footnotes to engage in nuanced, intramural scholarly argument), and I have supplied references at the end of chapters to make reading easier and more pleasurable, because less interrupted. Scholars who want to know the page number on which quoted material occurs will have to locate it among the references, where sources of everything quoted and cited can be found. I hope that it won't, but the book's style may put off the scholarly reader. I have tried to write clearly, with a sense of humor. I believe that one can take a subject seriously and enjoy oneself at the same time, and I hope that what's sauce for the author is sauce for the reader. Anyway, surely it would miss the point to write a stuffy book about slang.

I have a tendency to practice books aloud while I'm writing them, to the inconvenience of students and other friends. Thus I must apologize to the many students who suffered through early versions of stretches of this book, mostly at North Carolina State University from 2004 to 2006, and lately at Indiana University. Graduate students and other colleagues at Duke University and NC State suffered the most, particularly Jeannine Carpenter, Christine Mallinson, Sarah Hilliard, Jeff Reaser, Charlotte Vaughn, Angus Bowers, Drew Grimes, Michelle Pattie, Tyler Kendall, Phillip Carter, Kristy D'Andrea, Janelle Vadnais, and Libby Cogshall. The Great Walt Wolfram invited me to work among the linguists in North Carolina State University's English Department and the North Carolina Language and Life Project, and I am very grateful for those two wonderful years among those wonderful people.

Of course, they weren't the only ones who helped along the way to finishing this book. I also have to thank Lesley Scott and my Indiana University colleagues Linda Charnes, Rob Fulk, and Traci Nagle for their advice and contributions. Over many years I have benefited immensely from conversations about slang and language generally with Jesse Sheidlower, Tom Dalzell, Jonathon Green, Katherine Connor Martin, Ben Zimmer, Mark Peters, Anne Curzan, Ron Butters, Julie Coleman, Bill Kretzschmar, and especially Richard W. Bailey, Michael Montgomery, and Connie Eble. Much of this book is informed by those conversations, but I'd be hard-pressed to say exactly where or how. Many other intellectual debts will be clear from the references. The book would never have been conceived or completed without the support of my two favorite editors, the visionary Erin McKean and the supernaturally patient Peter Ohlin, as well as Christine Dahlin, Brian Hurley, Elyse Turr, and others at Oxford University Press who perfected and promoted the book.

My wife, Jennifer, hasn't read every draft of every chapter (that would be spousal abuse, and I'd be in prison), but she read most of them and read them patiently, helpfully, kindly. After all is said and done, I may not be smart enough to understand slang, but at least I was smart enough to marry her. I wrote this book, but, for all that she's given me, it belongs to her.

Indianapolis, Indiana
MAY 5, 2008

SLANG

"WHAT IT IS?"

THE ESSENTIALS OF SLANG

If I were to say to you right now, "Dude, I know where we can score some phat mongo," what would you do? Would you call the police? Would you come along to see what I meant by *mongo*? Would you look up *mongo* in the dictionary before we left, so that you knew what you were getting into? I mean, what kind of word is *mongo*? It doesn't sound like an English word. It certainly isn't a word you learned by studying for vocabulary quizzes in school. Is it a bad word for something good, or a good word for something bad?

Mongo sounds something like *mango*, a word borrowed into English from Portuguese in the sixteenth century along with the fruit to which it refers, but the two words aren't related. In *Old Possum's Book of Practical Cats* (1939), T. S. Eliot named a mischievous cat *Mungojerrie*, but nobody ever called him *Mungo* for short, and there's a whole vowel's difference between *Mungo* and *mongo*, anyway.[1] *Mongo* rhymes with *bongo*, *Congo*, *Longo*, and *pongo*, none of which sounds like run-of-the-mill English, with good reason:

---

1 Relative to the vowel in *mongo*, that in *Mungo* is articulated toward the center of the mouth and is lax; the vowel in *mongo* is produced lower and further back in the mouth's space and is relatively tense. Linguists would identify the two words as a minimal pair, that is, two words that differ in only one sound. Each of the rhyming words listed here, whether real or imagined, also constitutes or would constitute a minimal pair with *mongo*. Minimal pairs expose what sounds count as distinctive in a language (what linguists call *phonemes*). One phonemic distinction identifies two words with two meanings. Although

- *Bongo* (for the drum) entered American English in about 1920 from American Spanish.
- *Congo* is the name of a country in Africa and entered English around the year 1800.
- *Longo* is an Italian American surname.
- *Pongo*, modified from a Congolese word, once referred in English to various species of great ape, later to marines and soldiers, and later still, by Australians and New Zealanders, to Englishmen. P. G. Wodehouse named one of his characters Reginald "Pongo" Twistleton, a compliment neither to apes nor to marines.

English has no *dongo, fongo, gongo, hongo, jongo, nongo, quongo, rongo* (though it does have *wrongo*, the slangy American antonym for *righto*), *songo, tongo, vongo, wongo*, or *zongo*. The sound structure of *mongo* is unusual in English, perhaps only possible for an English word because speakers of English had gradually become accustomed to a few similarly structured borrowed words. *Mongo*, then, catches our ear and we ask, again, "What kind of word is that?" Is it for real, an item of SAT-approved Standard American English? Or is it some kind of wacky slang that falls far from the standard? If you looked it up in dictionaries, how would lexicographers label *mongo*: as *standard* or *nonstandard*, as *slang* or *jargon*, *dialect* or *colloquial*, or even *vulgar* or *taboo*?

When I was a contributing editor on the *Barnhart Dictionary Companion: A Quarterly of New Words* (henceforth, *BDC*), I sometimes disagreed with David K. Barnhart (the editor) and Allan Metcalf (the other contributing editor) about which of two fundamental labels, *standard* or *nonstandard*, we should apply to particular entries, and why. Each eighty-three-page issue of the *BDC* contained roughly 130 entries, arranged alphabetically, that identified, defined, and illustrated usage of words so new that they had not yet been entered in dictionaries, some of them slang, but most of them not.

While I was on the job, the *BDC* accounted for relatively new words like *amuse-bouche* 'small piece of food that "amuses the mouth" in preparation for a meal'; *bubble economy* 'marked economic expansion'; *chat room* 'address in a computer service for people to exchange messages in the manner of an informal conversation'; *DSL* 'telephone line designed to carry digital data'; *fashionista* 'person who follows the latest fashions'; *identity politics* 'association of one's political attitudes and beliefs with those of a group with which one feels strong

one sound is sufficient to distinguish two words, it isn't necessary: homophones, like *hear* and *here*, differ in no sounds but nonetheless have different meanings.

affiliation'; -*palooza* 'combining form meaning "large or grand of its kind" '; and *shipper* 'person who focuses on the romantic relationships within a story, especially a television series or motion picture'. If you've wondered why some people are addicted word-watchers, now you know: the words don't stay new for long.

It wasn't enough simply to lump together all of the words in an issue as "new"; *new* isn't a very descriptive label. The *BDC* tried to specify a word's "level" more precisely: if the word was labeled *standard*, it might also be either *formal* or *informal*; or the word might be labeled *nonstandard*. In its front matter, the *BDC* explained that *standard* identified the word in question as part of "the English language as currently used by educated people in polite conversation and writing," whether formal or informal. A word labeled *nonstandard*, on the other hand, belonged to "the English language as characteristically found in dialect, slang, jargon, vulgarisms, and usage often confined to special groups and institutions." So *nanobe* 'microscopic object thought to be a very primitive form of life' was labeled *standard*, and so was the combining form *Franken-* (from *Frankenstein*) meaning 'genetically engineered', as in *Frankenfood* and *Frankenfruit*. Words like *stubby* 'nonworking fire hydrant' were labeled *nonstandard*.

David and Allan always maintained that a term was "standard" if it was the only one available in English to cover a certain concept or thing. Thus the self-explanatory *alternative-fuel vehicle* is labeled *standard* in the *BDC*; so is *mega-dump* 'large landfill'; but so is *bed head* 'hair so messy it looks fresh from the pillow', I guess because English doesn't have another word for hair in that particular condition. Slang dictionaries agree with the *BDC*: none of the dozens on my shelves, including all of the big players, includes *bed head*.[2] But then, neither do any of the regular dictionaries, so *bed head* seems lost in some kind of lexical limbo. I thought then that *bed head* was slang, and I still do. Consider the *BDC*'s definition of the label *standard*: in polite conversation, would you say, "Mr. Henderson, you might want to brush out that bed head" or, in polite writing, "Please resolve any bed head before addressing the board of examiners"? I have my doubts.

---

2   The big players are J. E. Lighter's monumental *Historical Dictionary of American Slang* (1994–), of which two volumes have been published; Tom Dalzell and Terry Victor's *The New Partridge Dictionary of Slang and Unconventional English* (2 volumes, 2006), and Jonathon Green's *Cassell's Dictionary of Slang* (2nd edition, 2005). These wonderful dictionaries underlie much of this book, and I will refer to them constantly. If you really enjoy slang, you should own copies of them. But don't pick one of them up just before an appointment, or you'll be late.

Perhaps *bed head* is merely colloquial rather than slang. But, then, how do you know the difference?

I suggested that, in assigning labels, we should take sources into account, as well as the attitudes of those sources toward the words in question. For instance, unless *bed head* appeared regularly in newspapers of record and was registered in dictionaries as Standard English, I was inclined to hear it as slang. Though the *Manchester Guardian Weekly* had placed *megadump* in quotation marks, I was willing to accept it as standard, because the quotation illustrating the word was one among many without the marks, and the sources included general news outlets, like the *Toronto Star* and National Public Radio's *Morning Edition*. Nevertheless, Pamela Munro and her collaborators, in *Slang U.: The Official Dictionary of College Slang* (1989), Connie C. Eble, in *Slang and Sociability: In-Group Language among College Students* (1996), and John Ayto, in the *Oxford Dictionary of Slang* (1998), include *mega-* among slang combining forms.

I argued, however, that if a technical term occurred only in quotations from the *New England Journal of Medicine*, *Scientific American*, or a National Institutes of Health report posted on the Web, and then appeared in the *New York Times* between quotation marks, it might be labeled *nonstandard* until we had evidence of its general currency, as it seemed to be generally unfamiliar medical jargon, even if English offered no synonym for it. If a term had attitude, as in the case of *Frankenfruit*, it might very well be slang even though there is no word that stands for the phrase "genetically engineered fruit that might seem a monstrous aberration." After all, there's no single-word equivalent for "nonworking fire hydrant," either: why, then, does the BDC label *Franken-* as *standard* and *stubby* as *nonstandard*?

I never won any of these arguments.

Nonetheless, I had a point. Recently, Ted Botha's *Mongo: Adventures in Trash* (2004) introduced *mongo* to a relatively wide audience. *Mongo* isn't a new word: the *Historical Dictionary of American Slang* (henceforth, *HDAS*) records it from 1984, and rumor has it that the word had been around for at least a decade by then. Indeed, Grant Barrett, in *The Official Dictionary of Unofficial English* (2006), reports that "evidence from the unpublished *Lexicon of Trade Jargon*, compiled by the Works Progress Administration, has a form of this word from before 1938: *mungo*, referring to the person who salvages discarded items, rather than the things being salvaged."[3]

---

3 Perhaps there's a connection between *Mungojerrie* and *mongo* after all, in sound and spirit, if not in meaning or etymology. Mungojerrie and his colleague Rumpelteazer, we

Here is how Botha defines *mongo* in his book: "Some [collectors of sidewalk trash] also have a word for what they find, a word that is suitably playful and vague. It could be French, Chinese, or even African, but it is, quite appropriately, American slang, concocted in New York for any discarded item that is picked up, retrieved, rescued. That word is *mongo*." *HDAS* and all of the other dictionaries that enter *mongo* concur in this definition; all of them, including *The Official Dictionary of Unofficial English*, agree that *mongo* is American slang.

But is it? *Trash* is the word for what we leave at the curb; *plunder* must be taken with force. Does Standard English possess a term for stuff once thrown out and then retrieved? The typical definition of *mongo* doesn't include "rescue" as a constituent, but the word camouflages an intention on the part of one who "picks up" an item in someone else's trash. That item "deserves" to be saved from the trash; it has value, as determined by the rescuer. Even "retrieve" reflects intention beyond mere "picking up": picking up is easy, but retrieval takes some effort, and most of us don't waste effort on things we don't value. In an interview with Dick Gordon on NPR's *The Connection* (August 25, 2004), Botha explained that *mongo* is trash that appeals to the rescuer, that "sparkles" or otherwise catches the eye (or maybe Gordon helped to define it thus, with Botha's assent). Surely Standard English has no word for 'appealing trash' other than *mongo*. According to one way of thinking (that is, the way most often pursued in the *BDC*), *mongo* isn't slang after all, but a "standard" term, one that gives a whole new meaning to talking trash.

The evidence presented in the entry for *mongo* in the *HDAS* merely complicates the issue of to which "register," "style," or "level" of speech *mongo* belongs. The *HDAS* cites *The New Yorker* (September 24, 1984): "The walls sagged with what artists call found objects, and what [sanitation men] call 'mongo.'" Again, like found art, mongo is collected for a reason, in response to its aesthetic appeal. But if sanitation workers used *mongo* among themselves before anyone else, it was a term of art, so to speak, not standard or slang, but jargon, that is, language of vocation or avocation. Barrett's comment on *mungo*

---

are told, "were a very notorious couple of cats" and "were highly efficient cat-burglars as well." They didn't salvage discarded items, however, but were "remarkably smart at a smash-and-grab," and we can assume that people still wanted what they stole. *Mongo* is neither feline nor felonious, and although *mungo* appears to predate *Mungojerrie*, there is no reason to believe that Eliot, long resident in England, knew the word as Barrett records it.

supports *mongo*'s jargon origin. Barrett also notes that *mongo* "appears to be specific to New York City." Standard term, slang, jargon, or regionalism — which is it?

You might answer that the argument sounds like one that lexicographers would have over drinks. Who else would care? And anyway, *mongo* is obviously slang; everyone I ask about it, including the lexicographers, agrees that it's slang. But how do they know? On what bases do they judge? The hairsplitting history of usage just outlined does not support the label *slang* for *mongo* unequivocally, and it seems unwise simply to ignore the evidence. Do we know what counts as slang and what doesn't, not by thinking about it, but in the gut? Certainly, when I proposed that we score some mongo, you knew that something was up, you heard *mongo* as not just unfamiliar but edgy (*score* and *phat* probably pushed you a little closer to the edge). If I had suggested that we pop around the corner for some comestibles or appurtenances, you'd have backed away from the proposition, but for reasons different from those that made you wary of *mongo*. When you encounter the *slang* label in dictionaries, does it reflect reasoned conclusions about words or intuitions about them?

This book proposes a theory of slang: what it is, why it is, and how we know it when we hear it or see it — primarily when we hear it. I argue that slang is not merely a lexical phenomenon, a type of word, but a linguistic practice rooted in social needs and behaviors, mostly the complementary needs to fit in and to stand out. In addition, slang asserts our everyday poetic prowess as we manipulate the sounds, shapes, and effects of words; the pleasure we take in the slang we speak and hear is, at least sometimes, an aesthetic pleasure. And, though it plays only a bit part in the linguistic epic, slang may figure in our "linguistic competence," that is, the innate human capacity to acquire and use language. We can't tell the story of language unless we can account for all of its characters, slang included. This book provides slang's backstory.

Recently, in *The New Yorker*, John Seabrook asked America's preeminent sociolinguist, William Labov:

> What causes dialects to change? Not television, Labov said. The people he calls "extreme speakers" — those who have the greatest influence on others — tend to be visible local people: "politicians, Realtors, bank clerks." But isn't slang a bottom up phenomenon? "Slang is just the paint on the hood of the car," Labov said. "Most of the important changes in American speech are not happening at the level of grammar or language — which used to be the case — but at the level of sound."

Maybe. Most of us prefer cars with painted hoods, and, as I argue in this book, slang is less surfacey than many linguists suppose; it may be an integral part of the language machine. In any event, slang matters to us, and this book attempts to explain why.

SLANG BY DEFINITION

Native speakers of American English recognize American slang more or less automatically: the brain sorts and labels much more efficiently than any lexicographer. We know slang when we hear it, and we know how to deploy slang in our own speech, because social, aesthetic, and linguistic knowledge guide us. (Not every linguist would agree, but I believe that these three knowledges overlap significantly, and this book is partly about how they play well with one another.) When dictionaries define the term *slang* they attempt to identify the social, aesthetic, and linguistic characteristics or properties that distinguish slang from other language.

Here are four definitions of *slang* from prominent dictionaries.[4] You can see how, at their cores, they are similar, but each departs from the others in one or another detail. This book hopes to resolve some of those disagreements and, in doing so, to pick the useful threads of explanation and ravel them into a durable theory of slang.

> *Encarta World English Dictionary*: **1. VERY CASUAL SPEECH OR WRITING** words, expressions, and usages that are casual, vivid, racy, or playful replacements for standard ones, are often short-lived, and are usually considered unsuitable for formal contexts **2. LANGUAGE OF AN EXCLUSIVE GROUP** a form of language used by

---

4   The etymology of *slang* is quite interesting. According to Anatoly Liberman, in the first
volume of his *Analytic Dictionary of English Etymology* (2008), *slang* dates from 1756: "One
of the meanings of the word *slang* is 'narrow piece of land running up between other and
larger divisions of ground.' *Slang* must also have meant 'territory over which hawkers,
strolling showmen, and other itinerants traveled.' Later it came to mean *"those who were
on the slang' and finally 'hawkers' patter'; hence the modern meaning. The phrase *on the
slang* is a gloss on some Scandinavian phrase like Sw[edish] *på slänget (E[nglish] *slanget
has been recorded). *Slang* 'piece of land' is a word of Scandinavian origin, but its meaning
may have been influenced by Southern E[nglish] *slang* 'border'. *Slang* 'informal speech'
does not go back to F[rench] *langue* 'language', and it is not a derivative of N[orse] *slengja
'throw.'" This is the short etymology Liberman provides in the section "Etymologies at a
Glance"; the full article on *slang* runs to seven double-column pages.

a particular group of people, often deliberately created and used to exclude people outside the group.

American Heritage College Dictionary, 4th edition: **1.** A kind of language esp. occurring in casual and playful speech, usu. made up of short-lived coinages and figures of speech deliberately used in place of standard terms for effects such as raciness, humor, or irreverence. **2.** Language peculiar to a group; argot or jargon.

Merriam-Webster Collegiate Dictionary, 11th edition: **1:** language peculiar to a particular group: as **a:** ARGOT **b:** JARGON 2 **2:** an informal nonstandard vocabulary composed typically of coinages, arbitrarily changed words, and extravagant, forced, or facetious figures of speech.

New Oxford American Dictionary (NOAD), 2nd edition: a type of language that consists of words and phrases that are regarded as very informal, are more common in speech than writing, and are typically restricted to a particular context or group of people.

All of these definitions agree that slang is "in-group" language, the use of which designates who belongs to a group and who does not. The American Heritage and Merriam-Webster definitions provide *argot* and *jargon* as quasi-synonyms for *slang*; along with *cant*, they have been used interchangeably, not only in everyday speech, but also in thoughtful writing about language. *Jargon* is the oldest of the terms, entering English from French in the fourteenth century to mean 'unintelligible talk'. *Cant* started as a verb, probably in the sixteenth century, and referred to the beggar's whine (*cant* likely derives from Latin *cantus* 'song', and refers to sing-songy speech), though by the eighteenth century it referred to the language of gypsies and thieves, as well as beggars (in the minds of many, the groups overlapped).

Chaucer describes birds as chattering in jargon; we can't understand what they're saying because they're birds. We don't understand beggars and thieves because they don't want us to: they invent language to cover their nefarious activity. As Julie Coleman, who is currently writing the third volume of her definitive *History of Cant and Slang Dictionaries*, puts it, cant's "primary purpose is to deceive, to defraud, and to conceal," whereas jargon "typically belongs to professions or interest groups, such as doctors or train enthusiasts." *Argot* rose in the nineteenth century as a synonym for *cant*, just as the word *cant* was on the wane; of course, criminals continually developed language to confuse everyone who lived in the overworld, so *argot* either arrived in the nick of time to replace a dying word, elbowed *cant* to the periphery of English, or both.

Choosing among these supposed synonyms is itself an exercise in jargon, the jargon of linguists and historians of English. Though the arguments over terminology may sound as incomprehensible as a parliament of fowls, attempts to pin one term to one phenomenon are meant to clear things up. Certainly there's a need for precision. The *Oxford English Dictionary* suggests that *jargon* can be "applied contemptuously to any mode of speech abounding in unfamiliar terms, or peculiar to a particular set of persons, as the language of scholars or philosophers, the terminology of science or art, or the cant of a class, sect, trade or profession," which brings the speech of philosophers, rocket scientists, thieves, lawyers, Methodists, and beggars too close to one another for comfort.

In this book, criminals speak cant or argot when they're on the game; anyone pursuing a legal vocation or avocation, from doctors to model train enthusiasts, employs a jargon suited to that particular occupation; any other language that characterizes a group and identifies speakers with that group ends up slang by default. Is *mongo* slang? If art thieves strip your walls of mongo, *mongo* is argot; if sanitation workers pick up mongo at the curb, then *mongo* is jargon; when you and I talk about rummaging for mongo because we just read Ted Botha's book and we're all about the next big thing, then *mongo* is slang. Slang, jargon, and argot aren't essential characteristics of a word; one or another of them applies depending on who uses the word, in what situation, for what reasons.

The *Encarta* definition emphasizes the power of slang to exclude and goes a step further, asserting that the exclusion is often "deliberate," that speakers use slang to draw lines in the sand. *NOAD* agrees that slang can identify a group and its members, but no one has to draw the line between those who belong and those who don't—it just appears. The difference between these two descriptions of slang is significant. It's not clear that slang is always slung consciously. Those who object to "It was like totally awesome, and I was like, 'Dude, aren't you glad we came?' " view the slang features of the sentence as one speaker's mindless repetition of in-group markers. But can slang be unconsciously racy, playful, or irreverent? The *American Heritage College Dictionary* claims that substitution of slang for standard is a matter of choice rather than reflex. The apparent inconsistency has figured in attitudes toward slang for a long time, and it is a central issue in this book, as it originates in the tension between slang's social and aesthetic impulses.

We enjoy slang (those of us who do enjoy it) just for its casual, vivid, racy, irreverent, and playful elements, and some combination of those elements is what alerts the ear to lexical trouble: slang rebels against the standard (whether mildly, wildly, or somewhere in between), and each synonym it supplies must add some social meaning to the standard alternative's lexical meaning.

If you want to be casual, don't spend time or, as in standard English, *relax* with your friends: *hang out* with them; even better, just *hang*, or be cool and *chill out* or *chill*, or *chillax* — just sit around, like, *chillin'* with your friends. Does language follow attitude here, or make it, or perhaps a little of both? *Hanging* is just as purposeless as the purposeless fear ("Don't you have anything better to do than hang out with your friends?") and is thus an example of perfect slang. The metaphors are so casual as to be barely recognizable as metaphors. Some listeners hear clipped phrases and blends like *chillax* as lazy, as though the speaker had given up before completing the phrase or, dazed and confused, just forgot that there were two words, so that *chillax* is a slip of the mind, really, and not a serious word. In fact, clipping and blending are much more complicated and interesting social and aesthetic maneuvers than their detractors realize. If you hang for the rest of the book, you'll see why.

Nevertheless, casual is an approved attitude in the world that uses slang, and *casual* is itself an item of slang. This is how Jonathon Green defines *casual* in *Cassell's Dictionary of Slang* (2005): "**casual** *adj.* **1** [1950s+] (*US campus*) acceptable, satisfactory. **2** [1970s] clever, witty. **3** [1980s] not worth becoming upset about." And it gets even more casual than that! In the 1980s the first sense of *casual* intensified, as speakers clipped *casual* (rather innovatively) into the new form *cas* (or *caj* or *cazh* or *kasj*), meaning (according to Green) "a term of general approval for anything favoured, e.g., a close friend, an item of clothing, a rock band, a given activity." The smaller word is more potent, like liquor distilled or sauce reduced. Does *cazh* draw a line or cross it? Is it clipped two syllables too far? Is *cazh* so casual that it's in your face? That paradox is part of slang's project, too, and while it doesn't diminish slang's easygoing nature, it does complicate it.

Oddly, the casual can be vivid. Rather than *have sex* or *do it* or *get it on* or *copulate*, you can *shag* or *bang*. Even better, you can *horizontalize*, which has more syllables than *copulate*. It is totally casual, where *shag* is edgy and fun and *bang* is violent, and, along with *sixty-nine*, it suggests the posture of everyday sexual intercourse better than the everyday lexical alternatives. In fact, sex stimulates production of many vivid terms, from *donkey dick* to *hung like a cashew*, some of which, like *hairy clam* 'vagina', are olfactory as well as visual.[5] These are only a

---

5   In his excellent book *The Slang of Sin* (1998), Tom Dalzell records such pornographic escapades as "**Sixty-Ninth Street Bridge** A scene in a porn movie in which a woman upon

few examples of a slang tendency. Think of any human excretion or expectoration (forward, backward, feminine, drunken), and you'll easily come up with a list of your own to illustrate the point.

We are so sure that slang should be vivid that we even "invent" vividness for relatively pedestrian slang terms. In the past year or so I have heard several radio commentators question the use of slang *suck*, as in "You suck!" or "That sucks!" On the National Public Radio magazine show *Day to Day* a correspondent took comments on *suck*, its origin and appropriateness, from citizens on the street. Pretty much all of them thought that *suck* was vividly off-color, because they believed that it derives from *suck* 'fellate'. Ronald R. Butters has pointed out that, in a strict etymological sense, this assumption probably isn't true: historically, you can *suck eggs*, *suck rope*, or *suck wind* if you are 'disappointing' or 'worthless', and all of these precede use of simple *suck* to mean the same things.

It appears that, in order to explain *suck*, we PREFER the *suck* 'fellate' origin, a folk etymology, to the alternatives. But then something funny happens: because we BELIEVE in the folk etymology, it actually BECOMES an etymology for the word, because we think that we're using a term derived from *suck* 'fellate'; the supposed etymology is carried in the meaning we give to *suck* in "That sucks!" We WANT *suck* to be vivid and, in being vivid, mildly taboo. As Connie Eble demonstrates in *Slang and Sociability* (1996), slang terms are more than usually susceptible to mixed etymologies like this one. It does no good to stand on street corners, dictionary in hand, and proclaim the "true" etymology to nonbelievers. "Etymology is not destiny," Geoffrey Nunberg quips, and "phonetics always trumps etymology." In doing so, it may actually develop into an etymology. Mixed etymology is one of slang's "democratic" tendencies: the People's use has considerable authority and can change the course of lexical history.

We like our slang casual or vivid and sometimes both, but, as *suck* proves, we are equally committed to slang's racy, irreverent, and playful qualities. These three characteristics of slang are closely related, and if we turn to Jonathon Green's *Cassell's Dictionary of Slang* (2005) once again, we find all three busy in one lexical item:

---

whom oral sex is being performed by one man arches her back and performs oral sex on a second man" and "**triple play, triple crown** A scene in a porn movie showing a woman engaged in sex with three men simultaneously — oral, vaginal, and anal." A bashful Episcopalian boy, I depend on books for the vocabulary of acrobatic sex. There's a lot out there.

morning glory *n.* 1 [1900s–1980s] (*US*) something which or someone who fails to maintain an early promise, esp. in sporting contexts. 2 [1950s] (*US drugs*) the first narcotic injection of the day. 3 [1970s+] (*Aus.*) sexual intercourse before one gets up in the morning. 4 [1990s+] an erection on waking. [puns on SE *morning glory*, the plant *Ipomoea purpurea*]

Half of the *HDAS* evidence for *morning glory* has to do with horse racing, an activity that is indeed racy because it is the focus of gambling, legal and illegal, and because people who spend enough time at the track to worry about morning glories do not fit comfortably into polite society.

This is just as true for the member of polite society who can't resist going to the track once in a while as it is for the inveterate gambler. If you are as comfortable as a Quaker, you don't itch to gamble or to lose yourself on the fringe of criminality. As David Maurer once observed,

> There are the words and phrases used by those people who gamble on the races; these generally originate within the tightly organized professional gambling groups, then spread gradually to the ordinary citizen who likes to go to the races or place a bet with his local bookie. Often these terms are unmistakably criminal argot and may be derivative from or related to the argot of dice or card gamblers. Everyone who bets on horses at all learns a little of this argot, even though he may never penetrate beyond the sucker level.

And this lexical drift, the movement of words from argot to slang and sometimes into the English vocabulary at large, explains how *morning glory* moved from the racetrack to the fight ring into sports generally (the other half of the *HDAS* evidence supports this description), and then into slang unrelated to sports.

From racy, *morning glory* becomes playful, as a metaphorical and self-effacing term for the penis in bloom. And it is certainly irreverent to apply the folk name of a lovely flower to the first narcotic injection of the day. In each case but that of the Australian in Green's sense 3, *glory* is at least partly ironic: the horse that exercised well in the paddock at sunrise runs poorly in the harsh light of day; the narcotic high diminishes hit by hit; the man who wakes up alone will think, "Some glory." Slang's exuberance and wit often compensate verbally for the disappointments and insecurities that crop up and make living an uphill climb. When a word or phrase mingles irreverence and playfulness into something like defiance, whether toward authority (official or social) or life's vicissitudes, it's slang. You can bet on it.

It would be nice if all definitions of slang agreed in the essential elements: slang is casual, playful, racy, irreverent, or playful language that outlines social in-groups. But note that the Merriam-Webster definition characterizes slang quite differently: in slang, words are changed "arbitrarily," and what sounds playful to one listener sounds "forced" to another, the irreverent becomes "facetious," the racy is "extravagant." What have the folks at Merriam-Webster got against slang? What sounds appealing in the other definitions, even if the appeal was illicit, sounds awkward, nasty, and impolite in theirs. Importantly, the difference in definitions is not just down to Merriam-Webster's attitude, but reflects a broad difference of opinion among speakers about the social level of slang and its appropriateness or "correctness," at least in certain situations. Not everyone agrees that slang is cool: some consider it bad language for bad behavior; the behavior taints the speech. As should be clear by now, I disagree with some of the assumptions that underlie the Merriam-Webster definition, but the question of how "low" slang is remains to be answered by the rest of the book, and there is no doubt that slang presents itself as "low" often enough to earn a bad reputation.

The definitions quoted above also disagree about the stamina of lexical items we consider slang. Are they ephemeral, or do they persist in the vocabulary? And if they survive, do they survive as slang, or do they "ascend" from slang to colloquial English, relatively informal English that isn't invested in fitting in or standing out, as they lose their restrictive, in-group quality? The *Merriam-Webster Collegiate Dictionary* and the *New Oxford American Dictionary* do not commit themselves, whereas the *American Heritage College Dictionary* and the *Encarta World English Dictionary* characterize slang as "short-lived." But as with its role in the demarcation of social groups, or the question of whether it is arbitrary or thoughtful speech, poetic or forced, casual or extravagant, playful or facetious, slang's life span is problematic, and no simple estimate adds up. For instance, most of us are convinced that *like*, as in "It was like the best concert ever" or "He was like, 'It was the best concert ever,'" originated recently in Valley Girl slang, but Alexandra D'Arcy has recently reported that this is language mythology, because examples of both these *likes* can be found in rural speech in England . . . in the nineteenth century.

If, once upon a time, you and your friends were really bored (or really drunk), you may have attempted to relieve the boredom (or focus the drunkenness) by listing all of the synonyms you knew for *drunk*. Take *drunk, inebriated,* and *intoxicated* as standard English synonyms for one another; all of the others you listed were slang, at least when they started out. Rather than merely listing them here, let's consider them chronologically:

	← 1920	1930	1940	1950	1960	1970	1980	1990 →
annihilated						———	———	———
bent	———	———	———	———	———	———	———	———
blasted			———	———	———	———	———	———
bombed				———	———	———	———	———
faced						———	———	———
fubar							———	———
fucked up				———	———	———	———	———
gone		———	———	———	———			
gone Borneo							———	
hammered					———	———	———	———
jammed	———	———						
legless					———	———	———	———
lit/lit up	———	———	———	———	———	———	———	———
loaded	———	———	———	———	———	———	———	———
messed up					———	———	———	———
polluted				———	———	———	———	———
ripped						———	———	———
shit-faced						———	———	———
smashed					———	———	———	———
snockered					———	———	———	———
stoned				———	———	———	———	———
trashed						———	———	———
wasted						———	———	———
whacked / whacked out						———	———	———
wrecked						———	———	———

Several of these terms illustrate various essentials of slang, as proposed by the dictionary definitions. You may disagree, but I think that *ripped* is racy, *faced* is a deliberately casual, euphemistic successor to *shit-faced*, and *gone Borneo* is, in its way, playful and vivid. (Its way is convoluted: it derives from the once popular and ubiquitous circus sideshow "The Wild Man of Borneo," so it is vivid if you can imagine the wildness and playful when you realize that someone who has *gone Borneo* is a sideshow to an evening's entertainment.)

But the chronology is especially interesting: once most terms start, even *bent*, *smashed*, and *loaded*, all recorded first in the nineteenth century, they continue. Most don't have short lives at all. Some may hobble along in old age, of course, but they aren't buried in the lexical cemetery yet. In fact, *gone Borneo* is the only clear exception to the trend; apparently, it burned so bright in the 1980s that it burned out within the decade, and thus it is the perfect example of slang's ephemerality. Most of its synonyms, however, aren't ephemeral.

Nonetheless, each generation comes up with new words for the same old inebriation. Because lots of people who were drunk in the 1940s were *legless*, *smashed*, or *fucked up*, young people got *messed up*, *bombed*, or *snockered* in the 1950s in order to draw the generational line. In the 1960s their younger siblings felt the same social need and so added a few items, like *ripped*, *wrecked*, *hammered*, *trashed*, and *shit-faced* to the growing list. Often generations announce themselves by doing their thing and making up a word to use among themselves, without much concern for oldsters. Sometimes, though, new synonyms are overtly competitive: after their great-grandparents got *smashed*, their grandparents got *blasted*, their parents got *smashed* and *bombed*, and their older brothers and sisters got *hammered* and *wrecked*, teens in the 1970s and since have gotten *annihilated*. Not content simply to get *fucked up* like their forbears, kids in the 1980s appropriated an old military acronym, *fubar* 'fucked up beyond all recognition', to prove that their slang, if not their behavior, was extreme. Overenthusiastic drinkers in the 1940s *barfed* (*barf* is supposedly echoic or onomatopoetic); in the 1960s, some barfed, but others *ralphed* (*plus ça change . . . ralph* is also supposedly echoic); in the 1990s, they *hurled*. It's hard to decide whether visual *hurl* is more vivid than audible *barf*, as the words offend different senses.

Sometimes slang terms fall out of favor, though probably not out of use, and then rise again with slightly different meanings. For instance, a sixty-year-old might use *stoned* to mean 'drunk' even in the twenty-first century, but obviously *stoned* has more to do with *weed* than whiskey today — no one calls the habitual cocktail drinker a *stoner*. Similarly, *jammed* could mean 'drunk' in the 1920s, but it shifted gradually to mean 'coked up'. Of course, *stoned* later faced competition from *baked* (from the 1970s on) and *jammed* from *gacked* (from the 1990s on), suggesting that, for one reason or another, whether pursuit of novelty for its own sake or generational competition, if there's one slangy synonym for a standard term, there's also another.

Indeed, within generations several slang synonyms jostle one another for attention and use. No generation NEEDS more words to mean 'drunk', if by *need* you mean that there's a lexical gap that needs to be filled, a thing or concept out there for which English currently has no word. Slang is finely calibrated to social circumstances and social goals: you need the right slang synonym for *drunk* when you are talking to your parents, another when you are describing last night's festivities to a guy you don't know that well but really like, yet another with the friends who were with you last night. Given the hard social work to which we put our slang, a few more words can't hurt.

Having said all of this, I have to agree, from intimate experience with slang, that most of it disappears before we notice it. As Connie Eble puts it, "Taken as a whole, the slang vocabulary of a language is ephemeral, bursting into existence and falling out of use at a much more rapid rate than items of the general vocabulary." One of the great things about slang dictionaries like those mentioned so far (and there will be more to come) is that they stop time so that we can locate the slang of here and now among all other speech, or they recover artifacts of slang gone by.

But slang's short half-life isn't its biggest problem. As Eble points out, *slang* "is widely used without precision, especially to include informal usage and technical jargon, and the social and psychological complexities captured in slang vocabulary make the term difficult to define." You may be surprised to learn that "the aim of using slang is seldom the exchange of information. More often, slang serves social purposes: to identify members of a group, to change the level of discourse in the direction of informality, [and] to oppose established authority." In the market of social meaning, "slang is the linguistic equivalent of fashion and serves much the same purpose." Chapter 2 explores many social dimensions of slang, but before arriving there, it might be wise to distinguish slang even more precisely from jargon, argot, and colloquial use.

LANGUAGE OF PURPOSE VERSUS LANGUAGE OF BEING

On the face of it, jargon behaves very much like slang. For instance, if you work as a bartender in a national chain restaurant that serves lots of frozen, blended drinks (frozen margaritas, frozen daiquiris, and the like), you may end up the *blender tender* on Friday or Saturday night. Like many a slang term, *blender tender* is playfully constructed and it's casual, too, in the sense that it's a more casual term than Bartender at Station 6, or Bartender 4007, or whatever official term the restaurant and its automated ordering and inventory system uses to identify the human employee who tends the blender. Blending frozen drinks for eight hours isn't a pleasure, exactly; the humor conveyed in jargon compensates some for the numbing boredom of the work. A term like *amateur diner* is used among servers for the customers who eat out once a year, perhaps on Mother's Day, and who aren't sure what the menu items are or how to order them effectively. Customers provide servers with most of their income; one might think that they deserve some respect. *Amateur diner*, you'll note, is a little irreverent.

If both slang and jargon are playful and irreverent and casual, then why aren't they the same thing? The distinction lies in this: slang is language of a group with a shared interest but not a shared purpose. It's a language of being, not of vocation or avocation. As I said before, *hang* is perfect slang: *hanging* is just being, whether alone in your apartment or with a group of friends. You've probably had a Sunday morning cell phone conversation like this one:

FRIEND: I was thinking of heading over to Rittenhouse Square for some brunch — what are you doing?

YOU: Oh, you know, I'm just hangin' out reading the paper.

FRIEND: Well, we may as well hang together or we'll just hang separately.

Slang can belong to small groups (junior high school cliques) or big ones (all Americans under forty). If members of a group have things in common (and if they didn't, they wouldn't be a group), then they are bound to speak a common language that separates them in some fashion from the language of those who aren't in the group.

Jargon is language at work; the work group is the in-group. If you are a server in a restaurant, then you and your fellow servers have not so much common interests as common purposes, namely, to serve customers well and thereby make money for the restaurant and for yourselves. Everyone who eats in restaurants knows that servers are paid *tips* but may not realize that servers *tip out* (that is, 'pool and share tips') at the end of a *shift* with the rest of those who work in the *front* (bussers, hosts and hostesses, bartenders, etc.). To make big tips, servers persuade customers to run up big bills: they sell food and drink and they may suggest that you buy more so that you spend more, or *upsell*. You might be introduced to an appetizer you hadn't thought to order or a dessert you know you shouldn't order. Or, when you request a vodka martini, your server asks, "Would you like a Grey Goose martini?" Well, who wouldn't? You'd have settled for *well liquor* (the cheap stuff), but why not go *top-shelf*? You've earned it!

You're not supposed to know about *upselling*, or that you are an *amateur diner*, or that the servers call you a *camper* because you sit too long at your table without ordering anything. To make money, a server needs to *turn* tables and has only a few in his or her *station* or *section*. Imagine a *station* with four tables, two *four-tops* and two *deuces*. A *four-top* seats four people and a *deuce* seats two. Four people means four *covers* or *setups* ('place settings' to you and me), which means four meals to sell, or better yet, to upsell. Have you ever wondered why you aren't allowed to sit at the clean, unoccupied table for four, or (even worse) why you and your date weren't seated at that table, but the group of four that arrived fifteen minutes AFTER you did WAS seated, while you were forced to wait for a smaller table? It's all the business of making money in a restaurant: from a server's point of view, maximum covers at tables that turn often are the ideal.

But customers need not worry about the jargon spoken all around them while they chat, network, flirt, eat, and drink. It's not for them. Once in a while a server will approach my table with the familiar patter: "Hello, my name is Jared, and I'll be your server tonight. Before I take your drink orders, let me tell you about our specials tonight. For apps, we have . . ." Wait a minute, my internal monologue interrupts: don't use your jargon with me, Jared. Speak to me as a customer, not another server. I do not belong to your group; I do not want to understand the mysteries of your profession. Tell me about the *appetizers*, not the *apps*. "Now, what would you like to drink, sir?" "Thank you, Jared. I'd like a dry vodka martini, up, please." "Would you like a Grey Goose martini?" Sure, who wouldn't?

My purpose is to drink and eat; Jared's purpose is to sell and upsell. Jared and I do not share purposes, so we do not share the server's lexicon. When servers complain about their *sidework* 'cleaning or other preparation for serving', they complain to one another, not to me. When the restaurant is *on a wait* (that is, there are more patrons than available covers) and Jared gets *triple-sat* (that is, three tables have been seated simultaneously), he's suddenly *in the weeds* (not just swamped, but in the weeds). I'm waiting for my second martini, which will be a while coming, so I'm unlikely to be sympathetic. Jared has to vent his panic and frustration to those who feel his pain and share his purpose, namely, fellow servers. To this extent, restaurant jargon, any jargon, is social: servers achieve their purpose socially, and colorful, inventive language supports their social structure because it identifies who is in the know, who deserves pro forma respect as a member of the team.

If *amateur diner*, *camper*, and *in the weeds* are irreverent, playful synonyms for standard English phrases ('inexperienced customer', 'customer who sits at table too long', and 'unbelievably busy', respectively) and so resemble slang, well, I suppose they do resemble slang. But the social circumstances that provoke jargon are different from those that provoke slang: in jargon, there's something at stake beyond positioning oneself in the social circumstance. Jargon may be stylish, but it is not, as Eble suggests of slang, analogous to fashion: jargon has to roll up its sleeves and do real work. There is nothing playful about *on a wait*, *triple-sat*, or *four-top*; these are all shorthand for things that folks working in restaurants don't have time to say at length. For instance, when a server returns from a break, another says, in passing, "We're on a wait," not "We have more patrons than we can serve at one time." The second server is passing because she has just been triple-sat and she doesn't have time to explain, or she'll be *weeded*. Note that "I'm weeded" takes less time to say than "I am in the weeds."

In slang, clipping's *cazh*, but in jargon it's efficient. When a server behind you quietly says *Backs*, there's nothing casual in the message: it's a warning that said server is carrying a full tray and that no one within distance of a stage whisper should move. If you stand up, knock over the tray, and spill the food all over patrons, you'll not only make a mess, but each order will have to be prepared again *on the fly*, and everyone will suddenly be in the weeds with their tips on the line. The warning has to be quick because the server is on the move; it has to be short because it is uttered in public but not for the public to hear. Again, jargon is on the job.

In this situation, if you don't understand restaurant jargon, if you don't respond to it as a member of the guild, the results will be catastrophic. You will disrupt the common work of the restaurant, of course, but you also will anger everyone: customers, other servers, the *bussers* (they have to clean up the mess), the *runners* (they have more food to move from the *back of the house* to the *front*), the *expediters* (who have to call and clear more orders in the kitchen), and the *KM* (the kitchen manager), who will provide free meals to replace those you've ruined—free to the customer, but not to the restaurant. When it comes to sales and tips, everyone loses.

So jargon is practical: it's brisk and unambiguous, and it helps busy people do their jobs efficiently. But its use is also social: social relations within the restaurant depend on it, and efficient work toward the common goal depends on certain social relations. When restaurant jargon is slangy—full of fun, invention, and irreverence—it reinforces the restaurant in-group's camaraderie and alleviates the tedium of its shared labor.

Jargon is not exclusively the language of work; it is also the language of serious play. Sports and hobbies and activities with equipment, rules, strategies, and traditions have jargons. Stamp collecting, for instance, has jargon; you can find out about it at the Collectors Club of Chicago's philatelic reference site, AskPhil. A *spoon cancellation* is apparently a "duplex cancel used in England and Wales, named from the oval shape of the duplex portion." A term like *spoon cancellation* will not come up in general conversation — it's technical. And it belongs to a vast technical vocabulary: every stamp that's used on mail that moves is canceled; there are different cancellations in every country with a postal service at this moment, not to mention throughout the worldwide history of postage; there are terms for all of those cancellations, yet their number is not the total of cancellation-related terms, let alone the total of stamp collecting jargon. A serious philatelist must master all of the information articulated in the jargon.

Is *spoon cancellation* really jargon, or is it a standard English term? Surely we have no other term in the English vocabulary for this particular mark on a stamp. But how about the designation *Fine-Very Fine*, which is clearly extended from standard English senses of common words just for the purposes of stamp collectors? If a stamp is *Fine-Very Fine*, its design

> may be slightly off center on two sides, perfs are noticeably off center, imperforate stamp design will not touch any edge, some non-US stamps may be printed so that the design is naturally very close to the edges, used stamps will not have a cancellation that detracts from the design; ref. Scott Catalogue.

You can define a word only with other words, of course, but consider the density of jargon within this definition: *perfs* are perforate stamps, the ones you tear from a sheet along lines of perforation; once upon a time, you used to cut imperforates from a sheet with scissors, but nowadays almost all U.S. stamps are imperforate and peel away from a sheet. The *Scott Catalogue*, a standard reference on stamps and stamp collecting, is, in a case like this, jargon: you are supposed to know a good bit of the jargon before you even ask AskPhil.

Stamp collecting seems like a quiet, solitary activity, and usually it is, but committed collectors may end up in social situations focused on philately, like stamp auctions, where an auctioneer may give *fair warning* to let bidders know that an item will soon be *hammered down*, or sold at the current bid. Here, the jargon of stamp collecting overlaps with the jargon of auctioning any kind of collectible. But none of the terms mentioned here belongs to the nonstandard speech of just being, and people don't hang with friends and discuss philately unless they're all stamp collectors, and then they are talking with a shared purpose, namely, collecting stamps. Collecting stamps is very, very different from serving food in restaurants. But each activity has a purpose and a purposeful lexicon that helps to achieve it.

Jargon turns up in every corner of American life, and even those familiar with the ways of words can be taken by surprise. I followed snowboarding for a while (from a safe distance), the *freestylers* effortlessly *catching air* and doing *tricks*, *carving powder* that would spray up into the mountain sun. It was all so graceful and exciting that I didn't think much about snowboarding jargon, even though I couldn't interpret what I was watching without it. A *freestyler* is a *boarder* or *rider* who does ground and air *tricks* or 'fancy maneuvers'; *catching air* means 'leaving the ground'; *carving* is 'riding or curving on the edge of the board'; *powder* is the universal winter sports term for snow on which you can sport. Once I started to read snowboarding magazines (and then skateboarding and surfing magazines, because a lot of snowboarding jargon is borrowed from that of the other sports), I was soon buried in an avalanche of unfamiliar words.

Obviously, snowboarding was fun, not hard work like waiting tables, not the sort of activity that required a catalogue! Given the devil-may-care attitude adopted in public by riders, I didn't expect to read passages like this when I dipped into the surprisingly extensive boarding literature:

> Freestylers and half-pipe enthusiasts need plenty of lower leg motion so they lean toward short, lower highbacks. The freestyle highback stays out of the way of their legs, making it easier to twist and tweak during tricks. For the same reasons, free-stylers rarely — if ever — use a third shin strap.

It took me a minute to figure this out: *highbacks* are a type of *binding*, the apparatus that holds a boot onto the *board*. If you have a short, lower highback, you can exercise more control over your ankles and lower legs and do tricks with more style, for instance, by *grabbing* the board and *tweaking*, or twisting, the body. It's another example of the age-old field sports boot problem: how to maximize flexibility and support when each inevitably interferes with the other.

If you don't know your boarding lingo, you may not recognize the term *half-pipe*. You won't find it in most standard dictionaries, nor will you find it in slang dictionaries, so it's probably jargon: nonstandard language that is nonetheless not slang, even when it sounds slangy. *NOAD* is an exception, and defines *half-pipe* as follows:

half-pipe ▶**n.** a channel made of concrete or cut into the snow with a U-shaped cross section, used by skateboarders, rollerbladers, or snowboarders to perform jumps and other maneuvers.

NOAD may be following Barnhart and Metcalf in entering *half-pipe*, since the term is arguably *standard*—there's no other word in English that means what *half-pipe* means. Yet *half-pipe* is used only in boarding contexts, whether skate or snow: it's part of the equipment peculiar to those sports, and the name for the activity (the *half-pipe* or *half-piping*) that depends on the equipment. Note that the definition is a standard English explanation of a jargon term: snowboarders perform jumps and maneuvers, but *boarders* or *riders* do *tricks* (which involve, besides jumps, *slips*, *noses*, *spins*, *airs*, and other components). Of course, NOAD's definition can't go into particulars ad infinitum; the point of a definition is to abstract essential qualities of whatever is defined. But the definition demonstrates that either *half-pipe* or NOAD is out of its element.

Snowboarding, like all sports, is technical and develops a technical vocabulary so that practitioners can talk precisely and efficiently about things that matter to success. People who don't ride don't need to know that stuff and don't need to talk about it.

> Stand on your board and look at the rise or *kick* in the tip and tail shovels. Subtract these lengths from the board's *overall* length and you'll have the effective edge. In other words, the effective edge is simply the length of the edge that is actually touching the snow.

Boarders give names to important features of their equipment, and here the authors are conscious that a word like *kick* belongs to the jargon, so they italicize it, to warn the uninitiated. They don't bother to italicize *tip* and *tail shovels*, also part of the jargon, which suggests that, once you're deep in jargon, it's hard to remember what's special vocabulary and what's not.

But the unitalicized term of most interest is *effective edge*. Is it a "thing," like a *tail shovel*, or is it a "concept"? I opt for both (why make it easy?): every board's effective edge can be measured and physically touches snow, but *effective edge* is an abstract category of length and surface, like the ones you encountered in geometry and algebra. In fact, passages like this one remind me of nothing more than the "word problems" we did in school, problems that boarders solve in order to be good at what they do. They also discuss effective edge issues with other competent boarders and instruct new boarders on the importance of effective edge. Snowboarders may act like slackers, but they are pulling the wool over our eyes, probably so that we'll leave them alone and let them live on the edge, where they can cultivate their *edge awareness* 'knowledge of where the edge is and what it's doing'.

None of this implies that snowboarding is math and its jargon dull (or, for that matter, that math jargon is dull). In fact, the jargon can be as much fun as the sport looks; it can be just as casual, irreverent, inventive, and playful as any slang. If your left foot is in the front binding, you are riding regular; if your right foot is forward, you are riding *goofy* or *goofy-foot*. You can ride backwards, which is called riding *fakie*. You can do all kinds of *tricks*, some *freestyle* and some on the *half-pipe*, including (but far from limited to) the following:

- *Tail wheelie*: trick in which a boarder leans far back on a board and pulls its tip off the snow
- *Tail grab*: trick in which a boarder straightens the front leg (to straighten a leg is to *bone* or *bone out* that leg), pulls the back leg forward, and holds the tail of the board with the back hand
- *Ollie*: trick in which the boarder catches air by crouching, jumping up while bringing the front foot up and pushing forward, bringing both knees to the chest (in order to level the board), and then landing with both feet simultaneously on the ground
- *Nollie*: Ollie taken off the board's nose
- *Backside tweak air*: air in which a boarder straightens the legs at the beginning of the jump, then shifts weight slightly toward the tail while pulling the front leg up, grabs the nose on the backside edge with the front hand, and then tweaks
- *Chicken salad*: frontside air (*frontside* is simply what's in front of you, or the side of the half-pipe that is forward) in which a boarder grabs the board with the front hand between the legs on the heelside of the board, with the front leg boned out
- *Melancholy*: frontside air in which a boarder grabs the toe-side of the board with the front hand and bones out the front leg
- *Hoho plant backside*: invert (an *invert* is a jump in which the head is lower than the board) in which a boarder starts on the backside wall of the half-pipe with bent knees, shifts the upper body toward the tail, and, when the nose reaches the *coping* (the "lip"), jerks the body toward the tail, then pushes the board off the coping hard, plants both hands on the backside coping of the half-pipe, stretches the body upward to its full extension, and *stalls out* (holds the handstand for a long time)
- *Indy*: turn in which a boarder grabs the board between the toes with the back hand and bones out the front foot

- *Stalefish*: frontside air in which a boarder reaches between the heels with the back hand and bones out the back foot
- *Freshfish*: backside turn in which a boarder reaches between the heels with the back hand and bones out the back foot
- *Caballerial*: a 360 air that starts fakie but ends in a forward ride (in freestyling, a *half-cab* or 180 air of the same kind is typical).

There are probably some snowboarding philatelists. Generally, though, we think of stamp collectors and boarders as very different people who do essentially opposite things for recreation. But you cannot say that any of the above tricks is less technical, in its way, than the *Fine-Very Fine* designation for stamps. Success in one activity may require a different intelligence from that required in the other, but the jargon ends up just as precise and purposeful, whether murmured from a wingback chair by a crackling fire, magnifying glass at the ready, or whooped into big sky while carving up Montana slopes.

Obviously, snowboarding expects its jargon to be clever, irreverent, and casual, that is, slangier than that of philately. Note the persistent diminutive (*wheelie*, *ollie*, and the punning *stiffie* 'air in which boarder bones out both legs'), all sorts of playful items that originally referred to something more specific than the average etymologist can discover (*chicken salad*, *melancholy*, the *hoho* in *hoho plant backside*, and the *-fishes*), and blends (*nollie*, from *nose* + *ollie*, and *Caballerial*, from the name of its originator, Steve *Caballero* + ae*rial*). The tricks are hard, but the names make them sound *cazh*. Boarders like to execute the most demanding tricks with so much style that they look effortless.

At its best, restaurant jargon is just as colorful as boarding jargon. It also similarly gets the job done. No one in a busy restaurant can warn others on the *floor* at length about the obstacle course in which they are all working, so *Backs!* will have to do; a half-pipe routine would be over before you could explain the first two tricks to an observer in everyday language, so "She just did *backside tweak to fakie*" is the efficient substitute. Stamp collecting may be less pressured than serving and boarding, but sales catalogues can't repeat the definition of *Fine-Very Fine* every time it applies, so collectors learn and use the jargon to manage the hobby's complexity. And even stamp collectors talk about *perfs*, which is kind of *cazh*, when you think about it.

If we accept that it's more than usually slangy, we still haven't explained why American speakers so easily assume that snowboarding jargon is really just slang. I think that it's because most boarders are young; their slang gets mixed up with their jargon, and it's hard for stamp collectors to distinguish one from the other. Chris Daniele's comments in the magazine *SnowboarderGirl* (1999) illustrate the point (jargon in italics, slang in boldface):

> No *grab* in the history of snowboarding has inspired as much **trash-talking** as the *tindy*. For those who don't understand, allow me to explain: a *tindy* is a *grab* done on or behind your back foot on the *frontside edge* of your *board*. It's not an "*Indy*" *grab*. It's not a "*tail*" *grab*. It's a "*tindy*." Get it? It's not a real *grab*. It's a, "Hey look at me! I think I'm **rad**, but I don't really know what I'm doing!" *grab*. It's also usually done with a severely **retarded** *tweak*, which makes it look extra **lame**.

There are seven jargon words and four slang words, though some of the jargon is repeated and the slang is not. Some of the jargon, namely *tindy*, requires explanation, as jargon will, but the slang slips into the explanation easily because the speech is that of a boarder talking about boarding while at the same time being young.

When Melissa Larsen discusses boarding in Montana, in *Transworld Snowboarding* (March 1999), she spends whole paragraphs being young, and boarder jargon creeps in on occasion, just to focus her experience:

> The truth is, I couldn't **hack it** in Montana. Not many people really can, but at least I'm honest about it. Most of this story's pictures were taken of local *riders* by Stan Evans, a local photographer, over the course of an entire winter. The plan was for me to roll into town on the **down-low**, *solo-style* (i.e., no *imported pros* and media circus hoopla), **hook up** with Stan's **posse**, and just **chill**.

The balance of slang to jargon is reversed from that of the previous passage, but that probably wouldn't occur to someone who was neither young nor a rider. Both slang and jargon are varieties of in-group language and, by definition, are used by different groups. Most of us belong to more than one social group, and we don't necessarily stop demonstrating our allegiance to one just because we simultaneously demonstrate membership in another. So jargon and slang and other types of language co-occur in our speech; usually, however, we can distinguish them, if we care enough to take the time.

Much jargon could not conceivably be confused with slang, as it lacks all of the characteristics (delightful or annoying, depending on your point of view) that we associate with slang. If you look at the *UPS Stylebook* (1993), you'll discover a streamlined language of work that isn't casual, or irreverent, vivid, playful, or racy (it's far from racy). The United Parcel Service is a magnificently efficient company, and jargon helps it serve a high volume of *senders* and *addressees* successfully day after day. To manage that volume, UPS consolidates shipments to big addressees by packaging small packages in larger packages so that the small ones don't undergo repeated sorting. The order to follow this procedure is *bypass smalls*, and all of the OFFICIAL UPS slang is similarly clinical, pared to the communicative essentials. It's a language of fiat, handed down in a stylebook so that everyone "agrees" about how to address the work of UPS in official speech.

It probably will come as no surprise that the stylebook ends with a list of acronyms and abbreviations, some two hundred of them. Several of these are in general use, not unique to UPS, especially those related to computers or organizational structure, such as *RAM*, *ROM*, and *CFO*, but most by far have been invented by and imposed on UPSers. On one hand, this makes sense (though I am far from presuming that I know how to run corporate operations for UPS), because *splits* 'destination loads created for loading in hub operations' means the same thing to all UPS employees worldwide and is the reliable term. I don't know what that means, but I don't need to know. And fundamentally, there is no difference between *splits* or *expediter* or *highback*, as regards TYPE of speech. You can be distracted by the relative sterility of official UPS jargon, or by the relative slanginess of some restaurant and snowboard jargon, and imagine a functional difference when there isn't one.[6]

If official UPS jargon seems repressive and reminds you vaguely of William H. Whyte's *The Organization Man*, I take your point. You can bet that everyone who works at UPS is a member of the "team," or some other organizational entity that simulates familiarity and camaraderie, even though the jargon (among other things, I'm sure) bleaches that camaraderie of any color. Members of the "team" don't mind when they are subjected to *Master Standard Data (MSD)*, " a procedure that assigns predetermined time values to basic motions required

---

6   One thing about restaurant jargon that takes me by surprise, even after studying it for more than a decade, is its homogeneity: servers in California use terms familiar in Indiana, Ohio, New York, and New Jersey. An ollie in Maine is an ollie in Montana, and philatelists from Oregon and Mississippi both know what a *spoon cancellation* is. Slang is much less homogeneous (some items are universal in English, some are so local that only a few people use them, most fall somewhere between the extremes), and we can attribute the universality of jargon and its tendency to survive once introduced to the strong link between language and aspects of work or play. If the work or play doesn't vary, why would the language?

to accomplish any manual task according to the conditions under which it is performed," because they're just taking one for the team.

It would be difficult to follow UPSers around (for instance, you'd need special permission to ride in one of those brown trucks), but if you did, I am sure that you would hear UNOFFICIAL UPS jargon, the sort that builds the real camaraderie that supports the organization's efficiency and effectiveness. I suspect that unofficial UPS jargon resembles restaurant jargon more than it resembles the official alternative. Some of it would be directed at the official jargon and the corporate attitudes reflected in it. Work is social, and the language of work must serve social purposes on "natural" terms, originating with workers rather than a stylebook. Why put up with official UPS jargon? The answer is easy: fringe benefits. Save extreme sports for the weekend and you can play with language AND pay the hospital bills.

Though you can map the correspondence of any item of the server's lexicon to some aspect of restaurant work, though you can distinguish snowboarding jargon from slang in a snowboarder's speech even when they're jumbled up, and though most stamp collecting jargon and all official UPS jargon is plainly jargon and not slang, there are still problems of defining one relative to the other. For instance, when Pamela Munro and her colleagues compiled *Slang U!* (1989), a wonderful dictionary of UCLA student slanguage, they noted:

> A category of words that is often confused with slang is jargon: the specialized vocabulary of a particular group. While words which begin as jargon (in California, for instance, surfers' jargon) sometimes may be transferred to the general slang vocabulary of ordinary speakers, we have tried to eliminate true jargon from our Dictionary. (There is a sense, of course, in which many of the words on our list could be considered student jargon, since they refer to test-taking and other activities not usually practiced by the general population!)

It's true that *bubble* means something different for the university examinee than it does for the general population of English speakers. (It's what you fill in with a No. 2 pencil or, in this advanced era, a pen that writes in black ink.) But students live at school in ways that workers don't live at work: students are mostly just being when they are studenting, so their language ought to be slang rather than jargon.

At Winchester, one of England's great public schools, students have spoken a peculiar slang over so many centuries that it looks surprisingly like jargon. An item of Winchester slang is called a *Notion*, a term that is itself a Notion.

Notions are nothing if not playful, in just the way that slang spoken by students studying Logic, Latin Grammar, and Notions would be. Since sometime in the mid-eighteenth century, a student at Winchester has been called a *Wykehamist* (because the school was founded by William of Wykeham, bishop of Winchester, in 1382). *Wykehamist* is a Notion and, if you were one, you might once upon a time have been beaten if you were ignorant of either fact.

Actually, the term is more precise and jargonistic than I have just described. As you can read in Christopher Stray's edition of Charles Stevens's *Winchester Notions* (1998):

> **Wykehamist,** or **Wokehamist** (pronounced Wökehamist) (1) the school magazine, first published in 1866. (2) a present or past member of the school, the latter usually being called an Old Wykehamist or Old Wok. (3) A large spider. To be a Wykehamist (1917), a man had to have (a) spliced a hollis over Mill in a cathedral (i.e. thrown a pebble over College Mill wearing a top-hat). (b) been to Third Pot and Amphitheatre. (c) (i) been beaten three times; or (ii) been hotted into Otterburn by a man in a different div and House (for which purpose College East and West were rated as two Houses). But this last was not always considered a genuine method of becoming a Wykehamist.

So, if you were beaten three times for not knowing what a Wykehamist was, you would be one. Sounds like jargon to me, and so does the elaborate definition, which finds it difficult to avoid jargon. Also, slang terms aren't usually capitalized; capitalization smacks of authority, and slang is habitually rebellious, or, at least, nonconformist.

However, Winchester Notions are often slangy. For instance, *div* means 'division', and, because Wykehamists are not, like UPS employees, subject to MSD, they have plenty of time to say *division* in all of its syllables. Following Eble, *div* sounds more like fashion than necessity; it's casual, so would count as slang. Similarly, *disper* or *dispar* 'share of food' was clipped from Latin *dispertio* 'divide, serve forth', but came to mean 'unfairly unequal portion' (the folk etymology derives the term from Latin *dispar* 'unequal'; think English *disparity*). It's a casual term that acknowledges the hierarchical structure of teen social groups. And many a junior *commoner* (in this sense meaning 'member of the school not in College') often wrote such terms in a notebook stowed in his *scob*, or, as Stevens defines the term, "a double-lidded oak box, set at the angles of the squares of wooden benches or scrubbing-forms in School. One lid was kept up as a screen and the other was used as a desk to write on. In the box beneath, books and personal property were kept." *Scob* looks like an irreverent nonstandard synonym for desk, so slang rather than jargon.

Still, Winchester Notions are institutional, and only a certain degree of irreverence is permitted within institutionally approved grounds. The "level," slang or jargon, of Winchester Notions is confused because the social structure of young men living together is institutionalized as the school structure. Stevens apologizes at the outset of his dictionary: "Some of the Notions you will dislike as much as I do, because they represent the vocabulary of bullies at various stages in the history of the school." Stevens calls Notions a "dialect":

> Dialects survive because they enshrine words passed by mother to child, and by that child to the succeeding generation. Dialect is, in fact, mother-tongue, however small the area to which it applies: and the same is true of community-slang, composed as it is of a vocabulary passed by one generation to the next, to express subtleties of meaning known only to members of that community.[7]

As "all sorts of changes took place, buildings vanished, customs were discontinued, and large areas of the Notions vocabulary vanished with them." That is, language at Winchester changed with school circumstances (change typical of jargon), not simply because being requires change (change typical of slang).

The Notions was such a traditional feature of the school that new boys were "examined" in Notions by the prefect of school on the second Sunday of term. "The real test came on the last day of the first fortnight of term, when the Senior Praefect of each upstairs Chamber examined the Chamber in general, and new men in particular, in Notions." If Notions were slang, they would have been changing from generation to generation, not persisting by rote. There's nothing casual, irreverent, or playful about rote learning.

Notions dictionaries proliferated toward the end of the nineteenth century. Some have taken this to indicate the school's cultural "stability and pride," but, as Stevens observes, "The dictionary-making of the 1890s . . . responded to the denigration of Notions by outsiders. It was also, in part, a response to the perceived challenges of state intervention in the public schools." So Notions

---

7 Most linguists would resist using the term *dialect* for Notions, because a dialect is a version of a language, and languages have phonologies (sound systems), morphologies (systems of word structure), syntax (phrase, clause, and sentence structure), and semantics (meaning structures). The Notions are essentially a vocabulary, so more credibly a "community-slang," as Stevens puts it.

became more important to students at Winchester when they needed to assert an in-group identity more forcibly, as a sort of counteroffensive to the hostility they felt directed at them and the school. Notions had always figured as community slang, but when Wykehamists considered themselves an in-group of self-contained or isolated identity, rather than an identifiable group that mingled fluidly with the world at large, their language reflected the new rigidity of purpose and began to seem more like jargon than slang, without quite being one or the other.

The potential confusion (or interfusion) of slang and jargon is typical of schools. At Duke University, students undergo an arduous ritual in order to obtain tickets to the university's basketball games, because the number of available tickets is restricted by the size of the stadium and the number of nonstudent fans who obtain tickets by pleasanter means. Students gather in a tent city, called *Krzyzewskiville* after Duke's famous basketball coach, Mike Krzyzewski (the name is pronounced *shi she ski*, with the vowels pronounced as in *shin*, *shell*, and *ski*), or *Coach K*. Their activity is *tenting*, and their common purpose (not merely interest) is to get tickets and be a *Cameron Crazie* 'fan who sits in the student section of Cameron Stadium'.

A *tenter* is a member of a tent and cooperates with other members of that tent to keep the tent occupied according to the rules of tenting; the tent gets the tickets and distributes them among tenters according to prior agreement. Tenters may tent together regularly for a certain number of tickets, but not all tenters receive tickets for all games; the important thing is that all members of a tent conform to the tenting rules so that SOME members of the tent can attend the game in question. The Crazies set up tents in line in order to stay in line; that is, Crazies arrive days early, set up tents, and live out of the tents, according to certain rules.

The tents are registered and the number of people occupying the tent hoping to take a certain number of tickets is a matter of record. Members leave a tent unoccupied only when they don't anticipate *tent shifts* 'periods during which tents must be occupied to maintain their places in line'. The tents are checked periodically in order to test the seriousness of their members. Miss too many *tent checks*, and your tent will be *bumped*, or sent to the end of the tenting line (where no one gets tickets). In the last two days of tenting for a particular game, tenters are subject to *personal checks*; all members of a tent must be present for at least three personal checks, or the tent (and all its members) loses its place. If all members of the tent meet the personal check rule, then members will be given *bracelets* 'color-coded and numbered wristbands that ensure entrance to a game in the order of successful tents', that is, the tents that, for one reason or another, weren't bumped.

Tenters more interested in the activity of tenting than in obtaining bracelets are called *Camping Crazies* to distinguish them from tenters who suffer inclement weather, sleep deprivation, the inherent discomfort of tenting, and the indignity of tent checks and personal checks in order to attend a basketball game. For them, the social scene is the point and the language of tenting a sublexicon of the university's slang; indeed, even students who don't tent know the lingo, so *Crazie Talk* is "bigger" than a jargon. Nonetheless, most tenters view tenting as a purposeful activity, one that might develop a jargon over time; in any event tenting seems more purposeful than just being a Wykehamist, for instance. Crazie Talk identifies one as a Crazie, but if Crazies didn't share an objective, there wouldn't be any Crazie Talk. Wykehamists would have a slang, whether Notions or something else, just by virtue of belonging to the same group. Aaron Dinin, who includes a fine glossary of Crazie Talk at the end of his recent book, *The Krzyzewskiville Tales* (2005), defines *Crazie Talk* as "slang or jargon of the Cameron Crazies." Indeed, it isn't always clear which it is.

Though they are often distinct, we must admit that jargon and slang are sometimes so closely related as to be indistinguishable without sustained attention. The jargon that speakers enjoy lightens the burden of work or heightens the pleasure of other purposeful activity because it approximates the playfulness, irreverence, casualness, or vividness of slang. Jargon that speakers don't enjoy is clinically efficient or precise but will most likely be supplemented with jargon that promotes the social nature of work or play, if the work or play is, in fact social. In any event, whether language is slang or jargon (as contrasted with each another or with colloquial or even standard English) has little to do with the nature or quality of the words, but with whatever social purposes the words serve.

T. S. Eliot's famous Gumbie Cat, Jennyanydots, was a tabby social worker who saved the mice in her house from bad manners and behavior. She lined the louts up one day and ever after taught them music, crocheting, and tatting. One suspects that, before they ran into Jennyanydots, the mice were all chillaxin' in corners of unoccupied rooms, leaning against the skirting boards, speaking slang; once she got hold of them, though, they applied themselves to the useful, orderly employments to which she put them, and their conversation improved by reference to *picot loops* and *pizzicati* and similarly useful, orderly jargon.

LOWDOWN, OR POETRY ON THE DOWN LOW?

Slang has a bad reputation. Teachers and parents tell you not to use it because it leaves an impression of you that they think you don't want to leave. If the term *slang* carries negative connotations, it has some sketchy denotations, too. According to Dalzell and Victor's *New Partridge Dictionary of Slang and Unconventional English* (2006), *slang* can mean "sell drugs, especially crack cocaine" in the United States, obviously a fairly recent usage; but since as early as 1844 it has meant "berate someone with abusive language" in Great Britain; in Britain again, from an even earlier date (1789) to the present day, it has meant "exhibit or perform in a circus, fair or market, to perform on a stage." Drugs are bad, right? And "berating" is bad: contrary to what the definition seems to imply, you can't berate with kind words. Circuses and fairs are fun, but a little scary, like the clowns that inhabit them, because they are seedy sites of the con and the knowing glance. Of course, they are places where you can do things that you can't do in the legitimate world.

Lexicographers are cleverer than you may think: the evidence is often not in what they say when they define a word, but what they don't say. None of the definitions of *slang* reported from standard dictionaries earlier in this chapter suggests that slang is "low" or "seamy" or "seedy" or "trashy" or "nasty," and, though some slang surely can be characterized along these lines, slang isn't necessarily low or degraded speech. In fact, it can be poetic, even if it isn't poetry per se (remember punning, metaphorical *morning glory*). It needn't carry any social stigma at all, and most slang in the mouths of most young people isn't vulgar or an attempt to hide criminal activity, or anything of that sort. Slang may draw a social line between teen and parent, for instance, and it may be the language of being on one side of the line, being in which those on the other side do not partake. But not wanting your parents' noses in your business doesn't imply that you have anything other than adolescence of which to be ashamed.

Certainly, though, slang has been associated with low social elements in the past. As Tom Dalzell explains at the outset of his delightful book, *The Slang of Sin* (1998):

> Throughout [the book], I use the terms "sin" and "sinner" quite loosely, referring to conduct that is generally considered to be on the vice side of the scales. Do I truly believe that those who play pinball, shoot pool, or drink coffee are sinners? Hardly. I simply recognize that these activities, and those included as sins here, have been at times considered by society to be vices. . . . Sin and the seedy, vice and venery, the

underworld and the underside of life all produce one of the richest bodies of slang in the English language. It is no accident that many of the early slang dictionaries dealt heavily, if not exclusively, with the slang and cant of criminals and lowlifes, and patrons of sins.

We live in a permissive society — make of that what you will. Even if we prefer that our teens not join "boardwalk culture," many of them do, and we are inclined to indulge them, up to a point, say, at the Shore, once they have passed a certain age, once we can control them only by caging them, anyway. Some prefer not to pollute their bodies with coffee, but they refrain from public disapproval of others. When shooting pool meant trouble in River City, slang was even edgier than it is today.

James Sledd's classic description of slang starts in the pool hall but is subtler than it seems at first glance and applies pretty well today, even though most of what were once vices are now popular pastimes of the middle class:

> Typically slang is a para-code, a system of substitutes for statusful expressions which are used by people who lack conventional status and do not conduct important affairs of established communities. Slang flourishes in the areas of sex, drinking, narcotics, racing, athletics, popular music, and other crime — a "liberal" language of things done as ends in themselves by gentlemen who are not gentlemen and dislike gentility. Genteel pedagogues must naturally oppose it, precisely because slang serves the outs as a weapon against the ins. To use slang is to deny allegiance to the existing order, either jokingly or in earnest, by refusing even the words which represent convention and signal status; and those who are paid to preserve the status quo are prompted to repress slang as they are prompted to repress any other symbol of revolution.

Lots of people go to the track now, even women. Senior citizens fill buses destined for Atlantic City casinos. As activities, any of those Sledd mentions has its jargon, its purposeful language; being low undoubtedly requires low language, but it's harder to be low than it used to be. Sledd does not insist, however, that the disaffection that leads to slang be criminal; the inevitable disaffection of youth is sufficient. And surely every one of us denies allegiance to the existing order now and then, at least jokingly, even if she stops short of joining the revolution. Every one of us is convinced, rightly or wrongly, that she is one of the outs, with a grudge against the ins that she can only exercise socially in slang, the patchwork jeans she wears, the alt rock she listens to, the pork rinds she eats. Surely, at some level, all Americans must dislike gentility — gentility is undemocratic.

Even church ladies acknowledge this on occasion, when they eat fried chicken at the church social with their fingers.

J. E. Lighter, who knows as much about slang as anybody (and there are several Anglo-American scholars who know quite a lot), elegantly pares Sledd's somewhat polemical comment to its essentials:

> Slang deviates stylistically from other sorts of English; its hallmark is its undignified or indecorous tone. Indeed, this is the critical distinction between slang and the merely informal. Whereas the merely informal or colloquial imparts a natural, unstilted tone to discourse, slang is conspicuously divergent, taking the place of words that lie near the familiar core of standard English. The aim and chief function of slang is to lower and disavow the dignity of discourse.

John Ayto, in his introduction to the *Oxford Dictionary of Slang* (1998), agrees that "our longstanding love affair with the undignified bits of our language—the unguarded language of conversation, the quirky slang of in-groups, the colourful outbursts of lexis in extremis—has assured us a continuing tradition of collecting such words in dictionaries." Dalzell, Sledd, Lighter, Ayto, and any thoughtful observer of language agree that language can be unguarded, quirky, colorful, and most especially undignified without suggesting criminal activity or even shameful behavior. Even if you stand on your dignity once in a while, you are probably more comfortable when you are a little undignified. I know that the rest of us are.

However easygoing our social and linguistic attitudes may be now, the lines between acceptable and antisocial behavior were once easier to draw. Though slang is neither a modern nor an English invention, the first sustained treatment of slang in English, a dictionary, comes along relatively late. A *New Dictionary of the Terms Ancient and Modern of the Canting Crew* was compiled by "B. E. Gent." and published in 1698 or 1699. The first freestanding dictionary of cant in English (the earlier ones were parts of other books), it contained more than four thousand entries for words supposedly used by the criminal element. Earlier glossaries had also focused on cant, the language of beggars and thieves, and that early notion of slang as irremediably low has dogged its reputation ever since.

In the *Canting Crew*, the curious (or paranoid) could read about thieves' slang for money, including the general term *quidds* 'money', and terms for more specific denominations, like *pig* 'sixpence' and *smelts* 'half guineas'. After they had stolen your pigs, they would *snack* 'share, go halves' on them, an early version of bringing home the bacon. Dictionaries like *Canting Crew* purported to collect useful information about low life and language for cautious citizens, but they were at least equally sensational. Readers found out that thieves might be across the road from home, *casing* it, after which one rogue might say to the other (in one's hearing), "Friend John, or sweet Tom, 'tis a bob Ken, Brush upon the Sneak." If you had read *Canting Crew* you would know at once that you were in the presence of a *ken-miller* 'housebreaker' who had just advised a crony, " 'Tis a good House, go in if you will, but tread softly, and mind your Business." With that, you would notify the authorities and preserve your worldly goods. Or you would unless one of the thieves (they worked in teams, of course) decided to *amuse* you, which *The New Canting Dictionary* (1725), one of the many successors to "B. E. Gent." 's work, defined as follows: "TO AMUSE, in a *Canting Sense*; to fling Dust in the Eyes; to invent strange Tales to delude Shop-keepers and others, from being upon their Guard."

All of this is very Dickensian. Recall the speech of one Jack Dawkins, the Artful Dodger, on meeting Oliver Twist for the first time: "Hullo, my covey! What's the row? . . . I suppose you don't know what a beak is, my flash com-pan-i-on. . . . I'm at a low-water-mark myself—only one bob and a magpie; but *as* far *as* it goes, I'll fork out and stump. Up with you on your pins. There! Now then! Morrice!" *Covey* is the familiar form of *cove*, thieves' slang for 'fellow' from the mid-sixteenth century. Today the first sentence would translate to something like, "Yo, wassup dog?" and "What's the row?" to something like "What's the noise? What's happening?" A *beak*, as the Dodger goes on to explain, is a 'magistrate', and *flash* means 'hip, in the know, fly'. A *bob* is a 'shilling' and a *magpie* a 'halfpenny'; *fork out* is still in use to mean 'pay', and *stump* is merely a synonym for the same. *Pins* are legs and the command *Morrice!* means 'move on', like a Morris dancer. Most of the passage's unfamiliar terms originated in the late eighteenth century or early nineteenth; some of them (according to the *OED*) were brand-new in the 1830s, the very decade in which *Oliver Twist* (1838) was published, which means that Mr. Dickens must have been pretty flash himself.

Oliver has spent most of his life in a workhouse somewhere in England, far from the city and its vices. So when the Dodger knocks on Fagin's den of iniquity, gets the call and responds, "Plummy and slam," or '[everything is] as it should be', Oliver doesn't suspect a password. Nor does he ask why he is set to picking the monograms out of the scores of *wipes* 'handkerchiefs' hanging throughout the house. He doesn't ask anyone to explain what it means to say that a wallet is *well lined* 'full of money'. He is, says Charley Bates, one of the Dodger's associates, remarkably *green* 'inexperienced, naïve'. And then he goes out on the game with Fagin's lads:

What was Oliver's horror and alarm as he stood a few paces off, looking on with his eyelids as wide open as they would possibly go, to see the Dodger plunge his hand into the old gentleman's pocket, and draw from thence a handkerchief! To see him hand the same to Charley Bates; and finally to behold them, both, running round the corner at full speed.

As "B. E. Gent." explains, the Dodger has merely *"Tip[ped] the Cole to Adam Tiler* c. give your Pick-pocket Money presently to your running Comrade," and the whole incident proves the value of books like the *Canting Crew*. If Oliver had just read more about the language of thieves, he would have been spared a lot of mischief.

Many assume that slang originates in the need for people doing bad things to obscure their activities. It's not a sound assumption, exactly, as I've already suggested. It's not true that, if you're not doing anything wrong, you have nothing to worry about! A desire for privacy would not be obsolete just because we were all virtuous in our own eyes; we want privacy because we don't trust the eyes, or ears, of others and are unwilling to submit our private thoughts to their judgments. So we sometimes speak in whispers, sometimes indirectly, and sometimes both. Having made the point, though, criminal argot is no fiction, even if the earliest glossaries and dictionaries of it include plenty of fiction among the facts.

England's infamous rhyming slang is usually identified with argot, as historically it seems to have been. It may have developed in the late eighteenth century; by the mid-nineteenth century, it had been exposed. As Henry Mayhew wrote, in *London Labour and the London Poor* (1851), "The new style of cadgers' cant is done all on the rhyming principle." By the end of the same decade John Hamden Cotton's *The Slang Dictionary* (1859) recorded examples of rhyming slang. In fact, while some of this clever, diversionary speech has something to do with crime, and some of it is decidedly "low," much of it is neither and merely expresses its practitioners' linguistic exuberance. It is probably worth considering that rhyming slang started as a feature of the language of London's East End, once called Cockney. The term *Cockney* was disparaging and the association between East Enders and crime a result (at least mostly) of social prejudice.

For instance, *ginger pop* means 'cop', *Sweeney Todd* refers to the London constabulary's rapid response unit, called the Flying Squad (T. S. Eliot's Macavity, the Mystery Cat, was such a formidable criminal that he was, we are told, "the

Flying Squad's despair"), and *bubble and squeak* (the name of a potato and cabbage dish) stands in for 'beak' (which in turn stands in for 'magistrate'). You see how it works: the rhyming phrase need have nothing to do in substance with what's really meant (ginger pop is not a policeman, etc.), but the last word rhymes with the word that the speaker has in mind. Somehow, until the rhyming phrase conventionally replaces the word that's meant, the word that's meant has to be in the speaker's mind; more remarkable, it has to be in the intended hearer's mind, too, or the rhyming phrase won't make any sense. Speaker and hearer have to be on the same page, as we say today. Because argot is closer to jargon than to slang, a language of shared purpose, this meeting of the minds is plausible. But once rhyming slangers got going they couldn't stop, and they rhymed more from simply being than from purpose: *trouble and strife* meant 'the wife', and so did the sarcastic *Duchess of Fife*. *D'Oyly Carte*, from the name of the production company associated with W. S. Gilbert and Arthur Sullivan, came to mean 'fart'. In any case, the experts quoted at the beginning of this section are clearly right: the Flying Squad, a fancy London theater — these are statusful, relatively dignified things talked of in a way that mocks their dignity.

After a while those the rhymer tries to fool may catch on to the pattern and guess at true meanings. What can argot do to preserve secrecy then? The answer is to clip the rhyme from the phrase: rather than *ginger pop*, you can refer to a cop as *ginger*; by the same technique, *Sweeney Todd* becomes, more familiarly, *the Sweeney*. But such clipping may not reflect criminal intention at all. Consider *D'Oyly* to mean 'fart'; there's no crime to speak of, only impoliteness, but the rhyming word is clipped nonetheless. After a while, from frequent use, East Enders came to know certain rhyming phrases; some rhymes were coined on the fly, but others become conventional and fixed, until the rhyme was unnecessary, at least to the flash cove. The rest of us are confused, but that's not because East Enders are being dodgy; rather, it's because we aren't East Enders, because we don't belong to the group that defines itself in part by rhyming (and eventually not rhyming) slang. Rhyming slang is clever and trades on familiarity among speakers; so do clipped rhyming phrases, but more so.

If you really want to speak freely around those who shouldn't know your secrets, learn how to form back slang or center slang. When you are next in your local, order a *top o' reeb* instead of 'pot of beer', but hope that the bartender understands the slang, or you may be *eighty-sixed* 'thrown out', not just for the night but for the whole *kew* 'week'. Don't blame the bartender, though, who may not be the right *nosper* 'person' for the *bloomin' emag* 'bloomin' game'. Better that you be *ietqui* 'quiet' than play the *oolerfer* 'fool'. The last two are examples of center slang; the rest (with the exception of *eighty-sixed*) is back slang, though *nosper* falls between the categories. Obviously, the rules of center slang are especially complicated. Unless you are talking about something worth hiding with a friend who knows your business, everyday slang might serve your interests better. Do not ask for someone's number in center slang. To prevent a worse headache, don't attempt center slang on the morning after.

In a permissive society, is secrecy of the kind that classic argot, like rhyming, back, or center slang provides really necessary? It would be if you were doing something that most people consider terribly wrong and that might tip the ginger beer. A college student might admit to her parents that she occasionally smokes *pot* or *weed* and that she didn't drive home from a party because everyone got pretty *messed up*. The terms are intergenerational slang for 'marijuana' and 'drunk', and young and old, approving or disapproving, might agree that there isn't anything really worth hiding. The activities in question may be somewhat stigmatized socially, but they aren't stigmatized enough to prompt argot. In fact, the casual use of terms for unruly behavior suggests their slanginess.

Use of *methylenedioxymethamphetamine* or *methylenedioxyethylamphetamine*, abbreviated clinically to MDMA and MDEA, and known familiarly as *ecstasy*, is not talked about openly, except within very restricted groups—the stigma against use is too great and legal penalties for use too dire. The vocabulary of MDMA and MDEA use is slang resembling argot, partly because most of it certainly originated in argot. Here is a short list of slang terms for *ecstasy* in various forms (pill, powder, solution), and in various combinations with other drugs (heroin, LSD, PCP, Ketamine, etc.), mostly culled from Dalzell and Victor's *New Partridge Dictionary of Slang and Unconventional English* (2006), but supplemented with a few terms from other sources: *Adam, Adam and Eve, baby slits, Bart Simpson, bean, biscuit, booty juice, Californian, candy flip, China white, chocolate chip cookies, chocolate chips, clarity, cloud nine, coke biscuit, coke burger, crow's feet, decadence, Dennis the Menace, Dexedrine, diamond, disco biscuit, doctor, domex, double cherry drop, double stacks, double stack white Mitsubishi, dove, driver, E, East and West, e-ball, e-bomb, echo, eck, ecker, ecky, ecstasy, Edward, Egyptian, Elaine, erecstasy, essence, eva, Eve, exiticity, euphoria, fantasia, fast in, fido dido, fishies, flower flipping, gaggler, go, gum, happy, happy drug, happy pill, Harry Hill, H bomb, heaven sent, herbal bliss, hit, hug drug, hydro, iboga, ice, Kleenex, K capsule, lemon and limes, little fella, love doctor, love drug, Love Potion #9, love trip, lover's speed, Lucky Charmz, M25, mad bastard, madman, madwoman, Malcolm X, M and M, mitsubishi/mitsi, mizzi, New Yorker, nineteen, Number 9, om, parma violet, Partick Thistle, part timer, Pete Tong, phase 4, pill, Pink Panther, pit bull, Playboy, pollutant, power pill, red hot, rhubarb and custard, rib, ritual spirit, roca, roll, roller, running, saucer, Scooby snacks, sextasy, shamrock, slammin', slit, smiley, snowball, snowheart, space pill, Stacy, superman, Super Mario, tangerine dream, Thatcher, thunderdome, trumpets, tutu, ultimate xphoria, USP, V & E, vitamin E, VW, wafer, white robin, wigit, wild flower, Woody Woodpecker, X, X-Files E, x-ing, XTC,* and *yoke.*

Some of these terms are formed along lines well established by earlier drug slang. *Californian,* for instance, is the twenty-first-century clubbing parallel to the earlier clubbing term *Bolivian* 'cocaine', or the earlier *Acapulco gold* 'marijuana'. Other drugs have assumed personal names on the basis of shared initials or syllables, so that *Benzedrine* becomes *Bennie* (or the more formal, less obvious *Benjamin*) and *cocaine* becomes *Charlie* (in America) or *Cecil* (in the United Kingdom). *Edward* and *Elaine* for *ecstasy* thus come as no surprise; neither does *Stacy,* which, like *Mary Jane,* takes liberties with sounds and stress while adapting the common name of the drug in question.

Abbreviations of various kinds, not to mention innovative extensions of abbreviated forms, apparently have served ecstasy users well: *E* takes *ecstasy*'s initial, as does *Vitamin E*; *X* initializes the first syllable, as does the clever placement of ecstasy's first syllable as the final syllable of *Kleenex,* where no one expects a drug reference. The forms *eck* and *ecky* stop just short of taking the whole first syllable; so does *echo,* less obvious (better argot) than *eck* because it has a homophone in standard English, one that might come up in conversation. If everyone who might interfere with your clubbing (or raving) lifestyle thinks of your club drug as *ecstasy,* then you might refer to it as *M & M,* borrowing the less suspicious initials from *MDMA,* and then camouflaging them as an all-American confection. A night of *rolling* in the clubs, all *faced* on *M & Ms,* sounds more like a slumber party than a rave to the uninitiated.

Some abbreviated and extended forms are more successful than others. It's unlikely that the most obtuse parents, let alone the police, would fall for *XTC, ultimate xphoria, sextasy,* or *erecstasy,* a combination of Viagra and ecstasy, also known, abbreviatedly, as *V & E.* This last item, you'll note, is excellent slang. Though less colorful than *erecstasy,* it more effectively serves to identify an in-group because it's less obvious; also, it's casual, but wicked, a play on your parents' *G & T.* Everyday words used metaphorically to represent a pill, like *bean, biscuit, gum,* or *saucer,* work better than something flamboyant, like *ultimate exphoria.* You can even go with the literal *pill.* If that seems risky, too transparent to disguise from the 'rents, just ask a friend to invite *Harry Hill* to the club — *Harry Hill* to rhyme with *pill*, referring simultaneously to Henry Hill, the coked-up mobster antihero of Martin Scorsese's film *Goodfellas* (1990).

Unless you knew that they all somehow referred to MDMA, you would not otherwise associate most of the terms in this list with one another; they represent a wide variety of word types and types of word formation. Variety and ephemerality confuse parents, the law, club owners and bouncers, and nonusing youths who may inform on users or simply disapprove of use in ways that affect users' social status among their peers. There are 143 items in the list above, approximately 120 of which are distinct from one another. If we attribute these to the period 1985 to 2005 (according to *HDAS*, *ecstasy* and *Adam* are first recorded in 1985), then there are at least six terms for MDMA introduced for each year, and these account only for those recorded in dictionaries and captured ad hoc from a few other sources; there were likely many more terms briefly popular in the underworld that never surfaced into public awareness.[8]

The list of terms that did make it into dictionaries, however, is an odd mixture of argot, jargon, and slang; it demonstrates how easily terms can cross from one category into another or even occupy more than one category simultaneously, depending on who uses them, with whom, and for what reasons. Argot is slang that hides criminal activity, but it is also criminal jargon. Makers and dealers use any of these synonyms for MDMA professionally, purposefully, in order to sell drugs, make money, and evade legal restraint. A *candy flip* is one part MDMA and three parts LSD; *chocolate chip cookies* mix MDMA and heroin or methadone. It's important for dealers to know what they're buying from makers and what

8 The numbers given here are essentially fictional, and I wouldn't even give them were they not likely a gross underestimate of the terms actually once used as synonyms for MDMA. The *New Partridge Dictionary of Slang and Unconventional English* (2006) supplies most items in the foregoing list, and it marks the terms as "US" or "UK," supposedly indicating where they were used. There are many more terms marked "UK" than "US," but I am suspicious of the value of the labels because I have American evidence of several restricted to the United Kingdom. From what I can determine, Terry Victor, the dictionary's U.K. editor, had at hand a few British sources that listed many *ecstasy* synonyms and then labeled the entries as "UK" even though the term's provenance may have been wider, though *Fido Dido* (the name of a Spanish cartoon character), *yoke* (recorded in Ireland), and some other terms are more surely restricted than others. This is a problem of labeling not uncommon in dictionaries: the label locates a source that seems to exclude a range of use. But knowing where a word is used is not the same as knowing all places in which a word is used.

they're selling in the club drug market. If it weren't so insecure, MDMA dealers would keep their trade secrets straight in a handy color-illustrated reference, like the *Scott Catalogue*.

There is surely a social aspect to the development and use of such terms among makers and dealers. They identify one another by correct usage. Teachers try to convince students who buy drugs from dealers that slang is rarely correct usage, while dealers turn the standard of usage on its head, just as Sledd argued they would. They probably take collective pleasure in the creation of newly useful terms known only to them. Whoever decided to put red and black stripes on a tab of ecstasy and then call that manifestation of the drug *Dennis the Menace* (by association with the colored stripes on Dennis's shirt) must have felt doubly clever, like whoever coined *in the weeds* or *blender tender*. And, like servers, drug professionals probably derive incidental pleasure from using such terms.

Clubbers (or ravers) use any of the synonyms recreationally in order to provide for a good time and to discuss that good time (before, during, afterward). Of course, they also want to evade suspicion, which requires that speech restrict knowledge of their activities to the in-group of ecstasy users. But there is also a social aspect to that in-group's in-language: it's hip, or peculiarly in the know. The shared experiences and understandings, and the shared language that expresses them, are part of the recreation, part of simply being a clubber who rolls. It seems a stretch to view such language as purposeful in the nature of jargon: rolling is not a hobby, and the term *rolling* is not one item in a lexical web that articulates the body of knowledge necessary to pursue an avocation like stamp collecting or snowboarding.

Whichever category a term inhabits at the moment of speech, it strives for maximum effectiveness as camouflage. *E* 'ecstasy' is easily presented as though it were *e*- 'e-mail' ("Hey, you've got e — CU2nite"); *X* and *ex* ("I'll be there at 10:00 — your *ex* will be there"), *Kleenex* (as in "Bring lots of Kleenex"), and *gum* ("I've got enough gum for all of us") easily hide a life of crime, too. Parents overhearing your cell conversation may even applaud mentally when they hear you say that what you really need is *clarity*. But users (of slang and clarity) also like being in the know and sharing the know with in-group members, whether it's the feeling MDMA provides (hence, *ecstasy*), the symbol on the pill (*Pink Panther*, *Bart Simpson*), or the hip casualness of *biscuit* and *wafer*.

Certainly *wafer* will serve as an innocuous replacement for *tablet of MDMA*: the slang term may describe the physical resemblance between a tablet and a wafer; or it may be the pill you can't resist even though you know that you should, the wafer that blows your mind, analogous to the "wafer-thin mint" that blows out Mr. Creosote's stomach in Monty Python's *The Meaning of Life* (1983); or it may be an irreverent allusion to the communion wafer and the transcendence, the ecstasy or clarity or love, that it stimulates. All of these interpretations of *wafer* may be inventions after the fact, as with *suck*: products of discourse rather than etymology. Sometimes both camouflage and etymology prove ironic: PCP is also known as *embalming fluid*; as a result, kids who thought they were in the know started soaking joints in actual embalming fluid. Joints embalmed with PCP are called *sherms* (from the Nat Sherman brand of cigarette); joints embalmed with embalming fluid are called *fry*. Slang misapprehended leads to human tragedy. That won't improve slang's reputation, though slang itself is hardly at fault.

Many pill names are really brand names, meant to market ecstasy to users: they promise certain effects, they serve as the club underworld's safety seals of approval, and they entice users with that in-group feeling, a product of the playfulness, irreverence, and pop cultural relevance of the names. Some terms in the long list above are generic, referring to anything anyone offers as MDMA.[9] Several, though, verbally represent the emblems cut into pills, or their colors or shapes: *crow's feet, Dennis the Menace, dove, Fido Dido, Pink Panther, VW, white robin, Woody Woodpecker*, and perhaps *shamrock* belong to this group. So do *Partick Thistle* (a Scottish soccer team), *part timer*, and *Pete Tong* (a DJ associated with the rave scene), all fanciful expansions of the *PT* that marked the pills so named. These are all brand names in an integrated marketing campaign: they prompt association with the corresponding emblems, just as the emblems are meant to prompt the corresponding names.

All of these names for MDMA are nonetheless slang, not just because you and I know them but because we CAN know them, because, even if they originated in jargon, they are now available to all Americans for use in discussing the American scene. They are implicated in the culture, and being part of American culture involves knowing some of those terms and something about what

---

9   Sometimes a word that buyers think guarantees ecstasy is actually another drug, as when the compound PMA was sold as ecstasy under the name *double stack white Mitsubishi*. Sometimes names specific to other drugs, such as *China White*, which is somewhat specific for a variety of heroin, are used generically for MDMA. *Dexedrine* is a trademark for a brand of amphetamine (you can't get more specific than that), but is similarly generic for ecstasy. As names for drugs other than the one meant, these terms offer a strange sort of camouflage.

they represent. Obviously, knowing about ecstasy and raves and clubs doesn't involve doing drugs, let alone manufacturing them or selling them. But, let's face it, if you and I know about *biscuit*, *Kleenex*, and *M & M*, then they aren't very effective argot. Neither is *clarity*, which was outed in the *Miramonte High School Parents Club Newsletter* (November 26, 2001); neither is *go* since Doug Liman made a movie about an ecstasy deal gone wrong called, you guessed it, *Go!* (1999). If any of these terms still works as jargon as well as slang, that's up to the makers and dealers, who have to sort out what jargon is useful when it's no longer argot.

Somewhere on the line from the language of secrecy to the language of everyday being slang gathers a head of poetic steam and accelerates past colloquial speech. Slang is fast and exciting, and you can't sustain the speed and the rush, so you'll always slow into plain English again. But every word of the ride was worth it. The raver's lexicon includes a lot of poetic language, bits and pieces of what might add up to poetry if the raver were dedicated to poetic discourse rather than rolling and raving.

Consider *Adam*, a near anagram of *MDMA* that personifies the drug for purposes of veiled conversation. MDMA's consort drug is MDEA, and the *E* is expanded to *Eve*. A cocktail of MDMA and MDEA is *Adam and Eve*. But these terms amount to more than mere language play, more than convenient personifications (either of which is mildly poetic in itself). They allude to the temptation and fall of our first parents, to the illicit euphoria, clarity, and ecstasy that Eve experiences in *Paradise Lost*. It's fair to say that Milton's Eve gets totally faced on forbidden fruit.

If you doubt the poeticity of these names or their connections to canonical poetry, not so fast: *El Cid* is a synonym for *LSD* and *acid* that takes the first initial of LSD as an initial and then pronounces the second and third as an acronym in order to camouflage the drug with the name of a hero of medieval Spanish romance. Remember that ravers and trippers are sometimes university students or graduates: the supposed lowness of their drug use gets mixed up with their relatively statusful social position. Tossing off allusions to epic and romance while scoring drugs is certainly casually irreverent enough to qualify as slang.

Some slang for MDMA is affective metaphor: a pill can't be clarity or ecstasy, but words for feelings that pills engender, *clarity* and *ecstasy*, can shift to name the pills. Other terms, like *biscuit* and *saucer*, are superficial metaphors that compare two mostly unlike things along the few characteristics they share. Still others are very deeply metaphorical, in the sense that the drug is several meta-phorical steps away from the slang term:

Om is a sound made during meditation.

Meditation leads to peace, clarity, and perhaps even ecstasy.

Producing om causes the body to vibrate.

Meditative vibration resembles the physical and psychoactive effects of drugs.

(Buzz is a slang metaphor for those physical and psychoactive effects.)

Peace, clarity, and ecstasy are associated with a meditative buzz.

MDMA induces a physical and psychoactive buzz accompanied by sensations of peace, clarity, and ecstasy.

MDMA resembles om and the meditation in which om figures in just these features.

Om is an appropriate metaphorical synonym for MDMA.

In spite of the complexity we tease out after the fact, om most likely was not created after prolonged deliberation, as the result of a poetic "process," but in a flash of insight ignited by a sound, a sensation, a verbal association, or who knows what?

This sort of indirection is common enough in slang, for instance, in rhyming slang like Harry Hill (which is also casual, because it familiarizes Henry Hill), lemon and limes, and rhubarb and custard. Lemon and lime is rhyming slang for 'time'; lemon and limes, in turn, rhymes 'good times'. According to the New Partridge Dictionary of Slang and Unconventional English (2006), rhubarb and custard was inspired by the red and yellow colors of a specific MDMA tablet; the dictionary also suggests that the -barb in rhubarb might indicate the presence of barbiturate in the pill. But here is an equally plausible explanation: rhubarb is repeated by actors as background speech, and it has come to mean 'nonsense' as a result; custard cream, often clipped to custard, means 'dream'; rhubarb and custard is a 'babbling dream', like a night on ecstasy.

Hidden rhymes and deep metaphors are especially useful in argot; criminals expect secrets and are quick to catch on when slang is camouflage for illicit activity. But where nothing more is at stake than to which group you belong or the casual irreverence that helps you deal with starch and suits, metaphor doesn't have to try so hard: weed for 'marijuana', blow for 'cocaine', piss for 'lager'. Slang is so essentially and casually metaphorical that frequent use of a term bleaches the figurative color right out of it: hanging and chilling are metaphors for 'spending time' and 'taking it easy', that is, metaphors for just being.

The relationship between slang and poetics has long been acknowledged, especially as regards various species of allusion and metaphor. Though Noah

Webster defined *slang* as "low, vulgar, unmeaning language" (1828), Ralph Waldo Emerson advocated slang's place in American speech not long after, when he asserted in *The Poet* (1844), "Language is fossil poetry," for slang is the poetry in speech that has not yet ossified. "What can describe the folly and emptiness of scolding like the word *jawing*?" he asked in his *Journals* (1840). Walt Whitman took the hint and expounded the ideology of slang in his wonderful essay "Slang in America" (1885):

> Slang, or indirection [is] an attempt of common humanity to escape from bald lit-eralism, and express itself illimitably, which in the highest walks produces poets and poems, and doubtless in pre-historic times gave the start to, and perfected, the whole immense tangle of the old mythologies. . . . Slang, too, is the wholesome fer-mentation or eructation of those processes eternally active in language, by which froth and specks are thrown up, mostly to pass away, though occasionally to settle permanently and chrystallize.

Some people say that slang is an especially American phenomenon. The claim is exaggerated, yet it would seem that affinity with slang is embedded in the Amer-ican Romantic ideology that still contributes profoundly to American thought and the American way of life.

Henry Bradley, one of the OED's principal editors, wrote, "Among the impulses that lead to the invention of slang the two most important seem to be the desire to secure increased vivacity and the desire to secure increased sense of intimacy in the use of language." In 1931 Earle Welby favored viewing slang as linguistic rebellion, on terms somewhat allied to Sledd's: "Some slang originates in honor-able discontent with the battered or bleached phrases in far too general use"; it is "the plain man's poetry, the plain man's aspiration from penny plain to twopence coloured." H. L. Mencken took a similar view in *The American Language* (1936):

> Slang originates in the effort of ingenious individuals to make the language more pungent and picturesque — to increase the store of terse and striking words, to widen the boundaries of metaphor, and to provide a vocabulary for new shades of differences in meaning. As Dr. Otto Jespersen has pointed out, this is also the aim of poets (as, indeed, it is of prose writers), but they are restrained by consideration of taste and decorum, and also, not infrequently, by historical or logical consider-ations. The maker of slang is under no such limitations.

S. I. Hayakawa bleached the sentiments of Welby and Mencken some when he referred to slang as "the poetry of everyday life" in *Language in Action* (1941), but that book was a seminal college text and has helped to advance slang's cause. And Thomas E. Gaston titled (of all things) a filmstrip "Slang: The Poetry of Group Dynamics" (1973). It is not clear to what extent the slang impulse to enliven speech, the impulse to stand out, mingles with the slang impulse toward social intimacy, the impulse to fit in. At times they seem like oil and water, but at others the social and poetic motivations emulsify into one linguistic practice.

Connie Eble compares slang and poetry in "Slang as Poetry" (1988) and throughout *Slang and Sociability* (1996). J. E. Lighter, in his excellent contribution to *English in North America* (volume 6 of the *Cambridge History of the English Language*), explains metaphorical processes in slang but goes on to draw a bright line between "poetic" as a loose adjective to describe stylistic aspects of slang and "real" poetry:

> Even at its most radical, poetry celebrates continuity with the past; poets, after all, recognize poetry itself as a venerable artistic pursuit and place themselves somewhere within (or sometimes at the end of) that tradition. Slang, in contrast, rejects tradition; the lay public experiences slang idioms as novel (one of the chief reasons for using them) and thinks of slang as a twentieth-century phenomenon. . . . More tellingly, a central purpose of poetic language is to prompt introspective reflection; a central function of slang is to short-circuit reflection and to exalt snap judgments and habitual attitudes among social peers. Indeed, each time a slang term is repeated, unthinking evaluative norms are reinforced. Irrationalism has always had its voice in civilized life, and this frankly anti-rational function of slang is what underlies the objections so often expressed by educators and essayists.

Conversation and poetry are certainly different modes of discourse: the rules and aims of one are not identical to the other, and slang as you and I use it is not the same as poetic diction. While Lighter is certainly right about poetry as a product of reflection, and about slang as speech that short-circuits reflection, he may not give slang enough credit as inspired speech. No one labored over their inventions, yet *Adam and Eve* and *om* are susceptible to interpretation as though we had encountered them in poetry. As I demonstrate in chapter 3, slang poetics far exceed metaphor and features of sound, like rhyme and alliteration, that we usually associate with poetry.

So we might take seriously the proposition that slang is poetry on the down low, and sometimes lowdown poetry on the down low, but rarely, if ever, merely lowdown. As Whitman wrote of slang in *An American Primer* (1856), "These words ought to be collected — the bad words as well as the good. Many of these bad words are fine." Upon Whitman's admonition, John Stephen Farmer and William Ernest Henley, in *Slang and Its Analogues Past and Present* (1890–1904); Eric Partridge, in the *Dictionary of Slang and Unconventional English* (1937), *Shakespeare's Bawdy* (1947), and *Dictionary of the Underworld, British and American* (1960); Harold Wentworth and Stuart Berg Flexner, in *Dictionary of American Slang* (1960); Richard A. Spears, in *NTC's Dictionary of American Slang and Colloquial Expressions* (1989); Robert L. Chapman, in *Dictionary of American Slang*, 3rd edition (1995); Gary Simes, in *Dictionary of Australian Underworld Slang* (1993); Clarence A. Major, in *Juba to Jive: A Dictionary of African-American Slang* (1994); John Ayto, in the *Oxford Dictionary of Slang* (1998); Jonathon Green, in *Cassell's Dictionary of Slang*, 2nd edition (2005); Tom Dalzell and Terry Victor, in the *New Partridge Dictionary of Slang and Unconventional English* (2006); and J. E. Lighter, in the monumental *Historical Dictionary of American Slang* (1994–), just to name the most prominent among many, have recorded and accounted for slang in a variety of admirable and accessible ways. Browse through these works at your leisure. If you still can't wrap your stylistic imagination around the vital paradox that bad is fine, that what's low is exalted, you will never appreciate slang.

WHAT IT IS

As James B. McMillan put it in 1978, and as I said at the outset of this chapter, "A new slang term is instantly recognizable, either when created as slang (*egghead* 'intellectual') or extended from an argot (*frisk* 'search' or *heist* 'hold up')." Nevertheless,

> despite the efforts of such aficionados as Eric Partridge and H. L. Mencken and the editors of twentieth-century dictionaries, the basic problem of slang lexicology — definition of the class — has not been solved. . . . Until slang can be objectively identified and segregated (so that dictionaries will not vary widely in labeling particular lexemes and idioms) or until more precise subcategories replace the catchall label SLANG, little can be done to analyze linguistically this kind of lexis, or to study its historical change, or to account for it in sociolinguistic and psycholinguistic contexts.

Just as McMillan was pointing this out, Bethany K. Dumas and Jonathan Lighter asked the question, "Is *slang* a word for linguists?" They argued that it is, that there is an indispensable use for the term SLANG to name a body of lexemes that are distinct from standard English, jargon, and all other kinds of informal uses such a regionalisms and colloquialisms and which are identifiable primarily by the intent (or the perceived intent) of the speaker or writer to break with established linguistic convention.

Its "intent" or perception must be social, or personal, or both; thus *slang* is a word for linguists as long as it's understood in sociolinguistic or psycholinguistic terms. McMillan wanted a definition of *slang* divorced from slang's context; Dumas and Lighter understood that context is an essential component of any useful definition.

Mencken may have been at the back of everyone's mind. In *The American Language* (1936), he insisted that "what slang actually consists of . . . doesn't depend . . . upon intrinsic qualities, but upon the surrounding circumstances. It is the user that determines the matter, and particularly the user's habitual way of thinking." Slang isn't "in" words; it is an extrinsic feature of their use adapted by speakers to very precise human social and aesthetic needs and aspirations. In fact, at its origin, slang appears to have been used, not to label words, but to identify an attitude, an awareness of how to behave in the know, how to be hip.

The first quotation to support the noun *slang* in the OED may refer, the editors speculate, "to customs or habits rather than language." The OED culls its quotation from that roller coaster of a novel, *The History of Two Orphans* (1756) by William Toldervy: "Thomas Throw had been upon the town, knew the slang well." And the adjective entry includes a sense (2.b) captured in the Merriam-Webster definition quoted earlier in the chapter: "Loud, extravagant; more showy or obtrusive than accords with good taste. A passage quoted from the *Sporting Magazine* (1828) perfectly captures this sense: some Beau Brummel appears to the demimonde "[w]ithout the slightest appearance of slang or flash toggery about him." In 1842, looking forward to Sledd, the American writer Richard Henry Dana Jr. wrote in his journal of Dickens's *American Notes* that the book was "careless, pretentious, & with a kind of off-hand, slang-ey, defying tone, which a man with a well-balanced mind & the delicate perceptions & self-respect of a gentleman could not fall into." Slang is language with attitude — you can't separate one from the other.

After thinking further for nearly a quarter of a century about the definition that he and Bethany Dumas had published in 1978, and after decades of work on the *Historical Dictionary of American Slang*, Jonathan Lighter recently proposed a somewhat improved definition:

> *Slang* denotes an informal, nonstandard, nontechnical vocabulary composed chiefly of novel-sounding synonyms (and near synonyms) for standard words and phrases; it is often associated with youthful, raffish, or undignified persons and groups; and it conveys often striking connotations of impertinence or irreverence, especially for established attitudes and values within the prevailing culture.

Lighter is the best at writing definitions among lexicographers of his generation, and this definition of *slang*, written with such clarity, grace, and assurance, illustrates why reading through the *Historical Dictionary of American Slang* is such a pleasure. Yet every definition is an abstract of meaning, and we must fill in the details. Lighter's definition does not emphasize the roles that slang plays in the social dynamics of groups or in an individual's ability to negotiate discourse; it ignores the poetics of slang; and it overemphasizes slang's lexical character. Finally, as Whitman put it, slang is a "wholesome fermentation" of speech; slang is a necessary aspect of our linguistic well-being, rather than an aberration brought on by thoughtless speakers of deviant character. Subsequent chapters of this book reach beyond Lighter's definition to a fully articulated explanation of slang.

Dalzell and Victor, in the *New Partridge Dictionary of Slang and Unconventional English* (2006), have hedged a bit where Lighter confidently asserts slang's boundaries and domain. "Rather than focus too intently on a precise definition of slang," they write, "or on whether a given entry is slang, jargon or colloquial English, we take full advantage of the wide net cast by Partridge when he chose to record 'slang and unconventional English' instead of just slang, which is, after all, without any settled test of purity." Words like *hang* and *eighty-six* still smell of slang but have lost their pungency; we may call them unconventional words without worrying too much about whether they are slang in some cases, jargon in others, and colloquial American English in others still. So Dalzell and Victor are right to be cautious in the face of Lighter's definition, yet Lighter's definition is probably as good as it gets. All defining or not defining aside, slang is what it is. You'll know it when you hear it.

REFERENCES

T. S. Eliot's *Old Possum's Book of Practical Cats* is available in many imprints; here and subsequently, I refer to my battered copy of Eliot's *Complete Poems and Plays*

1909–1950 (New York: Harcourt, Brace and World, 1971), 156–157 ("Mungojerrie and Rumpelteazer"), 150–151 ("The Old Gumbie Cat"), and 163–164 ("Macavity: The Mystery Cat), in series. For an introduction to English phonetics relevant to *mongo*, and to many other topics in English linguistics raised in the course of this book, see Anne Curzan and Michael Adams, *How English Works: A Linguistic Introduction*, 2nd edition (New York: Pearson Longman, 2009). *The Barnhart Dictionary Companion: A Quarterly of New Words* was published between 1982 and 2001, first under the editorial leadership of Clarence L. Barnhart, one of America's outstanding lexicographers, and later under that of one of his lexicographical sons, David K. Barnhart. Publication has been suspended since 2001 while Barnhart considers new publishers and publishing formats. Together, Barnhart and Allan Metcalf wrote *America in So Many Words* (Boston: Houghton Mifflin, 1997); subsequently, Metcalf also wrote *The World in So Many Words* (Boston: Houghton Mifflin, 1999), both of which I recommend to word lovers (especially teachers). Pamela Munro and several of her students compiled *Slang U.: The Official Dictionary of College Slang* (New York: Harmony Books, 1989). Connie Eble's *Slang and Sociability: In-Group Language among College Students* (Chapel Hill: University of North Carolina Press, 1996) is the standard: learned, thoughtful, and eminently readable. I quote from Ted Botha's *Mongo: Adventures in Trash* (New York: Bloomsbury, 2004), 3. Grant Barrett's entry for *mongo* in *The Official Dictionary of Unofficial English: A Crunk Omnibus for Thrillionaires and Bampots for the Ecozoic Age* (New York: McGraw-Hill, 2006), begins on 235. A quick check of radio station WBUR's Web site indicates that archive files for *The Connection* are still available there. John Seabrook's article about William Labov, "Talking the Tawk," appeared in *The New Yorker* (November 14, 2005), 39. Definitions of *slang* are quoted from *The Encarta World English Dictionary*, edited by Anne H. Soukhanov, Kathy Rooney, and others (New York: St. Martin's Press, 1999); the *American Heritage College Dictionary*, 4th edition, edited by Joseph P. Pickett and others (Boston: Houghton Mifflin, 2002); the *Merriam-Webster Collegiate Dictionary*, 11th edition, edited by Frederick C. Mish and others (Springfield, MA: Merriam-Webster, 2005); and the *New Oxford American Dictionary*, 2nd edition, edited by Elizabeth J. Jewell, Frank Abate, Erin McKean, and others (New York: Oxford University Press, 2005). The etymology of *slang* comes from Anatoly Liberman, *An Analytic Dictionary of English Etymology: An Introduction* (Minneapolis: University of Minnesota Press, 2008); the short etymology is on xliv and a fascinating long version on 189–196. Julie Coleman is quoted from *A History of Cant and Slang Dictionaries. Volume 1: 1567–1785* (Oxford: Oxford University Press, 2004), 4;

she has recently published *A History of Cant and Slang Dictionaries. Volume II: 1785–1858* (Oxford: Oxford University Press, 2004); a third volume is in preparation. *Sucks* was the subject of the segment "That Sucks" by Alex Chadwick and Karen Grigsby Bates on NPR's *Day to Day* (August 1, 2003). We will return to Tom Dalzell's *The Slang of Sin* (Springfield, MA: Merriam-Webster, 1998) in chapter 3; the material here is quoted from 194–195. Ronald R. Butters's " 'We didn't realize that lite beer was supposed to suck!': The Putative Vulgarity of 'X Sucks' in American English" appeared in *Dictionaries: Journal of the Dictionary Society of North America* 22 (2001): 130–144. Geoffrey Nunberg is quoted from *The Way We Talk Now* (Boston: Houghton Mifflin, 2001), 96. David W. Maurer's classic article "The Argot of the Racetrack," along with many similar pieces, is reprinted in his *Language of the Underworld*, collected and edited by Allan W. Futrell and Charles B. Wordell (Lexington: University of Kentucky Press, 1981); the quoted passage appears on 198–199. For this surprising fact about the *likes*, see Alexandra D'Arcy, "*Like* and Language Ideology: Disentangling Fact from Fiction," *American Speech* 82.4 (Winter 2007): 386–419. Connie Eble is quoted from her article on slang in *The Oxford Companion to the English Language*, edited by Tom McArthur (Oxford: Oxford University Press, 1992), 940–943. Those interested in restaurant jargon can find all of the terms discussed here and more in my "The Server's Lexicon: Preliminary Inquiries into Current Restaurant Jargon," *American Speech* 73.1 (Spring 1998): 57–83. AskPhil can be found at www.AskPhil.org. My knowledge of snowboarding jargon depends on years of reading magazines like *Transworld Snowboarding, Snowboarding Life, Snowboarder, Snowboarder-Girl,* and *Strength,* with a little *Thrasher* and *Surfing* thrown in for good etymological measure, as well as books like Jeff Bennett and Scott Downey, *The Complete Snowboarder* (Camden, ME: Ragged Mountain Press, 1994); Christof Weiss, *Snowboarding Know-How* (New York: Sterling, 1993); and Bill Gutman, *Snowboarding to the Extreme* (New York: Tom Doherty Associates, 1997). I quote from *The Complete Snowboarder*, 5 and 9, in series; Chris Daniele's "Deconstructing the Tindy," *SnowboarderGirl*, 1999, 10; and Melissa Larsen's "Pickups and Patchouli," *Transworld Snowboarding*, March 1999, 103. United Parcel Service terms are taken from the *UPS Stylebook: Glossary of Terms* (United Parcel Service of America, Inc., 1993). Fortunately, William H. Whyte's *The Organization Man* (Philadelphia: University of Pennsylvania Press, 2002) is still in print — more people should read it. The quotation from *Slang U.* appears on 4. The material on Winchester Notions is taken from Charles Stevens, *Winchester Notions*, edited by Christopher Stray (London: Athlone Press, 1998). The entry for *Wyke-*

hamist is on 317–318, that for *scob* is on 254–255. Stevens is quoted from xi, xiii, xv, and xvii, in series; Stray is quoted from 13. Aaron Dinin's *The Krzyzewski-ville Tales* (Durham, NC: Duke University Press, 2005) may fall somewhat short of its Chaucerian inspiration, but Dinin's glossary of tenting terms is excellent. Tom Dalzell's *The Slang of Sin* is quoted from xi. James Sledd's classic description of slang appears on "On Not Teaching English Usage," *English Journal* 54 (1965), 699; Lighter is quoted from his article "Slang," in *English in North America*, edited by John Algeo, volume 6 of *The Cambridge History of the English Language* (Cambridge, UK: Cambridge University Press, 2001), 220–221. John Ayto is quoted from the preface to the *Oxford Dictionary of Slang* (Oxford: Oxford University Press, 1998), v. Material from *The Canting Crew* and *The New Canting Dictionary* is quoted from Coleman, *A History of Slang and Cant Dictionaries. Volume 1: 1597–1785* (Oxford: Oxford University Press, 2004), 80–81 114, and 112, in series. For examples of Jack Dawkins's slang, I have turned to *Oliver Twist* in *The Oxford Illustrated Dickens* (Oxford: Oxford University Press, 1996), 53, 56, 61, and 66. References to Mayhew's and Hotten's accounts of rhyming slang are borrowed from John Ayto's *The Oxford Dictionary of Rhyming Slang* (Oxford: Oxford University Press, 2002), viii; examples of rhyming slang come from that dictionary and from Eric Partridge, *Slang: To-day and Yesterday* (New York: Bonanza Books, n.d.), 273–276, and examples of back and center slang from Partridge, 276–278. Emerson is quoted in H. L. Mencken, *The American Language* (New York: Knopf, 1936), 556 n3; Whitman is quoted from *The English Language: Essays by Linguists and Men of Letters, 1858–1964*, edited by W. F. Bolton and David Crystal (Cambridge, UK: Cambridge University Press, 1969), 58. Bradley and Welby are quoted in Partridge's *Slang: To-day and Yesterday*, 4. Mencken quotes Bradley in *The American Language*, 563. Lighter mentions Hayakawa and Gaston on 224 in his article on "Slang" for the *Cambridge History of the English Language*. Eble's article on "Slang as Poetry" can be found in *The Fourteenth LACUS Forum 1987*, edited by Sheila Embleton (Lake Bluff, IL: Linguistic Association of Canada and the United States, 1988), 442–445; Lighter considers the connections between poetry and slang on 224–246 of his article previously cited; the quotation is from 226. James B. McMillan is quoted from "American Lexicology, 1942–1973," *American Speech* 53.2 (Summer 1978): 146; Dumas and Lighter had actually published their answer before McMillan's challenge had been posed, in "Is *Slang* a Word for Linguists?" *American Speech* 53.1 (Spring 1978), and are quoted here from 13. Mencken is quoted from *The American Language* (3rd edition, 1929) by Partridge,

Slang: To-day and Yesterday, 4–5. Richard Henry Dana is quoted from Lighter's essay on "Slang" in the *Cambridge History*, 227. Lighter's most recent definition of *slang* appears on 220 of the same essay. Dalzell and Victor are quoted from *The New Partridge Dictionary of Slang and Unconventional English*, 2 volumes (New York: Routledge, 2006), ix. Throughout this chapter and, indeed, throughout the book, I depend on the *Oxford English Dictionary* (2nd edition).

FITTING IN

SOCIAL DYNAMICS OF SLANG

Two friends stand in front of a mountainside inn holding between them a prize-winning fish. They went to the same prep school; they were fraternity brothers at the same university; they live in the same type of suburban neighborhood, one of them in Indianapolis, and the other in Cincinnati. Every year they pack their rods and flies and fish some river somewhere between the shining seas. They wear plaid shirts, khaki trousers, and barn jackets ordered from L. L. Bean; they endure frigid mountain streams in waders purchased from Lunkers. They have knives and needle-nose pliers in leather holders at their belts. As they grin their success at the camera, their teeth brightly reflect the advantages of dental insurance and orthodontia. When they were younger, they were a line drawing in Lisa Birnbach's *The Official Preppy Handbook*; these days they could figure in a cartoon in *The New Yorker*. You don't expect the caption to read "Unhand my fly fish, you wanksta!"

Actually, they are a line drawing on one side of a flash card in the series of slang flash cards designed by the novelty purveyors Knock Knock and sold in boutiques all over the United States. The first set of cards appeared in 2003, the second in 2005, copyright Who's There, Inc. Each attractively colored card has, on one side, a slang term; turn the card over and you find a dictionary-style entry (complete with pronunciation, etymology, definition, and sentences that illustrate usage) and a cartoon, like that of the preppy fishermen, with a caption that also illustrates how the word in question is used.

Every one of the cards pits the image against the word. The image is affluent, WASPish, a little removed from the American mainstream, but in the right direction. The cartoon figures are not those from whom you expect the accompanying slang; they are stereotypes of Americans we suppose have little contact with slang. Two women shopping hold a dress between them. The dress is not unlike the fish held between the two men, who might be their husbands, brothers, lovers, neighbors, or friends. The women are very like the men: same ethnicity, same socioeconomic status, same sense of style, both in clothes and (surprisingly) speech. "Can't you just see this with a huge splash of bling?" one of them asks.

In yet another card, a brunette in Chanel, hair pulled back, bag at her side, standing, rests her hands on an elegant desk; across from her a blonde in a paisley blouse sits on an upholstered chair, her legs crossed at the ankles, and says into the telephone, "I can assure you that the Tupperware party will be mad crunk." In another still, generic corporate officers, some in ties and some in pearls, gather around a table to inspect a graph. One of them points and explains, "This bar represents the day we cold dissed the shareholders." Seated, a very Caucasian middle-aged suit shakes hands with a standing woman colleague (who may be African American, but not too African American), and says, "It's been hella dope working with you. Your ruffled blouses are da bomb. Peace." *Peace* is highlighted in orange, which means that it's the subject of the particular card; *hella*, *dope*, and *da bomb* are highlighted in green, indicating that, if you don't know what they mean, you can find cards devoted to them somewhere else in the pack.

The pictures are out of cultural synchrony with the slang, and the slang is out of place in the style otherwise represented in the captions: *assure* and *Tupperware party*, as well as the phrase structure of "I can assure you that," do not belong anywhere near *mad crunk*. The dissonance is what makes the cards humorous. But the cards are also instructive, for clearly their message is about who OUGHT to use slang and especially who ought to use the variety of slang represented in those captions. For a certain audience, the notion of WASPs speaking like gangstas, that is, as though they participate in a certain African American subculture, is clever and funny. Whether all audiences find it equally clever and funny may tell us something about the relationship of slang to group identity.

The joke, like each card, has two sides: on one side, affluent "older" white speakers pretend that they are African American; turn the joke over, and the affluent "older" white speakers are revealed as affluent "older" white speakers. The cards are successful because the joke has it both ways. The dissonance any speaker of American English hears on the cards confirms that although white folks generally should not speak like African Americans, white folks think that experimenting with Street is cool. The assumptions on which the joke rests are several and complexly related:

- If you have mad slang skillz, then you fit in to the group "Black."
- If you think that talking occasional Street is bangin', if you speak slang like a suburban housewife wears bling, then you fit in to a hip group of whites—at least, the group of whites that thinks it's hip.
- Clumsy (that is, "inauthentic") use of Street may be fun and funny (even some African Americans may find it funny), but it absolutely means that you fit in to the group "White."
- Some African Americans may not find it fun or funny; they may think you straight dissin' them and their culture, fo' shizzle; they know that you don't fit in to their group, no matter how well playing with their language helps you fit in to other groups to which you do belong and (really) want to belong.
- If you invent a set of slang flash cards, intend the slang words on the cards to represent Street, or African American slang, yet use the phrase *hella dope*, you also belong to the group "White," because *hella* is not African American at all, but northern California slang in contrast to southern California *totally*.

In other words, slang is all about fitting in. "Fitting in," however, is not a lightweight notion; it is laden with linguistic, cultural, and political significance.

While slang outlines social space, attitudes about slang partly construct group identity and identify individuals as members of groups. There is a lot at stake in slang, and all speakers of American English are stakeholders, to whatever extent slang figures in their speech. Who, for instance, is allowed to use the slang component of African American English? In a sketch on *Mad TV* titled "Slang Gang" (January 4, 1997) Dr. Mambuca (played by Debra Wilson) convenes an undercover government operation reminiscent of the Mod Squad. Two young African American men named Bob (played by Phil Lamarr) and D. Bone (played by Orlando Jones) are effectively linguistic "agents" dedicated to protecting African American slang, presumably because the slang helps to preserve the island of African American identity against erosion by the American mainstream.

It's safe to say that Dr. Mambuca and her colleagues wouldn't find the Knock Knock slang flash cards fun or funny. The cards would be very alarming evidence of white folks' persistent appropriation of African American slang; indeed, they would be evidence that someone was cashing in on that appropriation. In one of the fastest paced monologues ever aired on television, Dr. Mambuca sprints through the history of African American slang jacked by mainstream American speakers (that is, white speakers). In Stage 1 of the appropriation, those speakers want to sound a little black; in Stage 2 they don't realize that they sound a little black; and, in Stage 3, they no longer sound black because the appropriation is complete and the slang marks, not racial difference, but some other difference — age difference, for instance, or it is slang so general that it barely indicates difference at all. It's slang on the cusp of colloquial, like *cool* or *hip*. Postmonologue, Dr. Mambuca confers with her young colleagues about new slang to disseminate on the Street, then she sends them off to disseminate.

Appropriation of African American slang by mainstream culture has gone on since the early years of African American slang; it is still going on. A decade after "Slang Gang" aired, television returned to the issue in a manner subtler and more forceful, perhaps because more resigned, but no more accepting. In an episode of *The Office* titled "Casino Night" (May 11, 2006), the warehouse manager, Darryl Philbin (played by Craig Robinson), has apparently taught the regional manager, Michael Scott (played by Steve Carell), that **fleece it out*, **mach 5*, and **dinkin' flicka* mean . . . something in African American slang.[1] Michael uses it to prove that he's down with . . . something. The issues of race, class presumption, and corporate status are so confused as to be funny, which is the point.

As Darryl puts it, "I taught Mike some, uh, some, phrases to help with our interracial conversation. . . . You know, things us Negroes say." *Some, uh, some* alerts us to the joke; *interracial conversation* slyly appropriates a little managerese, a jargon of which Michael is a barely competent speaker, in spite of his position; *Negroes* makes clear where Darryl thinks Michael really stands. The passage is almost an inversion of slang: it contrasts the savvy, informed, political, and mildly subversive African American worker with his all too anxious to be hip, and yet not even close to hip, white manager. In fact, it imitates the tendency of the cards to mix African American slang with upper-middle-class white speech, for exactly the opposite purpose, with exactly the opposite effect. The term closest to slang in Darryl's passage is *Mike*. Of all characters in the show, Darryl is the only one who calls Michael *Mike*: he teaches Michael the fake black slang with which Michael attempts to patronize him; in the nickname he has the last,

---

1 The asterisk, which you'll see occasionally throughout this book, is a conventional marker for hypothetical forms without evidence in historical use or for impossible forms, that is, things that can't be said in a particular language, like **Be things that said can't* in English.

rebellious word. Interestingly, though, Darryl is not the office deviant; rather, he exposes the link of language and prejudice. Since James Sledd (quoted in chapter 1) wrote in the 1960s, the world is turned upside down.

According to the box for the original set of Knock Knock slang flash cards, the cards are self-help tools of language learning and social improvement: "Are you over thirty? Nerdy, uncool, or simply suburban? Get hip in mere days!" A bold claim, indeed, but, Knock Knock insists, "Slang Flashcards use old-fashioned teaching techniques to start you 'talking street' almost immediately. Study alone or with a friend—then get a load of your bad self!" The instructions recommend that, after you have read through the cards and "allow[ed] the words and meanings to wash over you in a relaxed, easy manner," you should prompt yourself to "compose new sentences" with the word side of the cards, "thereby flexing your newly developing Slang muscles." Use both sides to "quiz yourself on meanings." Once you feel proficient enough, practice using newly acquired slang "as much as possible in everyday life—practice is the key to correct usage and the seamless incorporation of Slang into your existing vocabulary." Of course, at first, the people with whom you usually associate will respond with alarm, but "don't be disheartened if others don't understand what you say—remember, they haven't yet had the benefit of Slang Flashcards. Gently explain what a word means rather than ridiculing their unhipness, and soon your colleagues and friends will be speaking street right along with you."

The Knock Knock theory of code-shifting is naïve, to say the least, though it's important to note, in fairness, that it's meant to sound plausible but false, a parody of optimistic, self-help advertising. You don't have to be a sociolinguist to know that we don't "learn" slang that belongs to groups other than our own. Slang surely migrates from group to group, and just as surely, many items of American slang, such as *bad* 'good', *bangin'* 'good', *cool* 'good', and *hot* 'good', originated in African American slang. Individuals are agents of this change: they mingle with members of less familiar or unfamiliar groups, occasionally migrate from one group to another, back again, or on to an entirely new group. But the "learning" that goes on in such situations is not rote, textbook, flash card, or even remotely planned and probably not even conscious learning.

Speech is not merely a tool of communication but a fundamental human characteristic implicated in social and personal identity. Humans are social animals; if you don't belong to at least one group, then you aren't a fully realized person. Inevitably, you identify with a group and its speech; in turn, you will be identified by that speech, until someone outside the group successfully appropriates it. The first white woman who cheered on a friend with *You go, girl!* raised eyebrows and expressions of disbelief. But *You go, girl!* isn't as black as it once was. It can still belong to a group, African American or otherwise, but it no longer as reliably distinguishes one group from another, and certainly not in the culturally significant way that it did when it belonged exclusively to the slang of African American women.

When white speakers borrow a feature like *You go, girl!* the borrowing doesn't alter the relationship between social groups and language. As Dr. Mambuca realized, it just means that maintaining group identity requires some history, focus, effort, secret agents, and, above all, a strong sense of group identity and an equally strong sense that it should be maintained. The Knock Knock flash cards appear to suggest that non–African American speakers can speak Street by borrowing lots of African American slang, item by item. In fact, no one will accept as authentic the use of such slang by white mainstream speakers unless the white mainstream speaker "code-switches," or moves seamlessly from one variety of American English (mainstream American English) to another (African American Vernacular English).

To switch from one code to another credibly, however, a speaker must identify with the groups to whom the codes belong. Many African Americans (like Darryl Philbin, from *The Office*) switch easily between African American Vernacular English (including its slang) and mainstream American speech of whatever region (southern African American speakers don't shift from African American Vernacular English to mainstream northern speech) because they participate in both speech groups regularly and naturally. When African American speakers move from African American Vernacular English to mainstream American speech, they don't borrow mainstream speech as though it weren't their own — both varieties are their own. Some African American speakers do not participate in mainstream culture and don't shift codes easily; similarly, most white speakers (like Michael Scott from *The Office*) don't shift into African American Vernacular English; they could do so credibly only if they genuinely identified with it.

Most blacks participate in mainstream culture; most mainstream white speakers do not participate in African American culture. The reasons, historical and contemporary, are too many and too complex to negotiate here; thoughtful readers will already know them. The mainstream thinks, like the Borg in *Star Trek: The Next Generation*, that all will be assimilated and that resistance to that assimilation is futile. For one reason or another, and to varying extents, all of us, and all of the groups to which we belong, including the putative mainstream, work relatively hard to maintain difference. And difference will be maintained; what's futile is resistance to difference.

All of our speech is about fitting in — not the same thing, by the way, as saying that all of our speech is only about fitting in. Slang is about fitting in to groups marked against the mainstream. But "fitting in" is not absolute. The Borg "fit in." Actually, they plug in to The Collective and don't have minds and motives of their own. Without regard for grammatical number, they have a mind of their own. We all have minds and motives of our own, though, even teenagers do, no matter what their adult detractors assume. And fitting in, though often accomplished below the level of consciousness, is not automatic, nor is it total. Fitting in requires the expression of style, but some style is individual. No one respects someone whose style is only about EXACTLY fitting in. If in just one token of dress or speech, each of us has to mark out personal space within the group space.

The exchange between fitting in and expressing individual style contributes to the development, not only of language, but also of all other expressions of group and individual identity. Slang, the instrument of both group and individual, is dynamic, a medium of exchange. But there's no question of getting to an end, a goal, or a result; slang is not teleological. Or, you could say, dynamic is the result. Dynamic is what you see and all you get. This chapter is about how both slang and perceptions of slang are mediums of fitting in, the basis of establishing and maintaining group identity on terms that allow the stylish individual to negotiate his or her identity, as one depends on the other.

BOYZ IN THE HOOD SPEAK SLANG, SOCCER MOMS DON'T

The title of this section reflects a common perception about slang and who speaks it. The Knock Knock slang flash cards are funny, to those who find them funny, or not funny, to those who find them a coy, mainstream (mainly white privileged) appropriation of African American culture, because so many people take for granted that slang is natural in urban, male, African American speech and barely impinges on the speech of white suburban women. As a matter of one kind of fact, the perception is simply untrue, or at least exaggerated, and can lead to unfairness and even to harm: African American speech is often stigmatized as slang, while at least some of those busy stigmatizing never recognize the slangy content of their own characters.

But because slang is more than a set of lexical items, because it is, as another kind of fact, a social phenomenon, perception means a lot. We don't distinguish among group identities, or identify with a group, on the basis of facts; instead, we rely on perceptions only partially informed by facts. So although a clinical assessment of slang exposes its supposed African Americanness as a language myth, that doesn't mean, paradoxically, that the myth is "untrue." Slang is all about fitting in to one group or another, but fitting in (and keeping others out) are as perceptual as they are anything. Perception is actually linguistically, historically, and culturally significant: African American slang is more slangy because people believe that it is, even though African American urban youth are not necessarily more prone to slang than are suburban white moms. Indeed, the perceptual element is essential to slang: slang is stylish, rebellious language, and it isn't slang until someone recognizes it as slang.

African American slang is everything that slang is supposed to be, plus soul. African Americans took English *bad* and used it to mean its opposite, as well as 'stylish, sexy, wonderful, formidably skilled'. The word, to those hip to it, was casually racy and irreverent, and vivid in its emphasis, more vivid the longer the vowel. African Americans taught the average (read "white") American how to play that *funky* 'soulful' music, have a *ball* 'party, celebration, big time', and shake his *booty* 'rump', to *get down* 'dance, sing, or whatever enthusiastically' in the face of all the *changes* 'marked adjustment of attitude, difficulties, anguish' that *bring down* 'diminish, depress' even the best among us. At the same time, African American slang preserves the image of the *macaroni* (now the *mack daddy* 'sweet talking man'—*mack* either from earlier English *mackerel* 'pimp' or through Louisiana French *maquerel* for the same—or *playa* 'player') walking into a juke joint all *zooty* with a sharp *brim* 'man's hat'. *Macaroni, mack daddy, booty*—that's playful language, and if enough of it accumulates in a passage of speech or writing or in the hustle and flow of conversation, it has a certain sound, a sound of its own, an African American sound. African American slang is *bad*—hold that vowel long enough to evoke every one of the slang senses embedded in the word.

African American English has slang, but is it an especially rich source of English slang generally? It's difficult to know how to measure "especially rich": it could mean that African American speech provides American slang with lots of items, or that the items it provides are very significant (used frequently, used prominently, etc.), or both. Even the notion of "source" is more complicated than it seems at first. African American English, though not the source of a word, may nonetheless be the source of the word as slang; a colloquial or even a standard term once shared in several or even all varieties of English could survive among African Americans longer than among other English speakers, shift its level from "standard" to "slang," and then reenter mainstream English as a slang term, because anything white speakers borrow from African American speakers shouts difference, and the act of borrowing in itself rebels mildly against the white-dominated status quo.

In the *New Dictionary of American Slang* (1986) Robert L. Chapman suggested, "Close analysis would probably show that, what with the prominence of Black people in the armed forces, in music, in the entertainment world, and in street and ghetto life, the black influence on American slang has been more pervasive in recent times than that of any other ethnic group in history." In *Slang and Sociability* (1996) Connie Eble analyzed the African Americanness of Chapman's slang lexicon and noted that while about five hundred terms were associated with African Americans, sixty were terms for African Americans used by non–African Americans, and only six of the remaining 435 or so unarguably have African language etymologies. Most of those 435 are no longer absolutely restricted to African American use, if they ever were. Indeed, as Eble writes:

> Many terms from more than fifty years ago are still in use in informal varieties of American English, sometimes with a slightly different meaning — for example, *uppity, white trash, truck, Joe Blow, reefer*, and *latch on to*. The two decades with the greatest number of entries are the 1930s … and the 1960s. … Almost all of the terms that rose to popularity in the 1960s are still in general informal use, though many speakers may no longer be aware of their African American origins, for example *bug* 'to pester'; *the nitty-gritty* 'harsh reality'; and *ripoff* 'theft'.

In other words, the stuff in Chapman's dictionary does not exactly support his introductory claim, omitted in a subsequent edition.

In his extensive introduction to the first volume of the *Historical Dictionary of American Slang* (1994), Jonathan Lighter does not comment on whether the African American contribution to American slang is ESPECIALLY significant. As Eble puts it, "On the surface the vocabulary items seem to depict a group of lower status as appealing and worthy of imitation. Yet a closer look shows that the borrowings from African American vernaculars are fairly cautious and are filtered by the stereotypes held by mainstream society." That the value of African American slang would be determined by mainstream American society (or that mainstream society sees itself as arbiter of that value) hardly seems fair, but such unfairness suffuses American cultural and political history, and I'm willing to bet that it comes as no surprise to most African Americans.

African American slang has an impressive history within African American culture, regardless of what the mainstream or any other group thinks of it. One way to measure that history is to examine Clarence Major's *Juba to Jive: A Dictionary of African-American Slang* (1994), which really records African American slang from *A* 'that which is emphatically correct' (as in, according to Major, "You fucking A, man") to *zooty* 'stylish' — well, actually to *Zutty*, the nickname of jazzman Arthur James Singleton, from which *zooty* derives. And there's a lot in between those entries: Major includes 660 words in his dictionary, 557 if you subtract cross-references. Of those 557, 226 (roughly 41 percent) appear to have entered the vocabulary from 1950 to 1990, and 217 (39 percent) entered in the first half of the twentieth century.[2] The remaining items are attested in the nineteenth century (68, or 12 percent) and from 1600 to 1800 (46, or 8 percent).

The relation of African American speech to other American speech isn't easy to determine: even if you know who used a word first, that term can change identities several times during its lexical lifetime. Nevertheless, some terms are historically more African American than others. According to Major, African Americans in Louisiana used *mizzy* for 'stomach ache' from the 1840s to the 1890s; in historical terms, I suppose, the word was a passing fad, but it reminds us that ephemerality is relative and that slang isn't always a flash in some pan. More recently (and more ephemerally), in the 1950s and 1960s a man could *sound on* 'flirt with' a woman, an item neither recognized nor borrowed by speakers of mainstream American English. White speakers don't use *mo' better* 'improving', according to Major a term of Gullah origin used from the 1700s to the 1950s and then revived in the 1990s, but some recognize it since Spike Lee released *Mo' Better Blues* (1990). None of these words is used much beyond the bounds of specifically African American culture: no white man is going to *get over* 'seduce, copulate with' a woman, any woman, by sounding on her — there's a problem of authenticity that charm just cannot solve.

Today, though, under the influence of hip-hop culture, Americans (not just adolescents, either) use *bling* and *mack* and *pimped out* in ways that would call

---

2   Unlike Chapman, Major finds a significant distribution of African American slang items across several twentieth-century decades, from the 1930s (seventy items), through the 1940s (eighty-three items), 1950s (fifty-nine items), and the 1960s (seventy-three items), and into the 1980s, with the rise of rap (fifty-two items). Of course, in both cases, the method of collecting was loose, and minor differences in dating could easily shift the balance of items from one decade to another.

Dr. Mambuca into action. Obviously Dr. Mambuca hasn't heard about Zwinky .com, a virtual world in which you can "turn yourself into a 3D image," dress "yourself" up in clothes of various styles from a virtual closet, and purchase what you like at shops linked to the site (once you've registered, so that purveyors of goods and services can assess your personal information and serve you better). Zwinky television ads are carefully multicultural, and the jingle talks about *bling* and how you can "be anyone," which is true, I guess, as long as you stay inside your computer.

Dr. Mambuca, some would suggest, needs to chill and "get Zwinky," put all of that cultural history behind her and be like everyone else, or at least the five million of us who get Zwinky so far. According to this opportunistic fabrication, kids today have shed history and cultural difference and supposedly share slang as though there were no groups to include or exclude them. Having displaced themselves virtually, these kids live (I'm not kidding — the Zwinks have to establish their trademark) in a consumerist "Zwinktopia." In Zwinktopia there is one and only one group, and everyone speaks the same language; unrealistically, that language contains a lot of what we consider slang, slang without any socially differentiating value. In the real world, though, the world of history, groups are significant, and slang is significant to the nature and integrity of groups.

The relevant history started long ago, but records of African American speech from before 1800 are rare indeed, so Major's long reach back into the history of American speech is a welcome achievement and credibly asserts the significance of African American slang. For instance, *chinchy* 'stingy, mean' was introduced into African American slang from colloquial English sometime around 1650; it remained in use among African Americans until the 1950s, long after it had disappeared from British or even general American English. African American maintenance of *chinchy* suggests something about the importance to African Americans of fitting in (and keeping others out) on the basis of shared language, not just at any one cultural moment, but over centuries of oppression. Words participate in cultural identity.

Chinchy is a good example of how complicated the history of English is and of African American slang's place in that history. No one said the relationship of words and culture was easy. Even though *chinchy* seems African American to Major, as it would to anyone of his generation, there's only half a reason in history to believe so. English has *chinchy* to mean 'miserly, stingy' from the early fifteenth century, and the *-y* suffixed adjective derives from an even earlier form *chinch* 'miser/miserly', both noun and adjective, dating from before 1300. The

English word was borrowed from Old French *chiche* 'parsimonious', the unetymological *n* inserted by speakers later, in both English and French.[3] If this is the *chinchy* that African Americans spoke until the 1950s, it was an English word adopted by African American speakers through contact with the sort of English speakers who used the word in the seventeenth and eighteenth centuries.

The OED also enters *chinch* 'bedbug' as an English word from sometime before 1625 but points directly to its origin in Spanish *chinche* 'bug'. *Chinch* in the Middle English sense 'miser' disappears from the record in the sixteenth century, but, just to confuse matters, the record of *chinch* and *chinchy* having to do with insects picks up at about the same time, and later is attributed specifically to African American use. The OED cites John Southall's *Treatise of Buggs* (1730) to this effect: "He asked if Chintses (so Buggs are by Negroes and some others there called) had bit me?" The term is clearly associated with the West Indies throughout the modern period: the OED cites Griffith Hughes's *A Natural History of Barbados* (1750) on *chinch* 'bug'. But *chinch* for 'bug' was also used early on in American English by white folks, like George Washington, who wrote in his *Diary* (1786) that he "examined the corn in several parts of this field and discovered more or less of the Chinch bug on every stalk."

Chinch 'bug' may have entered George Washington's English from earlier English, which may have borrowed the word from Spanish or Portuguese, and the word may have entered either of those languages via African languages in the course of the slave trade. Or *chinch* may have been reintroduced into English in North America when slaves used it among American English speakers. Major claims that *chinchy* 'miserly' derives from Bantu *tshinji*, but it's more likely that American *chinch* 'bug' derives from that word, and that the African American adjective meaning 'miserly' derives from Old French through Middle English and into English vernacular, from which it was borrowed by slaves as they learned English in America. *Chinch* from *tshinji* eventually became obsolete, unable to withstand the inexorable advance of modern pesticide. *Chinchy* 'miserly', on the

3 Clever readers will wonder whether *chinch* 'bug' or *chinchy* 'parsimonious', especially the latter, have anything etymological to do with *chintz* 'painted or stained calico cloth' or the adjective that derives from it, *chintzy* 'of cheap quality; stingy'. They do not, in spite of the fact that *chinchy* and *chintzy* are sometimes synonyms. Though *chintz* entered English from Hindi in the early seventeenth century, at roughly the same time as *chinch* 'bug' and while *chinchy* 'parsimonious' was still in use in England, *chintzy* 'of cheap quality; stingy' is not recorded until the mid-nineteenth century, by which time in England, *chinchy* had fallen from use.

other hand, survived well into the twentieth century. I wish that it had lasted longer and that mainstream speakers had appropriated it from African American slang to replace its venerable but volatile standard synonym, *niggardly*.[4]

Importantly, this does not make *chinchy* 'miserly' any less African American, especially in the twentieth century; it has survived in African American speech much longer than in colloquial English generally. To adapt a category from one of the great scholars of American English, Allen Walker Read, it is an "African Americanism by survival." Over the centuries, *chinch* 'bug' and *chinchy* 'miserly' mutually reinforced their African American identities. Our perception of to whom *chinchy* belongs has nothing to do with etymology but with the social circumstances that guide speakers to use one word rather than another in order to distinguish themselves, as members of a social group, from those who are members of other social groups. Its African Americanness is a matter of present perception; it's not a property of the word itself but of the word in use. Yet there's a lot of non–African American history and use underlying this presently African American word.

Those who used *chinchy* in 1950 were almost certainly African Americans: use of the word affirmed membership in that social group, and Americans who identified or were identified with other social groups avoided *chinchy* and marked their own social territory with different slang. The power of words to maintain social distinctions like this one isn't the stuff of ancient history, but an inevitable social manifestation of language, as true of tomorrow as of yesterday and certainly true in America today. As John and Russell Rickford explain in their excellent book, *Spoken Soul: The Story of Black English* (2000):

> One of the many fascinating features of black vocabulary is how sharply it can divide blacks and whites, and how solidly it can connect blacks from different social classes. In 1992, sociologist Teresa Labov published a study that examined the

---

4 For a particularly memorable reason to eschew *niggardly*, recall the case of David Howard, as Randall Kennedy describes him in his remarkable book *Nigger: The Strange History of a Troublesome Word* (2002), "the white director of a municipal agency in Washington, D.C.," who informed his staff that he would have to be niggardly with the agency's money while it was under budgetary stress. The word *niggardly* was widely misunderstood to bear some relation to the N-word, and Howard resigned. *Niggard* 'miser' like *chinch* 'miser' occurs in the record of English early in the fourteenth century; it is probably related to Old Norse *hnøggr* 'miserly', but its exact etymology is unknown. As Geoffrey Nunberg observed of the controversy, "Phonetics always trumps etymology." Had we lost *niggardly* in the 1950s and replaced it with *chinchy*, we'd be in a better place.

extent to which adolescents used and understood eighty-nine slang terms. Of all the social variables she considered, race turned out to be the most significant factor, with blacks much more familiar with terms like *bougie* ('an uppity-acting African American'), *busting out* ('looking good') and *fresh* (for 'cool'), and whites much more familiar with terms like *schlep* (for 'to drag along') and *bombed* or *smashed* (as a synonym for 'drunk'). That the black respondents knew the black terms is significant: they were college students at predominantly white institutions.

Other social variables were also important, of course: the students were not MERELY white or MERELY black, but belonged to several intersecting social groups at once. That's exactly why the preeminence of racial identity here is so arresting.

The lines between white and black aren't always black and white, however. For instance, Major identifies the intensifier *absofuckinglutely*, *mosey* 'walk slowly, meander', and *fixin to* 'prepare; imminent' as items of particularly African American slang in *Juba to Jive* (1994), but none of these originates in African American speech, nor is more prevalent in African American than in general American slang or regional varieties of American English. Major's perception of speech in the world guides him to define African American slang a little more broadly than is clinically justifiable. As the Rickfords say, it's remarkable how well words define groups, yet that has less to do with the volume of African American slang than with what's relevant to group identity when we attempt to draw boundaries on the social map. Speech is a more or less permanent human characteristic, so where there's social difference, words, among other linguistic features, help to maintain that difference.

It should come as no surprise, then, that an identifiable African American slang serves its community well and also exerts some influence on American slang generally. Some items of that slang have always been more or less exclusively African American in use, for instance, *ace boon coon* 'closest black friend' and *boon coon* 'close friend' (though the *boon* here may be from Scots or Ulster Scots *boon* 'above' as in *boonmost* 'uppermost', extended metaphorically to mean 'most important', as when something is "uppermost in your mind"); *back* 'to an extreme degree' (as in "She talk slang back"); *boojie* 'bourgeois; uppity'; and *boot* 'to make aware' (as in "Let me boot you to my slang").

Other words begin in general use and end up African American or start as African American and end up used by people of all groups. So, though *badmouth* 'bear false witness, curse' is undoubtedly a loan translation from an African phrase and must have been used early in its American career exclusively by Gullah-speaking slaves in South Carolina and Georgia, it features in every American's slang today, its African American history completely lost to common awareness. A word like *biddy* 'young woman', on the other hand, specializes to an African American sense from more general and generally used *biddy* 'woman' (Amy March talks about "Yankee biddies" in Louisa May Alcott's *Little Women*). It may in fact have become a pejorative term for young African American women: SlangSite.com defines *biddy* as 'girl who works at a fast food restaurant'; given certain stereotypes and a tough job market for urban youth, this may or may not reflect a sort of racial unconsciousness. Early African Americans learned from what they heard; they adopted the dialectal pronunciation of the Scottish and Irish immigrants all around them, so that *bug* 'bother, annoy' became *boog*. Though it started as an African American development from a common English word, many Americans today could say that they were not just thirsty but *bone* 'thoroughly' dry. And some younger Americans who aren't African American nonetheless borrow *ballistics* 'vivid, forcefully delivered, as in rap lyrics' from their African American contemporaries.

Buddy entered English in the late eighteenth century through African American speech; no one knows where it came from, though. Let's propose, for the sake of argument, that *buddy* is adapted from a West African word of which *buddy* is the only historical trace. Were this true, *buddy* would not have been slang when it first entered America; it could have been slang only when it entered the English of native English speakers, that is, when it was a borrowed synonym for 'friend' and not a remnant of native African speech among Africans newly in contact with English speakers. How did it become slang? Perhaps overseers derisively, condescendingly used it when speaking to slaves, but, as words will, *buddy* slipped into colloquial speech without the attitude. White English speakers began to "misuse" it among themselves.

Anyone can use *buddy* today; though it sounds old fashioned and socially neutral, it has lost any characteristic African Americanness. One might even question whether it is slang. At the earliest stage of its American history, it might have been playful (both phonetically and socially); it might have been racy, a word taken from slaves and so not socially approved in polite society. Today, though, it sounds mostly like a familiar synonym for *friend*: "He's my buddy" and "Hey, buddy, good to see ya!" That is, until you walk into a big box store and a salesperson or greeter says, "Hey, buddy, can I help you?" Then *buddy* carries a vestige of social rebellion, as the clerk refuses in a word to accept my superior social position as the bearer of cash and credit. It's a little like a server in a restaurant asking if my table would like to order any apps, a familiarity just inappropriate enough to grate on my goodwill, just innocuous enough to evade response. "No thanks, comrade," I reply to the greeter, as I steer a cart into the aisles.

Brother 'fellow, comrade in arms', on the other hand, often carries political meaning today, associated with the civil rights movement and discourse of the black Baptist tradition. Cornel West always closes his conversations with Tavis Smiley on *The Tavis Smiley Show* with "Always a pleasure, my brother." West uses the term generously; indeed, he seems to end every public conversation with this tag line, perhaps to transcend racial politics, or perhaps to implicate whites as well as blacks in racial political struggle and the improved social understanding that struggle should engender. But *brother* in this specific sense is an identifiably African American term because its meaning is partly determined by the racial identity of the speaker; it means what it means to African Americans because it acknowledges and constructs common African American heritage, a heritage of struggle, that non–African Americans do not fully share so cannot mean when they use the word. *Brother* is an even more conscious and political gesture of inclusion when extended to non–African Americans. Significantly, it is extended when African Americans extend it.[5]

The African American identity of *brother* is affirmed by contrast with other terms of address, for instance, with *man* and *dude*. *Man* has some strong African American associations, as when the white power structure is identified as *The Man* ("Don't let the man bring you down, brother"), which entered American English in the 1930s, or someone really exceptional is identified as *The Man* ("Cornel West is The Man"), which appears by the 1950s but derives from a more general sense of 'right person' recorded from 1535 forward. The phrase *my main man* improves on historical *ace boon coon* and also functions as a term of address,

---

5 Most uses of *brother* in this sense should be heard as *brotha*. For a while, *bro* was a casually transgressive substitute, but it has gone the way of *cat*, from 'cool/hip guy' to just '(any) guy', as when Colonel Scott Henry, the Infantry Training Brigade commander at Fort Benning, says of recent U.S. Army recruits, "I'm still of a mind-set that I need to have quiet to write a paper or an evaluation, to collect my thoughts, but these young cats can handle it." Perhaps *cat* is currently an item of U.S. military slang, but it's hard to view it as rebellious in Sledd's terms when Army colonels use it. Similarly, *dawg* 'guy', which *American Idol*'s Randy Jackson uses indiscriminately for black, white, Indian American, girl, and guy, so that the word is now more discourse marker than noun. *Yo, dawg, check it* is all just one big phrase to get everyone's attention, meaningful as a whole, but relatively meaningless in its parts.

as can the slightly less demonstrative *my man*, both post–World War II forms. To the extent that white folks have started to use these African Americanisms, the terms have lost some of their African American identity, but all of them are associated with African American culture, and white speakers are at least vaguely aware that their use is rebellious, in departing from the mainstream, exactly because it's racy. In this regard, *girl*, as in "Girl, you ain't all that," is perhaps more closely identified with African American speech, though the catchphrase "You go, girl" got pretty white, at least for a time. You don't hear it much anymore, so either Dr. Mambuca went to work or its vogue simply passed, another casualty of ephemerality.

As a term of address and exclamation, *man* is old, as old as Old English in the former case and (once again) especially characteristic of speech in northern England, Scotland, and Northern Ireland during the past few centuries. In the earliest texts *man* might be construed as 'humankind' (in the *OED* the contexts are all religious and suggest relations between man and God), but Chaucer uses it in *The Canterbury Tales* sometime in the 1390s as a parenthetical term of address: "Oure hors is lorn, Alayn, for Goddes banes / Step on thy feet! Com of, man, al atanes!"[6] Over time the term of address became an unemphatic emphatic, as in "Pull yourself together, man!" as well as a more intensively emphatic emphatic, no longer a term of address, often associated with African American speech, as in Zora Neale Hurston's novel *Jonah's Gourd Vine* (1934): "Man he kin cold preach! Preached over in Goldsborough las' night and strowed fire all over de place."[7] Historically it's difficult to know when exclamatory *man*, which dates

6   In Modern English, these lines might read "Our horse is lost, Alan. For God's sake, get on your feet! Come along, man, right now!" The tale in question is *The Reeve's Tale*, in which two foolish university students think themselves too clever to be outwitted by a miller. The miller lets their horse loose, and while they chase it, he cheats them after all. Not to push the influence of northern English on African American speech too far, but the two students speak in recognizably northern dialect of Chaucer's time, and this *man* may have been a dialectal feature, at least, as Chaucer heard it. In his entry on *man* Lighter notes that, from 1500 forward, the slang interjection was "evident in Scots E[nglish]," though some earlier, standard (that is, non-Scots) uses "are not conclusively distinguishable fr[om] present usage." The northern association may reach far back into Middle English, in other words.

7   This evidence from Hurston is even more interesting for her use of adverbial *cold* than it is for her use of *man*: the former is relatively infrequent because, like *bone* and *back* mentioned earlier, it is identifiably if not exclusively African American slang. Lighter's entry for *cold* in the *Historical Dictionary of American Slang* identifies this sense as associated

from the early nineteenth century, is a shift from earlier uses described above or the clipped remnant of other exclamations, like *man alive!* and *man, oh man!* The etymology is surely mixed, but that makes little difference to anyone using *man* in the twenty-first century.

As Lighter observes, "In casual direct address, particularly at the end of a sentence, *man* has long been common in Scotland, Ireland, and parts of England and Wales, as well as in the West Indies and in other areas of Anglo-Celtic colonization. The usage has been notable in working-class U.S. Black E[nglish] for over a century." These general slang senses of *man*, then, are shared among English speakers and have been shared among them for a long time, even though they were hip in the 1950s forward, no doubt partly because of African American use, which greatly influenced what counted as hip (and still does). International awareness of English speech probably has had an effect, some the result of contact among established and immigrant groups, some the result of media.

Though I have outlined the history of *man* at some length, Lighter is absolutely right to insist that "the subtleties of intonation, emotive associations, cultural context, etc., that distinguish modern 'slang' usage from older dialectal and 'prestige' uses of vocative *man* clearly illustrate how social rather than historical considerations determine speakers' recognition of a usage as 'slang'." As with *bad*, the slanginess of *man* depends not only on slang meanings but also on the expressive elaboration of the vowel. It's an odd admission for a historical lexicographer that a word's history has so little to say about to whom it belongs and that speakers' perceptions of the word as social marker matter most, but Lighter, an honest lexicographer, readily admits the truth.

In the *Historical Dictionary of American Slang*, Lighter cross-refers *dude*, the slangiest of the alternatives considered here, with *cat*, *guy*, and *man*, but notably not with *brother*, because it does not share that word's politicized semantics. Geneva Smitherman and Clarence Major include *dude* in *Black Talk* (2000) and *Juba to Jive* (1994), respectively, but Lighter does not associate *dude* with African American speech particularly. To the extent that *dude* and other shared slang participate in the English of African Americans, there's nothing wrong with including them in books devoted to the lexicon of that variety, but Lighter's evidence demonstrates more than a century of wide social, cultural, and regional distribution for *dude*.

---

with rap music and dates it from 1986, but clearly the term had been around for more than half a century before that.

In 2004 Scott F. Kiesling published an excellent account of *dude*, examining it from every linguistic angle. Kiesling notes that "the use of *dude* as an address term developed in the 1930s and 1940s from groups of men, 'Urban Mexican-American *pachuchos* and African-American *zoot-suiters*' . . . known for their clothes consciousness. These groups began to use *dude* as an in-group term, and it was soon used as a general term of address among men," after which *"dude* followed a well-worn linguistic path from stigmatized groups such as urban African Americans and Mexicans to whites through African American music culture." Today, as Kiesling notes, the avatars of *dude* are characters in films such as *Fast Times at Ridgemont High* that serve as what the sociolinguist Penelope Eckert calls "sociolinguistic icons." Once an item of African American slang has been borrowed by whites to sound hip, the word may have been bleached so white that many African Americans avoid it. Do they really want to sound like Jeff Spicoli, the stoner surfer dude from *Fast Times at Ridgemont High*? Do African Americans ask, "Dude, where's my car?"

The answer is that some do. Dr. Chris Turk, a character in the television sitcom *Scrubs,* would, but then he's a surgeon whose best friend is a white guy who sometimes tries to sound black, and his own "authenticity" is called into question. In the episode "Her Story" (2004) he is challenged to explain some rap lyrics, misunderstands *lo-lo* 'custom designed low-riding vehicle' as *Ho-Ho* 'trademarked name for a snack cake', and is taken to school by "the two whitest girls on earth." It's hard to find items of African American slang that remain just that forever, or mainstream slang that African Americans can't use in some social situation or another. Words can mark the boundaries between social groups reliably without belonging to one or another group absolutely. Knowing what is slang and what isn't, and what slang identifies one group rather than another, requires a sociolinguistic sixth sense.

Intuitively we expect African American culture to generate more slang because it is in a constant state of antagonism with white America, constantly resists authority, not for the fun of it, but for existential reasons. As Sledd argued in his classic article, "On Not Teaching English Usage" (1965), discussed in the previous chapter, slang is a useful instrument of rebellion. In *Juba to Jive*, Major writes that African American slang "is the classic example of a secret tongue," reflecting the historical African American

need to maintain a rapidly changing vocabulary unknown to the larger, mainstream culture — known generally or loosely as white America. The need for secrecy is part of the reason for the rapid change. Since the days of slavery, this secrecy has served as a form of cultural self-defense against exploitation and oppression, constructed out of a combination of language, gesture, body style, and facial expression. In its embryonic stages during slavery, the secrecy was a powerful medium for making sense out of a cruel and strange world.

Actually, Geneva Smitherman, in *Black Talk* (2000), more precisely aligns African American speech with Sledd's theory of slang, for she focuses on "resistance" rather than "self-defense":

> Africans in America have always pushed the linguistic envelope. The underlying tone of resistance in the language may explain why African American linguistic innovations are so often dismissed as slang. It's an easier concept to deal with than confronting the reality that the words represent. Slang, after all, is rather lighthearted and harmless, and it's usually short-lived — here today, gone tomorrow — but the social critique embedded in Black slang is SERIOUS AS A HEART ATTACK.

While most slang pulls up short of infarction, it's often lighthearted but edgy, harmless insofar as words aren't sticks and stones, and less ephemeral than we are led to expect. In the end, all slang is social critique. But African American slang is more noticeably slang, I think, because its critique is especially warranted: the seriousness of what prompts the critique is displaced onto the language of critique.

Although slang is a language of resistance and rebellion, not all language of resistance and rebellion is slang. Similarly, as Smitherman observes in *Talkin and Testifyin: The Language of Black America* (1977), "Black slang is Black Language; but not all Black Language is Black slang." In fact, there may be less black slang than folks, white and black, think there is. We perceive black language as slang when it isn't. As Smitherman argues, "There is a popular tendency to think of the Black Semantic contouring of White American English as ethnic slang. Though many terms are 'slangish,' to dismiss Black Semantics as simply slang talk is a linguistic fallacy. The concept of 'slang' does not begin to cover the broad range of semantic referents in the Black English vocabulary." Smitherman was careful to title her dictionary of African American English *Black Talk* rather than *Black Slang*.

African American English is as old as America. The first African slaves arrived in Virginia in 1619; slaves had to learn English to survive in an English-speaking community. African American Vernacular English (AAVE) is the historical social dialect spoken by African Americans; like all dialects, regional and social, it isn't an example of "bad" English, but varies from other varieties of English (including the "standard" variety) in its sounds, syntax, narrative and conversational strategies, semantics, and vocabulary. As Smitherman claims, "The vocabulary of soul crosses generational and class lines and is grounded in black people's common linguistic and cultural history." You could just as easily say, Yankee vocabulary (sounds, grammar) crosses generational and class lines and is grounded in the common linguistic and cultural history of Yankees. As Walt Wolfram puts it, "To speak a language is to speak a dialect of that language." If you speak the same dialect as others, you belong to the same social or regional group; if someone's dialect is unfamiliar to you, you suspect that he or she doesn't belong in your group, and you don't belong in his or hers. Nobody gets to not speak a dialect.

And many African Americans at least sometimes speak a dialect with features systematically different from mainstream speech. AAVE expresses habitual aspect, for instance, in a stressed *be* (usually represented BE). In standard American English, habitual aspect has to be expressed indirectly: "She is usually/typically at home at this time of day." To say "She is at home today" means that she really, actually, physically is at home. In AAVE the stressed BE works (and causes problems for white speakers) as follows:

> TEACHER: Bobby what does your mother do every day? (Teacher apparently wanted to call Bobby's parents.)
>
> BOBBY: She be at home!
>
> TEACHER: You mean she *is* at home.
>
> BOBBY: No, she ain't, 'cause she took my grandmother to the hospital this morning.
>
> TEACHER: You know what I meant. You are not supposed to say "She *be* at home." You are to say "She *is* at home."
>
> BOBBY: Why you trying to make me lie? She ain't at home.

In fact, Bobby's answer is grammatically precise, and he insists on its correctness: "She is home on Sundays" is habitual; "She is home as we speak" is not. It's *is* that's imprecise, not BE. As Smitherman points out in *Talkin That Talk* (2000), from which I have extracted the above example, "Dig it: white middle-class kids don't have to be 'versatile' in Black English," and neither do their teachers.

Sometimes grammatical information such as aspect is conveyed in an adverb or auxiliary rather than in a verb form. In "All the homeboys be steady rappin," an example borrowed from John Baugh's *Out of the Mouths of Slaves* (1999), *steady* signifies intense, consistent, and continuous action, somewhat more than "is rapping steadily" would signify in standard American English. In "She come going in my room, didn't knock or nothing," *come* is emphatic and expresses the speaker's indignation, according to Arthur Spears in his seminal article on *come* (1982), though Baugh suggests that it can convey a much broader range of emotion. But what is the difference between these words in AAVE and supposed items of African American slang, like *back* ("She talk slang back") and *cold* ("He can cold preach?")? The answer is: not much. Mainstream speakers of American English would find it hard to draw the line between dialect and slang in cases like these, and it's possible to circumscribe all of it as Smitherman's "black talk."

African American English has developed over more than three centuries; it has maintained features from African languages, borrowed features from various other dialects of English, both preexisting and concurrent, and developed in and of itself. It diverges markedly from standard American English, and, as a result, it isn't always easy for young speakers of AAVE to learn standard American English in school. Few members of their actual speech community speak the standard variety; in fact, few members of any speech group actually speak the standard variety, but for historical and social reasons their home dialects differ from the standard dialect less markedly, so shifting from one to another dialect is easier, less frustrating, less noticed by mainstream speakers, and less likely to turn heads in social evaluation. All of these complications and their negative effects prompted the Oakland, California, Board of Education in 1996 to propose the use of AAVE, or Ebonics, as a bridging language in classrooms, as a possible language of instruction so that students without firm command of the standard variety could learn a variety of subjects, including standard American English.

This is not the place to argue the merits of the Oakland proposal; an extensive literature supports it quite effectively. Here it's important to note that many opponents of the proposal caricatured AAVE as slang and in doing so meant to stigmatize it. Infamously, Brent Staples wrote in the *New York Times* (January 24, 1997), "In theory, teachers would use street talk as a 'bridge' to help children master standard English. But as practiced elsewhere, so-called 'Ebonics' instruction is based on the premise that street English is as good or better than the standard tongue. This means that students could use urban slang in their schoolwork." In 1998 Theresa Perry described the controversy this way: "The way the Ebonics case was coded in TV news accounts also played an important role in generating negative reactions from African Americans. As TV commentators and reporters talked about the resolution, the image that was projected over and

over again was that of a Black male speaking Black slang in a school context."
Several of those who testified about the school board's resolution before the U.S.
Senate similarly objected to the notion that students would speak slang in school;
so did prominent African American authors such as Earl Ofari Hutchison. In *Bad
Language: Are Some Words Better Than Others?* (2005) Edwin L. Battistella pre-
sents a balanced set of reactions without losing hold of the linguistic facts:

> [California English professor Ron] Emmons's comments reinforce a key idea: just
> as Standard English speakers shift styles to be effective in a range of settings, so
> too do African-American English speakers. A *New Yorker* article on a speech class at
> the Julliard School finds a student there making the same point. African-American
> vernacular, she says, "makes us feel stronger, together — the fact that we can talk in
> a way that other people wouldn't understand." But the student acknowledged the
> need for Standard English as well adding, "If I only knew slang, how far could I go?"

There's nothing wrong with slang per se: slang is an inevitable manifestation
of variety in language. Students in school, of whatever race, ethnicity, religion,
or income level, will speak it. And as America's leading sociolinguist, William
Labov, testified before the U.S. Senate, AAVE

> is a dialect of English, which shares most of the grammar and vocabulary with other
> dialects of English. But it is distinctly different in many ways, and more different
> from standard English than any other dialect spoken in continental North America.
> It is not a set of slang words, or a random set of grammatical mistakes, but a well
> formed set of rules of grammar and pronunciation that is capable of conveying com-
> plex logic and reasoning.

Indeed, Smitherman proves the point by shifting frequently between AAVE and
dissertation English in her books, especially *Talkin That Talk* (2000). The problem with African American English, as well as slang, is that people react to it as
evidence of difference; when they do so they are reacting as much to the difference as to the language. As Smitherman argues, they prefer to focus on the language rather than the social conditions that foster discrimination.

How far can you get if you speak AAVE? As far as people will let you get. How
much slang do African Americans speak? In a sense, as much slang as people
think they speak, because if people hear African American speech as markedly
vivid, playful, racy, rebellious, and all of that, and for historical and social reasons they well may, then regardless of the lexical "facts," they may end up interpreting speech as slang when slang is really only part of what they're hearing.

Importantly, as the story of the Julliard student illustrates, African Americans often accept this interpretation of AAVE. The confusion of AAVE and slang, the assumption that slang is disruptive and marks low character, and, for both reasons, the perception that African Americans speak more slang than those who speak other varieties of American English are shared broadly in American culture. If this book changes any or all of these positions among its readers and our collective perception of slang changes, then the book has done some good.

Even if African Americans speak less slang than some assume, do young urban African men speak more slang than suburban soccer moms? The answer, again, is complicated. Younger people generally use more slang than older people, so yes. But it's not clear that men use slang more than women, though, until very recently, pretty much every commentator on slang assumed they did. Katherine Connor Martin (2005) locates the central problem: "Since a sense of masculinity permeates the slang concept, the conclusion that women use slang less than men is circular. As Dale Spender has noted, this sort of circular reasoning, in which assumptions about gendered language use are built into the very methodologies intended to test them, has frequently plagued studies seeking to compare men's and women's speech."

Because the raw, irreverent, socially low speech of, as Sledd put it, "gentlemen who are not gentlemen and dislike gentility" is historically associated in our imaginations with men in bars, men in brothels, men talking to men but not to their sweethearts or mothers, and because women who use slang therefore seem especially rebellious because they are acting like men, we overlook women's use of slang, or hear it less as slang because it's used by women, much as we hear elements of AAVE as slang because they are used by black folks, and black speech is slangier than other speech, and around the loop of perception we go, once again.

But women's slang has been there all along. "Jo does use such slang words," observes her sister, Amy March, in Louisa May Alcott's *Little Women* (1868–1869). The stereotype plays out in the ensuing exchange:

> Jo immediately sat up, put her hands in her apron pockets, and began to whistle.
> "Don't, Jo; it's so boyish."
> "That's why I do it."
> "I detest rude, unlady-like girls."
> "I hate affected, niminy piminy chits."

Amy thinks slang is for boys; so does Jo, and so do readers of the novel, who are drawn to Jo's transgressive behavior. They are often disappointed when, by novel's end, superficial markers of rebellion dissolve in experience, duty, and even grudging femininity, all of which may just prove that slang isn't for girls, let alone women.

It's certainly true that Jo uses lots of slang. When Meg wishes she had a silk dress for a dance, Jo remarks, "I'm sure our pops look like silk," where *pops* means 'poplin dresses'. While at the dance, she asks her next-door neighbor, Laurie, " 'I suppose you are going to college soon? I see you pegging away at your books — no, I mean studying hard,' and Jo blushed at the dreadful 'pegging' which had escaped her." What dreadful language for a young lady to use in public! You wouldn't accuse someone of *pegging* at a frat party, and lots of Jo's slang is old-fashioned, daring for her time and place, but hardly so now; nevertheless, attitudes expressed toward them within the book signal readers to recognize them as slang, however quaint they may seem.

Some of Jo's slang, however, resembles that of late twentieth- and early twenty-first-century American girls. She explains to Laurie, "In a place like this I'm sure to upset something, tread on people's toes, or do something dreadful, so I keep out of mischief and let Meg do the pretty." Later she toasts her sisters, "All fun and no grubbage," by which she means 'no work,' or grubbing around. Shifts from adjective to noun ("It gives me a happy" or "What's with the glum?") and *-age* suffixing (*fundage* 'money', *foodage* 'food', *postage* 'Internet chat room posts', *sparkage* 'romantic connection') have been popular in recent college slang and are straight out of *Buffy the Vampire Slayer*, though, obviously, they've been elements of American slang for a long time.

Though Jo is the avatar of slang and the attitudes expressed in it, her sisters use it too, when it suits their purposes: " 'Your humble servant, James Laurence'; only think of his writing that to you. I'll tell the girls; they'll think it's killing," says Amy. Meg suggests that, if Jo wants to do something nice for Meg's lover, John Brooke, she should "begin to do something now, by not plaguing his life out," which also sounds very contemporary, since some phrasal verbs are slangy today: *freak out* ("Dude, stop freaking me out") or *plague out* ("Dude, stop plaguing me out," that is, 'stop bugging me like a plague of locusts'). Even the narrator uses slang: "The girls had never been called angel children before, and thought it very agreeable, especially Jo, who had been considered 'a Sancho' ever since she was born." Angels are blond and fair skinned, and Jo is tanned by virtue of an active life, but *Sancho* is little short of *dago*, slang a lot less easy to forgive than any of Jo's lapses. In other words, *Little Women* should lead us to a set of conclusions: in nineteenth-century New England, slang was framed as masculine; girls spoke it unconsciously but heard it consciously and socialized one another out of its use by the time they became adults; women well past adolescence, like Alcott when she wrote *Little Women*, used slang anyway.

Little Women is not an exception, and not all nineteenth-century literary works frame slang as masculine, though it does tend to thumb its nose at gentility, wherever it's spoken, whoever speaks it. Elizabeth Grant of Rothiemurchus was the living embodiment of genteel. She wrote a manuscript account of her interesting life, passed down to her children, titled *Memoirs of a Highland Lady* (1845). Nevertheless, at the age of forty-seven, she could let fly with comments like the following:

> Jane and I were very much with our young friend the Princess. Her mother's very handsome house looking into the Park near Cumberland gate was a very agreeable change to us, and we were so at home there we were quite at ease among all the family circle. Jane was still the favourite, the one most paraded, most spoke of, but I was the one applied to when help was wanted, in fact the real A. No. 1 whatever they pretended.

At forty-seven she was writing to her children about her relations with a princess, and the first term that came to mind to describe her own status in the relationship was *A. No. 1* 'the best'. This calls many assumptions about slang and gender, slang and age, and slang and social class into question.

Grant doesn't use slang frequently, but she doesn't seem reluctant to mix it into her mature, upper-class style. She could write, quite unselfconsciously, "He was a remarkably handsome man then as now, and quite a crack preacher, all London flocking round any pulpit he consented to mount." When she was young, she knew how to misbehave; for example, after baiting her, she "looked archly at [her] governess, who poor woman, seemed in the moon." Words like *crack* 'excellent' and *in the moon* 'confused, vacant, detached' (not recorded in slang dictionaries but closely related to the more or less standard English adjective *moony*) seem harmless enough today but were a little racy, especially from a woman's pen, a hundred and fifty years ago.

And, like Alcott, Grant occasionally anticipates *Buffy the Vampire Slayer* and the contemporary slang maneuvers associated with it: "The Latin class was very respectable, the arithmatick very creditable of course, the recitations had to be applauded, and Lachlan Cameron was rewarded for action as well as emphasis — Jane having John Kembled him to the utmost of her ability — by receiving a handsome Copy of Goldsmith's works." John Kemble was a famous actor of the time, and *John Kembled* means 'coached his acting'; this sort of shift from proper name to verb was a staple of slayer slang: "Does anyone feel like we've been Keyser Soze'd?" Xander asks in the episode "The Puppet Show" (1997), where *Keyser Soze* the verb, meaning 'definitively manipulated, outmaneuvered' derives from the name of the sinister character at the center of Bryan Singer's film *The Usual Suspects* (1995). Certainly slang like this is likely to be short-lived, since those using it and hearing it have to have the cultural referent in mind.

One suspects that Grant's bad language associated with low behavior. The governess in question, Miss Elphick, may have thought so: "Poor Miss Elphick, she had troubled times. Her first grand stand was against the backgammon — shaking dice boxes in a publick inn! We were very polite but we would not give in, assuring her we always were accustomed to shake dice boxes where we liked out of lesson hours." The Grant sisters had learned this loose behavior by bad example. At a ball at Margate, for instance, they saw "large, fat Dowager Aldermanesses [widows of city dignitaries], with a fortune in Mechlin [Belgian funeral lace] and diamonds on them, [who] sat playing cards with tumblers of brandy and water beside them; the language used possessed a grammar of its own." These are feminine versions of Sledd's gentlemen: they drink, they game, and they speak with a grammar well suited to drinking and gaming. It's only a prejudice against such things that allows us to overlook them or read past them, preferring our perceptions to the historical realities.

It should come as no surprise, then, that in twenty-first-century America, though they speak somewhat distinct slangs, men and women are equally slangy. Here is an extended example of women's slang that begins to make the case. The (now defunct) women's magazine *Jane* regularly featured a "dating diary." The August 2006 installment is titled "The flirt buddy vs. a friend with benefits." Even though the magazine catered to the interests of women in their twenties and early thirties — young soccer moms — slang is plenty present. The title of the column itself is composed almost entirely of slang: *flirt buddy* and *friend with benefits*. It's a short column, only 488 words long, and only 38 of those are clearly slang, more or less splitting the difference between 7 and 8 percent. There's no reason to believe that the rate of slang in a *Jane* article resembles the rate of slang in conversation, though it might come closer to the rate of slang in personal narrative, stories we've thought out a bit ahead of time in order to titillate and amaze our friends. Articles in *Jane* are selling an identity in which writers, readers, and advertisers share. They're a type of performance speech.

Though it isn't exclusive to women, much of the slang in this particular installment of the dating diary isn't what we expect to hear in discourse among men. The author, Erin Flaherty, includes the following among her 488 words (some more than once, which is why they don't add up to 38):

- *flirt buddies* 'friends or acquaintances who, though not romantically involved, flirt'
- *fuck buddies* 'friends or acquaintances who, though not romantically involved, copulate'. The article is about the hazards of converting a flirt buddy into a fuck buddy.
- *booty call* 'request, by telephone or otherwise, for sex with a reliable friend; what you give your fuck buddy, when you feel the need'
- *hang out* 'spend time' and *hook up* 'copulate'; the former is for flirt buddies, the latter for fuck buddies
- *ridiculously* 'extremely' and *extreme* 'total'
- *hot* 'sexually attractive', sometimes ridiculously
- *perma-laid* 'constantly engaged in sexual relations', a condition of the ridiculously hot
- *mage double whammy* 'absolute winner', in which there are no wizards, but *mage* respells *maj*, clipped from *major*
- *fella* 'fellow' and *gent* 'gentleman'; a gentleman, that is, who is not a gentleman and dislikes gentility
- *getting me down* 'depressing me'; what fellas and gents do to the single woman when she's you
- *trippin' the light fantastic* 'dancing'; old slang from an old song, "The Sidewalks of New York" (1894), from an even older source, John Milton's poem "L'Allegro" (1632): "Come and trip it as ye go / On the light fantastic toe"
- *the shizzy* 'the shit, i.e., stuff, things'; very hip and a lot younger than *trippin' the light fantastic* (more on *-iz-*, *-izn-*, and *-izzy* in chapter 3)
- *sack* 'bed', where you have "a garden variety" *screw* with your fuck buddy
- *joint* 'marijuana cigarette', smoking which gets you *spaced out* 'high'
- *deal* 'cope with, manage'; *bailed* 'left, exited, quit'; what you do when you get out of the sack and find your fuck buddy spaced out (possibly more female- than male-associated slang, as discussed later in this chapter)
- *pass* 'forgo'; what you do after you bail and deal
- *blah* 'uncommitted, uninteresting'; how he sounds when he calls and you pass
- *yeah*, *no shit*, exclamations of experience
- *babe*, *wanna*, casual (lazy) word's HE uses without irony, as opposed to the narrator's *fella* and *gent*

There's reason to be suspicious about this slang in the aggregate: *shizzy* is very hip-hop and pretty hip, whereas *trippin' the light fantastic* is very literary, in a roundabout way; *fuck buddies* is a little vulgar, as are *screw* and *no shit*, but no one would find *blah, yeah, bail, deal, pass*, or *hang out* guilty pleasures to say (*hot* and *ridiculous* are a little problematic, as their raciness depends on just how they're said).

But this odd collection of slang reflects the soccer mom's social position: she is educated, picks up lyrics from old songs in martini bars, knows gamers (her husband may be one), likes some hip-hop (she was born, let's say, in 1974); she's old enough to say things that sound weird to young people and young enough still to absorb language of the moment. Her slang is mixed because her experience is mixed. She belongs to the group of women with similar experience — she knows it and they know it from the slang they share. By the way, men don't talk about flirt buddies; they worry less than they should about the distinction between hanging out and hooking up. However much slang in the "dating diary" overlaps the masculine and feminine domains, some is surely feminine. Assessing the slang that identifies a (fairly large) social group, like "soccer moms" or readers of *Jane*, can't proceed item by item: in *Jane*'s "dating diary," slang is situated in a feminine discourse partly constructed by the slang itself.

The "dating diary" is not an isolated example. *Jane* is slangy from cover to cover, issue after issue, and I have trouble finding articles, long or short, in which there is no slang (there are a few). Many align with slang right from the title: "She Totally Bangs," punning on *bangin'* 'excellent' at the outset of an article on "forehead fringe"; the "Striptease Special" profiles seven *celebs* who "talk about boobs, butts, and who they'd love to see in the buff." Or "Be Your Own Muse in the Boho Spirit of June Miller," or "Luke Wilson Would Dump a Girl If She Cheated." It isn't just that the writers and editors use slang; it's that the readers know it, too, or more significantly, that they EXPECT it. The magazine, composed of its readers, writers, editors, advertisers, and content, defines a mature but hip social group, perhaps struggling a bit to stay hip, but no one said getting older would be easy.

Even if there's a performance aspect to writing like *Jane*'s, it's not all talk, and this is, perhaps, part of what's changed about women's speech in the past half-century or so: the casual rebellion formerly characteristic of Flaherty's *gent*, who turns out to be a gentleman who is not a gentleman and dislikes gentility, is just as characteristic of the women. Remember that when Flaherty wakes up after a night of hooking up, she finds the gent "puffing on a joint." She bails, and we never find out whether she was racy enough to get stoned with him when they were flirt buddies. In the same issue, Anna Marrian decides to hook up with a guy she used to babysit, a guy ten years her junior (he's nineteen at the time of the event, so don't panic): " 'Pretty boring party, huh?' he said . . . 'Wanna go smoke a spliff?' 'Sure,' I said, sounding a tad too eager. I wanted to prove to him that I could be as cool as any 19-year-old, that I wasn't his nanny anymore." At twenty-nine, Ms. Marrian could have a couple of budding soccer stars in the back seat of her SUV. Instead, she smokes spliffs and does a guy who "look[s] like an underwear model with his snug briefs and toned tummy." If you get stoned and engage in "illicit" sex, let's face it, you're going to end up using slang to talk about it.

One reason we get caught in the gendered-language loop mentioned earlier is that we tend to stereotype slang as low, vulgar language. In *Fanboys and Overdogs: The Language Report* (2005), Susie Dent reports an account of slang by Jonathon Green, editor of *Cassell's Dictionary of Slang* (2005). Green claims that, if you sift the approximately 100,000 items of slang he identifies into categories, "5,700 refer to crime and criminals, 4,700 to drugs, . . . 1,700 to the act of sexual intercourse, 1,350 to the penis, . . . 1,200 to the vagina, . . . 730 to beating and hitting, . . . 220 to vomiting," and so on. We tend to associate the supposed coarseness of such language with boys being boys, but there are a couple of problems with that perception.

First, consider the following headline from *Jane*: "Want the instant fame a nip slip or coin-slot shot can provide without showing any skin? We've got the lingerie for you!" That's graphic in ways that the Episcopalian altar boy still ringing bells and lighting candles inside me can't discuss. Women can be just as vulgar as men, but if men record the slang and expect to find it where they look among men, they may overlook the degree to which slang overlaps the sexes. Conversely, there are whole categories of "clean" slang, in which women may outperform men, left off of Green's list, like *bail, hang out, yeah, flirt buddy*, and *no shit* (which does not belong in Green's "defecating and urinating" category). I can't estimate how often terms in his inventory are used: as recounted in the preceding chapter, there are lots of terms for MDMA, but some have been used longer and more often, or either longer or more often, than others. The availability of terms doesn't certify the terms of their use, so a woman's term, like *flirt buddy*, might be used considerably more often than masculine *morning glory*.

Spliff, joint, hook up, and all the rest are part of the code that identifies readers of *Jane* as hip, young, new millennial women. Reading *Jane* fortifies hip when hip is on the wane; single city women (not all of them, of course) marry, move to the suburbs, and are suddenly, unaccountably soccer moms. Some subscribe to *Jane* (they probably started when they were single city women) in order to live vicariously through an alter ego, a hybrid of what they were before they became soccer moms, and what they had become when they started to read *Jane* during a Saturday morning pedicure. That doesn't make the slang fake, just complicated. The *Jane* group is not extraordinary; it's a convenient, compact example of women's slang that sociolinguists have begun to investigate across generations and cultures.

For instance, when Diane Vincent studied religious profanity in Québec French (her book on the subject was published in 1982), she found that use of that profanity had changed within a couple of generations: older men used profanity more than older women, but younger women employed it about as much as younger men. Older people and a significant number of boys surveyed (34 percent) thought that profanity was normal for men but "ugly" in women's speech. Regardless of their disapproval, however, women seem to have indulged in profanity just as often as men; in Vincent's study, older women reported that profanity is used as often among women as men. I have put the case this way for a reason: although Vincent's older respondents claimed that their parents used little profanity, girls were much more aware than boys of their mothers' swearing, much as Elizabeth Grant was aware of dissolute, gambling widows overlooked by male lexicographers. One of two things must have occurred: either profanity was spoken among women to the exclusion of men, or boys simply responded as they thought they should, according to a time-honored gendered view of appropriate speech: men swear more than women because we think they do.

Recent studies suggest that as we enter the twenty-first century, slang belongs to men and women equally. As Wong Man Tat Parco put it in his thesis on the use of Cantonese slang among Hong Kong youth, "In terms of the frequency of slang use, the present research findings suggest that females are by no means passive slang users nowadays. Therefore, the traditional belief that males are slang dominators and females slang eschewers . . . does not hold true at present time any longer." This would seem to reflect a redefinition of gender roles in the developed world from the 1960s forward: the girls in question are their feminist grandmothers' progeny, the little sisters of riot grrrls. So if we suspect that some soccer mom readers of *Jane* may read more slang than they speak, the same may not be true of their soccer-playing daughters.

In a very thorough examination of the Corpus of London Teenage Language, (COLT), Anna-Brita Stenström, Gisle Andersen, and Ingrid Kristine Hasund attempt to show "that slang words, dirty and vague words are not distinct categories, but that we are dealing with words that are typically multifunctional, so that different functions are often intertwined. A reflection of this is that not only ordinary slang words but also the majority of the vague and dirty words met with in COLT conversations are labeled 'slang' " in all kinds of dictionaries. The authors come to this very intelligent and helpful conclusion: "Slang does not only consist of what we generally perceive as slang, words like *booze*, *chap*, *fag* and *grub*, but also vague words such as *stuff* and *thingy*, dirty words like *bitch*, *cunt* and *wanker*, and small words like *sort of* and *you know*. Many of these words are difficult to place in a fixed category, but they are all part of slangy language." The range of words thus described captures much of women's language usually ignored in the study of slang; when it's included in slang, the perception that women speak considerably less slang than men, let alone young, urban African American men, is confounded.

The contrastive patterns of use across age categories revealed by COLT are especially interesting. Per one thousand words, boys begin their teen years producing 5.7 "traditional" slang items; by the time they leave their teens, the rate has dropped to 3.3 items. Girls begin well behind boys, at 1.1 items per thousand, but leave with a rate of 5.6, well on their way to enjoying *Jane* or the United Kingdom's equivalent magazine. Boys ages ten to thirteen spew "dirty slang" at a rate of 3.4 per thousand, but by nineteen are considerably more polite, producing only .8 items of filth per thousand spoken, perhaps because they are mixing more with girls, hoping to impress them, and harboring the illusion that girls don't like slang. Nothing could be further from the truth: girls ages ten to thirteen produce barely any "dirty slang," at .4 items per thousand; by the time they leave their teens, at age seventeen to nineteen, the rate has increased dramatically to 2.4 per thousand. Boys swear at the rate of 4.0 per thousand at age ten to thirteen and after they're twenty, somewhat less in between; when they're seventeen to nineteen girls swear more than their male peers, at a rate of 3.1 versus 2.0 per thousand, but their rate drops below 1.0 once they enter their twenties.

Where girls represented in COLT pretty clearly have boys beat is in what Stenström and her colleagues call "vague expressions" (for instance, *sort of* and *thingy*), quotatives ("She goes, '*Go* is sometimes used as a quotative, innit?' "), intensifiers ("*Go* is so a quotative"), and tags ("She goes, '*Okay* is a good example of a tag, innit?' "). Males and females in COLT use "vague expressions" at similar rates, 8.6 per thousand for the boys and 8.1 for the girls, though their inventories of such expressions is slightly different, with *thingy* and *sort of* shared, but *loads of* ("It was loads of fun") typical of boys and *and everything* ("It was fun and everything, but only sort of") typical of girls.

Girls are ahead of boys at the rate of 3.81 per thousand to 2.44 when it comes to quotative *go*; they marginally outdistance boys, too, in the use of intensifiers, .52 per thousand to .48. And they not only use more but, on average, different tags from boys: girls are ahead on *eh* (.17 vs. .16), *right* (.68 vs. .61), and *innit* (.90 vs. .56); boys are ahead on *okay* (.48 vs. .36) and *yeah* (1.91 vs. 1.25) — they're in a gray area.

Some will doubt whether tag questions like *okay* and *innit* should count as slang, and it's true that they are in a gray area. We don't think of a professor, standing in front of class and ending sentences with *right?* ("So, John of Gaunt was in a sticky situation, right?") as a slang speaker speaking slang at that moment. And perhaps the young women tag questioners of London are, in that feature, less slangy than I am suggesting, too. As a reality check, though, watch Albert and Allen Hughes's documentary *American Pimp* (1999) and listen for tags. There's really only one, and it suffuses the film: *know what I'm sayin'?* In its basic function, *know what I'm sayin'?* isn't profoundly different from professorial *right?* and schoolgirl *innit?*

But I think many viewers will hear *know what I'm sayin'?* as slang, an item of the late twentieth-century American underworld lexicon. All of the men who use it in the film are pimps, and all the women are prostitutes; we expect people like that to use slang, so we hear it. All of the pimps are African American men; we expect black guys to use slang more even than white urban teens, certainly more than professors and women. We hear slang when we are prompted by nonlinguistic facts to hear it; in other words, our conception of slang is partly perception, and our perception partly based on preconceived notions. In 1976 Harry McGurk and John McDonald, two Australian psychologists, tested the extent to which what we see affects what we hear. They showed their test subjects video of speakers saying one sound while simultaneously playing them an audio tape of a closely related but different sound; the subjects reported hearing a third closely related but different sound. The result of conflicting visual and aural information is called the McGurk effect. If we hear tag questions in the speech of black pimps as slang, yet tag questions from the mouths of babes are merely colloquial, we experience a similar effect.

Girls and women may have used slang less than boys and men in the past; as they grow into adulthood, men may continue to use slang more than women — at least, certain types of slang. But given the variety of evidence to the contrary, it's difficult to sustain the assumption. Similarly, depending on what you measure, African Americans may use more slang than whites, or African American men may use more slang than white women, or young, urban African American men may use more slang than suburban soccer moms. Or, depending on what you measure, which depends on what you hear or read, as well as what you count as slang, they don't.

But all of us, young and old, black and white, urban and suburban have slang, and, with your eyes closed, we can tell black guys chillaxin' with their buddies from young soccer moms dishing about the latest issue of *Jane*. We share more slang than separates us, but what separates us tells us and others where we fit in, or perhaps, where we hope to fit in, and where we don't. It supports social mythologies natural to the formation of group identity but potentially harmful because they don't correspond to the truth and, as firmly embedded assumptions, obscure and obstruct the truth about the way we speak now. As a social marker, though, slang works: you know that you're among the old, tired, gray, and hopeless, rather than hip, vivid, playful, and rebellious, if only in spirit, when you hear no slang. Slang is a tell even in its absence.

YOUTH: AN INTERLUDE

Though slang marks many types of social groups, most of us associate it with youth, especially with adolescence, and research like that of Stenström and her colleagues on COLT confirms our intuitions. As Mary Bucholtz has written, slang is "the most noticeable linguistic component of youth-based identities," so, as we are inclined to do with African American slang, we may overestimate it, especially as we get older. Old people don't like new things, and they can't help but notice that young people are disruptive, or at least different. But whereas relatively few Americans have been African Americans, all adult Americans have been teenagers, so our sense of slang's centrality in youth and youth's centrality to slang is informed, not only by observation, but also by personal experience.

Slang is fresh and improvised, for the most part young language, and therefore it cleaves to youth—they're joined at the hip, so to speak. Once upon a time, we were all casually clever, inventive, playful, vivid, rebellious speakers. Along the way to how we talk now, though, something went terribly wrong! Our perception may be driven partially by nostalgia, but we have no doubts that patterns of language use change considerably as we age. Oddly, the slang in dictionaries often seems more mature than adolescents are likely to use. How many teenagers spend their afternoons at the track, smoking crack, or shooting smack? (The answer is "Too many," but you understand the statistical point.) Dictionaries include lots of words without indicating how many speakers use them or how often, which distorts our picture of slang's social role: old slang used by relatively few people from long ago takes up as much space as new slang used by lots of people right now. Young people slang their way through their teens and twenties, profligate with profanity, tag questions, and everything in between; it's as though there were no limit, no balance to pay off. But, sooner or later, responsibilities mount and we quail at the linguistic risk. Life's usury trims away our use of slang.

What's true of slang is true of linguistic productivity in adolescence generally. In the course of learning how to use language socially, young people promote variation and change until they hit what William Labov calls "the adolescent peak," after which they calm down into adulthood. Adults devote their time to managing a wide variety of responsibilities (family and work chief among them), but, as Marcel Dinesi notes, "Talking occupies most of the teen's time," so teenagers have plenty of reason to invest in talk and plenty of opportunity to experiment with language and its social effects. In his book *Forever Young* (2003) Danesi also suggests that slang is not confined to youth, that adult culture is increasingly influenced by youth culture: "Adolescent slang is everywhere, alongside adolescent fashions and lifestyles," he writes. "It is unprecedented, to the best of my knowledge, that an entire culture takes many of its discourse cues from youth-generated slang. Words such as *loony, nuts, psycho, babe, chick, squeeze, dude, sloshed, plastered, make out, scram, split, chill* and many more, have become so much a part of our everyday vocabulary that we hardly ever realize that we have taken them from teen slang."

Certainly adults use slang (one suspects that they always have to some degree). Their use of it today may be unprecedented, but it's certainly extensive enough to warrant the language of *Jane*. Danesi's list of exemplary slang items is problematic, though, and may not support his case as fully as he hopes. Are *loony, psycho,* and *scram* ("All right, now, scram you big palooka") really current among teens? Do twenty-first-century teens *make out* with their *main squeezes*, or do they *mack on* and *hook up*? We may prefer that they get *sloshed* or *plastered* rather than *fubar* 'fucked up beyond all recognition', but they're more likely to associate *sloshed* with their parents — or my parents, who would be their grandparents. However much adults today emulate adolescents and attempt to appropriate their slang and other elements of teen style, they will not succeed enough to fool adolescents, those who really control cool.

Teens feel social pressure from all directions, and resisting it insofar as authority will allow is a natural response. All experiments with style, from skirt length to tattoos to slang, test the limits of authority and resistance. Though Lyn Mikel Brown has a particular group of girls in mind, the following comment aptly characterizes the role of language in fashioning adolescent identity:

> The Acadia girls, too, occupy this liminal reality; they, too, struggle against the gendered boundaries pressing upon them. But unlike the Mansfield girls, they embrace their education as the medium for refusal and resistance. The ease with which they manipulate the conventions of language speaks to their comfort with, indeed, their pleasure in, the privileged middle-class world of school they occupy. Experiencing the limits of "appropriate" speech and behavior, they create new, unofficial ways of expressing themselves. Robin, for example, introduces new words, as yet unpopulated with the intentions and meanings of the dominant culture, as a way to express her strong feelings and to carve out room for those pieces of her experience that are unfit for the public world of her classroom.

The boundaries need not be those of gender. Though young women learn to manage the gendered boundaries, African American teens struggle against boundaries of race, and urban teens struggle against the almost physical boundaries of class. While the Acadia girls "embrace their education as the medium for refusal and resistance," there are lots of other media effective for those purposes, and language is always one of them, because, as Brown suggests, it is always the focus of social measurement and approval. If, unlike Robin, you cannot think of any new words "unpopulated with the intentions and meanings of the dominant culture," you can nonetheless bend the existing language to your purposes. One could go on and on with examples of the new and the bent, but the preceding chapter is full of youth slang that perfectly captures pieces of experience unfit for the public world but necessary for the teen freshly engaged in experience and aching to talk about it.

As Geraldine Bloustien declares in her ethnography of Australian teen girls, "Cool equals self-possession." Allowing the pressures of growing up to get you down is both psychological and social defeat, and part of surviving adolescence is determining who you are, possessing yourself, so that no one else has the chance to impose an identity on you. "Cool" is a very elastic concept: at times, it refers to restraint and reserve, a resistance to being judged that depends on refusing to expose oneself to scrutiny, that is, on being inscrutable. But as long as a teen is comfortably extreme, self-possessed in outright rebellion, well, that's cool, too. "Cool" is fraught with paradox: you have to be above what others would do, if doing it would define you as following the crowd, but at no time can you simply ignore the crowd and its norms. Never having the guts to challenge the powers that be isn't cool, but constantly raging against the machine isn't cool, either. Finally, it doesn't do you any good to be inscrutable if people don't notice your exquisite inscrutability; nor does it do you any good if your outrageous behavior allows others to pigeonhole you. One of the greatest pressures bearing on adolescents is the pressure to establish an individual identity while learning to fit in to groups. If you are aggressively only individual, you disrespect your group; groups disrespect their members if they obliterate all emerging individuality.

Mostly, youth rebels against authority and revels in the pleasures of rebellion. As Samantha Moeller, the founding editor of *Missbehave*, explains, the relatively new magazine caters to "more edgy, street-savvy women ages 18–32," readers somewhat younger than *Jane*'s, who carry the teen propensity toward slang into the still youthful twenties.[8] In *Missbehave* you will encounter items like this one, which is all about (1) being bad, but (2) not being so bad that you can get into serious trouble, and (3) flaunting it, which is where slang comes in:

> Yo drunky, put down the Sparks and pay attention. Okay, so you know there's nothing funny about DUIs, but did you know there's plenty fun to be had with the Alcohawk portable breathalyzer? Minutes after your last swig of vittle you can play the fun and educational drinking game we've affectionately dubbed, "Who's Drunker Now?" . . . We can't help your questionable beer-goggled tastes, but with this nifty number you can anticipate if the dude you've pulled will pee all over your million-count sheets. What a champion. Cop yours for $69.99 at breathalyzer.net.

If you are a parent, you've heard this type of talk before: "Well, okay, we got wasted, but at least we didn't drive anywhere," in which case underage binge drinking is obviously, obviously a virtue.

Some of this slang, like *yo*, *swig*, *dude*, *pee*, and *cop*, is familiar and smells vaguely of the back alley and criminal activity, though apparently, if you're of

---

8. In fact, *Missbehave* is an excellent example of women's slang coming into its own, resisting the traditional stereotype that slang belongs to boys. Eric Sass, in "Mags Shift from Laddies to Ladies, Target Young Girls" (March 30, 2006), writes that *Missbehave* "moves in a milieu that marries hip-hop street culture and the cultivated hipster sensibility embraced by many young women with disposable income in urban environments. Interestingly, according to Moeller, this style demographic was first served by men's magazines." Sass quotes Moeller as saying, "There's all these men's magazines that show this kind of stuff—and we're saying hey, it's time for the women's side too." Where the style goes, so goes the slang, regardless of gender.

a certain mind and attitude, it's *plenty* fun. Some of it is new enough (or nonce enough) to evade the dictionary record so far, like *drunky* and *vittle* (is this an alcoholic beverage, or does it refer more precisely to bourbon or corn mash whiskey, associated in the urban imagination with hillbillies, vittles, and such?) and *pulled* (which Dalzell and Victor's *New Partridge Dictionary of Slang and Unconventional English* [2005] locates in the United Kingdom and defines as 'engage in a casual or recreational quest for a sexual partner', though in this case the "quest" seems to be over and *pull* refers instead to what happens between the sheets before the partner pees). *Missbehave* clearly appeals to readers somewhere between *Seventeen*'s innocent consumerism and the sedately slangy *Jane*.

Missbehave is written in slang, but it's about style and how to express it, not just in language but also in fashion, music, and just general attitude: it's an extended advertisement for how to stand out by fitting in. You can get a good sense of what Jeepney clothing looks like, for instance, not just from the photograph of a young woman wearing it, but from the language used to describe it: "Etymology lesson, bitches. For those who don't know, the Jeepney is a vehicle specific to the Philippines — leftover Jeeps from World War II tricked out as a form of public transportation. Get it? Jeep + Jitney? Awesome." This clothing is tough and in your face; it's old school improvised, just like slang! Jeepney clothing "flips and reverses the T-shirt game with a grip of badass Ts dropping this spring." The author of this squib, Samantha Moeller herself, identifies the brand with the brand name with the style: "Going forward," she proposes, " 'Jeepney' is going to mean 'lookin' real good.' Like, 'Hate me now! I'm feeling dumb Jeepney in my new T and matching Dunks.' Best believe you'll find a nice match for those kicks you've been hoarding all winter." I read this and I don't feel dumb Jeepney, just dumb. I can't keep up with the onslaught of youthful invention and the deft application of *Jeepney* to a whole way of being, which is clearly a very cool way of being, even if it is defined by T-shirt style. And how did Ms. Moeller get etymology into an article about finding the right T to match those kicks? If she didn't write so well, she'd be in danger of becoming an English professor.[9]

---

9   I don't know anything about Ms. Moeller's plans to parent or not, but she's seriously in danger of becoming a soccer mom! At this writing, according to an article about *Missbehave* by Gillian Reagan in the *New York Observer* (July 24, 2007), Moeller is thirty or thirty-one years old. I calculate soccer momhood as follows: graduate from college at twenty-one or twenty-two, enjoy an independent life for a few years, say, until twenty-six, then have a child or two, who, by the time you are thirty-five, are on the soccer field.

But I'm not supposed to understand youth slang; it's designed to keep me at a distance. Even if, in all of my lexicography, I manage to understand it, I'm still not going to get it. As Rosalind Wiseman warns in *Queen Bees and Wannabes* (2002):

> Don't use the slang your daughter uses. There's nothing more ridiculous to a teen than an adult who tries to be hip by using teen slang. Slang changes so fast that it's impossible to keep up anyway. Nevertheless, some parents think that if they use it, they'll relate to their daughter better. Not true. It only looks like you're trying too hard — and there's nothing worse to a teen. If she uses a word you don't understand, ask her to explain it to you. She may laugh at how clueless you are, but it demonstrates that you respect and are interested in what she has to say and how she describes her world.

Good advice, though it may miss the point: the young are not necessarily angling for our respect, which, given how clueless we are, may not be worth much. Nevertheless, I can't help but be interested in what they have to say and how they describe their world, even if a lot gets lost in translation. A young acquaintance of mine in North Carolina a couple of years ago, Eleanor Costley, had taken to using *Dig it?* as a conversational tag. She was, I think, in fourth grade, precocious and talking like a hep cat from the Beat scene or Geneva Smitherman — who knows how that happened? Sure, I dig it, but I can't explain why without its being beside the point.

Young people are the group with the most and most extreme slang; adults are the ones who've lost their slang along with their hair, teeth, and sense of humor. It can't be helped. As Abe Simpson memorably put it, "I used to be with 'it.' Then they changed what 'it' was. Now, what I'm with isn't 'it,' and what's 'it' seems weird and scary to me." Well, Ms. Moeller, "It'll happen to you."

NEGOTIATING WITH SLANG

The Knock Knock flash cards pretend to teach Street, but they can't, because they commit what we might call the Synonymic Fallacy. You are already familiar with this fallacy if you relied too heavily on a thesaurus in school, assuming that you could insert any synonym listed for a word in any sentence in any paper

---

For all I know, in a couple of years Moeller will have a junior fullback on her hands. By then, however, she'll have left her magazine's youthier demographic behind.

on any subject, without considering subtle differences in meaning or, above all, tone. So, you can't credibly write things like, "Catherine the Great wore mad bling at her coronation" or "In a world fraught with international misunderstanding, multilateral negotiation is the shiznit." To use slang effectively, that is, appropriately within a group-defined social circumstance (and, to some extent, all social interaction is group-defined), you have to grasp intuitively what works, what credibly identifies you with the conversational group, what presents the social face you want others to see, and what accomplishes the social work you have in mind for any given conversation.

When it comes to negotiating social status, you can't fool any of the people any of the time. One African American man can react approvingly to another's prowess with "You one ba-a-a-a-d muthafucka!" If you are a white guy, you can drill night after night with your slang flash cards, but you won't hit the note when you blow: you will say "You are one bad motherfucker." You will sound like Dave Chappelle's caricature of a white guy talking, and people are going to suspect that you are, in fact, a white guy. You need to know the slang that counts in identifying with the interests of one group or another, but you also need to know how to use the slang authentically and effectively, something that flash cards and dictionaries and, frankly, books about slang will not help you to do.

Our social identities are determined, to a degree, by things beyond our control, but that doesn't mean that we're automata. We want to fit in, we want to perform well socially, according to the social script, but we get to write parts of that script as we fashion ourselves into public characters. Slang doesn't just mark a social identity: it also facilitates style. At our most stylish, we get noticed, we stand out. So choices we make about when to use slang, what slang to use, and how to use it effectively subtly negotiate fitting in and standing out. On one hand, style identifies us with a group: what everyone's saying is like what everyone's wearing; on the other, style ensures that everyone in the group sees us as distinct, that we're not someone (or anyone) else.

On a practical basis the problem isn't whether to borrow items of another group's slang into one's own, or to make a big splash with an astonishing new word. Though borrowing obviously occurs, it isn't an everyday event, and it has to be calibrated carefully to a leader's status and a group's openness to change. Establishing new slang is within a group leader's purview, but leaders can't get too far ahead of their group without losing authority. The Queen Bee may micromanage her group's slang, but she can't ignore the group's macromanagement of identity, even if she can't control it; borrowing can enhance status within the local group, but the local group has no interest in erasing global distinctions between old and young, male and female, black and white. Indeed, quite the opposite.

Saying the wrong thing or saying the right thing in the wrong way, just generally lacking social finesse, can mean social isolation. If you are uncool because your speech exposes you as uncool, then you lose control over your identity: others will determine that identity, and you are literally no longer "self-possessed." Queen Bees can't have their followers making verbal fools of themselves because it reflects badly on the group and, therefore, the leader. In *Mean Girls* (2004), the film adaptation of Wiseman's *Queen Bees and Wannabes* (2002), Gretchen, who is generally a follower, keeps trying to work a new item, *fetch* 'awesome, excellent', as in "That is so fetch," into her group's lingo. The Queen Bee, appropriately named Regina, thinks *fetch* (clipped from *fetching*) is stupid and shuts Gretchen down: "Gretchen, stop trying to make fetch happen. It's not going to happen."[10] Put in these terms, it's surprising that we survive conversation and the social risks it entails. Indeed, some of us survive less well than others; the less conversationally adept have a hard time in school, and there aren't, in fact, any flash cards to help one cram for the next day's test of one's social savvy.

To watch slang in action, it helps to narrow our focus from all slang to one slang feature as it operates in one text. So let's consider phrasal verbs, like *bail out*, *freak out*, *hang out*, and *wig out*, as well as their clipped alternatives, *bail*, *freak*, *hang*, and *wig*. And, because it's a very manageable text, one in which the slang sounds authentic, let's consider how those verbs are used in the television series *Buffy the Vampire Slayer*.[11] In fact, let's narrow the focus a little more, to the first

10 Contributors to the online Urban Dictionary have paid no attention to Regina, compiling an entry with forty-one definitions of *fetch*, twenty-six of which have to do with the *Mean Girls* sense and refer to *Mean Girls* in the entry. Several of these insist that *fetch* has long been in use to mean 'cool, awesome' in the United Kingdom, but the dictionaries to trust do not bear this out. These contributors, well intentioned as they are, are an army of Gretchens determined to "make *fetch* happen," but getting it into "the Dictionary" is back-asswards, and *fetch* is no more common in speech today than it was before the film was released. Oh, and the other meanings recorded for *fetch* were 'spunk, cum, jism', 'euphemism for the F-word', and 'retrieve'.

11 *Buffy the Vampire Slayer* ran for seven seasons, five of them on the WB Network and the final two on UPN, from March 1997 to May 2003. Episodes and dates are not particularly important to my approach here, so I won't belabor them. Those completely unfamiliar with the show and its language may want to read my *Slayer Slang: A "Buffy the Vampire Slayer" Lexicon* (2003), but, to summarize briefly, Buffy Summers is the Slayer: she battles

three seasons, during which Buffy and her friends attend Sunnydale High; they start college in Season 4, and arguably, as evidence and argument earlier in the chapter suggest, speakers over the age of eighteen use different slang differently from those just a phase younger.

In every instance in which you could use either a full phrasal verb, like *bail out*, or its clipped version, *bail*, you have to choose which better suits the situation. You have to gauge this on the basis of several factors simultaneously: How do those to whom you are speaking see you? Is your relationship formal or familiar? Are you too old to belong in their group? Are you the right gender? What do you want from them as a result of what you say: acceptance within the group, a concrete result or action? The choosing here need not be fully conscious: we produce most of our speech unconsciously (we rarely think about how to pronounce the words we use, or how to compose a sentence), but we can be thoughtful on occasion and consciously produce speech to suit our sense of decorum, class, and generation. Style oscillates along the consciousness line.

There are lots of phrasal verbs in English, and plenty of them are represented in *Buffy*. Of course, you have to have some sense of which phrasal verbs can be clipped safely, and not all of them can. Here are some examples of clippings that wouldn't work, with full phrasal quotations from *Buffy* episodes:

- WILLOW: "I hear he NODS OFF a lot." "I hear he nods a lot" would confuse matters, failing as it does to distinguish between dozing and agreeing.
- CORDELIA: "Do I HORN IN your private discussions?" "Do I horn your private discussions?" doesn't make any sense!
- BUFFY: "I think it's great that you have this pen pal, but don't you think you're RUSHIN' INTO this?" There's a subtle difference between rushing something and rushing into it.
- BUFFY: "Digging on the undead doesn't exactly do wonders for your social life." Though you can *dig* the undead as well as *dig on* them, in the sense 'approve,

---

all sorts of evil forces, but especially vampires. The Slayer (there's only supposed to be one in the world at a time), is "chosen," often against her will, to serve destiny and has supernatural powers. (At the very end of the series we discover that those powers are demonic.) Like all Slayers, Buffy has a Watcher, Rupert Giles, who guides her, trains her, teaches her, and protects her. It's unusual in the history of slaying, but Buffy has friends who help her (they call themselves the Scooby Gang): centrally, these are Willow Rosenberg, Xander Harris, and Cordelia Chase, though, in later seasons, the group expands and contracts.

admire, crush on (but not crush)', someone might think that you were talking about exhumation rather than romance if you clipped.

Given the sexually charged atmosphere in which they're spoken, the following would be awkward conversations if the verbs were clipped:

- ANGEL: "I can't. Unless you invite me, I can't COME IN."
  BUFFY: "Well, OK, I invite you . . . to COME IN." Those who love each other but cannot consummate that love shouldn't talk about "coming."
- XANDER: "Hey, Snyder, heard you had some fun Friday night. Have you COME DOWN yet?" Principal Snyder is a frustrated little man, but not as frustrated as the clipped form would imply.
- JENNY: "Rupert, I know you're concerned, but having you constantly POKIN' AROUND, making little puppy dog eyes, wondering if I'm okay . . . you make me feel bad that I don't feel better." Though he hasn't got around to it, pokin' is on Rupert Giles's mind, but he doesn't want Jenny Calendar to confront him with her suspicion of that fact.

Only certain full phrasal and clipped forms count as slang. Everyone uses *wrap up* (a gift), *sneak up*, *paired off*, *track down*, *bounce back*, *pick up*, *grow up*, and *slipped out*, and though they're hardly elevated language, they don't mark speakers as male or female, young or old, or member of any particular group at school. Socially adept speakers know when listeners will accept a clipping and when they won't.

In cases like *bail out/bail, chill out/chill, creep out/creep, freak out/freak, hang out/hang, pissed off/pissed, show up/show,* and *wig out/wig,* both the full phrasal forms and the accompanying clipped forms are slang. (Meg March's *plague out* never seems to have developed a clipped alternative: there's no "Don't plague me [out], man" or "Why you always plaguin'?" though there is "Don't plague me [with] trivialities!") Using any of these forms entails two slang decisions: first, you have to decide to use *bail out/bail* rather than 'leave', to use slang at all, rather than a standard synonym; second, you have to decide to clip or not to clip, depending on which best achieves your conversational goal or manifests your style. Judging by the ear, one might conclude that clipped forms are favored in current slang. In all of the cases listed, the full phrasal and clipped alternatives have been available simultaneously since the 1960s (*freak out/freak,* for instance) or 1970s (for *bail out/bail*), whenever the clipping came into vogue. The prominence of clipped forms in current slang is probably a somewhat deliberate choice of a younger generation to distinguish itself from an older one, but, as we'll see, it's much more complicated than that.

Certainly, youngsters prefer that oldsters not tread on their slang territory, just as Wiseman argued in *Queen Bees and Wannabes* (2002). In the episode "Band Candy" Buffy has recently returned home after running away—she had had to slay Angel, the vampire she loved—and she finds both her mother, Joyce, and her mentor, her Watcher, Rupert Giles, overbearing. She proposes a little freedom, but they're not having it:

> JOYCE: The last time you made a decision on your own, you split.
>   . . .
> BUFFY: You can't babysit me all the time. I need you to back off a little.
> GILES: All right, come, come, let's not freak out.
> BUFFY: Freak out?

The passage turns out to be ironic, as *split* and *freak out* are items of Giles's and Joyce's 1970s slang, and the "band candy" Buffy is required to sell in order to support the Sunnydale High marching band soon drugs them (adults throughout the town, in fact) into something like adolescence. Buffy refuses to accept even the full phrasal form *freak out* from Giles: her tone when she questions it mingles dismay, disbelief, and outrage. She reacts as she does not only because he usually talks like the stuffy Oxbridge educated librarian and super-responsible person he is, but also because of his age: old people aren't supposed to use slang. By contrast, Jenny Calendar, once Giles's love interest, can get away with clipping because she's a hip young teacher, barely older than her students, considerably younger than most of her teaching colleagues: "Willow . . . I might be a little late tomorrow. Do you think you could cover my class till I show?" Jenny may well have subscribed to *Jane*, had she lived long enough, maybe even to *Missbehave*.

Though gender is not so important to this example, it is important, as we've seen, if not to the amount of slang a speaker uses, at least to the nature of a speaker's slang: though much is shared among them, men and women use different slang for different purposes. On the basis of *Buffy* evidence, a speaker's gender predicts, not only the tendency to use clipped forms of phrasal verbs, but to use phrasal verbs at all, even those that can't safely or idiomatically be clipped. In fact, in Seasons 1 through 3, women produce both clipped and full phrasal forms three times more often than men. If the show even approximates natural use of these forms, it seems safe to say that variation in full phrasal verb forms and their clipped alternatives is a significant feature of feminine discourse, present but less significant in masculine speech. In the show men never clip among themselves, though they do in conversation with women, especially when fitting in to groups dominated by them.

Buffy is a leader, of sorts. She is isolated (much of the show is about the loneliness of the adolescent heroine), but she is also extraordinarily powerful, an icon of "girl power" who untrivializes that originally pop-based phenomenon. Buffy the Vampire Slayer is no Spice Girl. The Slayer's world is a girl's world: the Slayer is always called when a girl and, given the risks of vampire slaying, she usually dies a girl; Buffy dies twice, in fact. Buffy is at the center of the Buffyverse, her best friend is a girl, she has a sister, and many of the extended Scooby Gang are rising young women. Xander is a friend of girls, and he spends a lot of time talking to them; sometimes he talks like them, but aware that masculinity isn't always his most prominent characteristic he occasionally acts and talks in manlier ways. Sometimes he clips, sometimes he doesn't, depending on what about his gender identity he wants to emphasize at the moment.

All of this is to be expected: throughout decades of work on the social factors contributing to linguistic change, William Labov has adapted a model of personal influence in social change proposed by Elihu Katz and Paul Lazarsfeld in 1955. Ultimately, we learn, certain middle-class women lead social change, including linguistic change. Labov is primarily concerned with sound change, for instance, how vowels merge with one another in a dialect's phonology. But the model works for slang, too. Buffy exerts a great deal of personal influence in her world: she initiates almost all of the innovative language in the show, not item for item, but by establishing the patterns on which other characters create new words. Buffy may lead the other characters in clipping of phrasal verbs overall, but she is not the first to clip in the series. That honor belongs to Cordelia Chase, Sunnydale High School's Queen Bee (or "Queen C," as her vanity license plate announces), who is a leader in her own right.

Cordelia's group, the Cordettes, is a stereotyped version of the cool group. Its members are so subordinate to Cordelia that that they can't really be considered "self-possessed," but Cordelia is self-possessed enough for all of them. She rules her group with a tongue of steel — what she says goes. She tumbles from that exalted social position, however, when she becomes too involved with Buffy's friends, the Scooby Gang; she changes groups, gradually and unexpectedly, for reasons that she can't begin to explain. (Before the transformation is complete, though, she has a poignant discussion with Buffy about the loneliness inherent in leadership, a theme that runs through the series.) The Scooby Gang is a more loosely organized group, one in which individuality is respected and encouraged; the series story arc includes much discussion of who is in whose shadow and how to get out from under it, issues that never occur to the Cordettes. But that doesn't imply that life in the Scooby Gang is easier than in other high school groups; the Gang's language models and reflects intragroup conflicts, enacts the stress of deciding when to fit in, when to stand out.

Whatever their differences, because Cordelia and Buffy are young and female phrasal verbs and clippings figure in their shared idiom. They use the forms in conversation according to motives subtler than race, ethnicity, gender, or age. For instance, when Cordelia says to Buffy, "You'll be okay here. If you hang with me and mine, you'll be accepted in no time," she is exhibiting her casual control of things, asserting her cool, in the clipped form. Her theory of leadership is apparent in the phrase "me and mine," and the implication is that Buffy will not be okay unless she assimilates into the "mine." Cordelia is in the habit of pushing the linguistic envelope just a bit, and her verbal style establishes a sort of social base line for Buffy:

CORDELIA: And, if you're not too swamped with catching up, you should come to the Bronze tonight.

BUFFY: The who?

CORDELIA: The Bronze. It's the only club worth going to around here. They let anybody in, but, it's still the scene. It's in the bad part of town.

BUFFY: Where's that?

CORDELIA: About a half a block from the good part of town — we don't have a lot of town here. But, uh, you should show.

Cordelia's informality is double-edged: it's meant to be appealing, to insinuate that Buffy wants to be part of Cordelia's crew; it's also proof that Cordelia takes liberties with language, a declaration of status.

Interestingly, at least early in the series, others at the school, including the uncool, unpopular students who become Buffy's best friends, defer to that status:

CORDELIA: Are these guys bothering you?

BUFFY: Uh, no.

WILLOW: She's not hanging out with us.

Willow is not cool, and she does not tread on Cordelia's social territory, which is marked by certain types of slang; instead, she differentiates herself from

Cordelia and her followers by using the full phrasal *hanging out*, and, in doing so, she speaks a little more formally and politely, meant as a deferential gesture. It's not that Willow's incapable of clipping: she chooses not to clip here so that she doesn't compete with Cordelia for the right to use certain slang, just as she stays out of social trouble by not competing with Cordelia for Buffy's friendship, though she's delighted when Buffy chooses her over Cordelia in the end.

Authority, as much as humility, is often a matter of tone. To be emphatic, to demand an appropriate response, Buffy clips: "What I need is for you to chill." Isn't it odd that people who use *chill* emphatically are far from chilling themselves? The short form conveys, among other things, that Buffy doesn't have time for the full phrasal form—it's a matter of survival. Conversely, the full form can convey a reassuring gravity, empathy communicated in willingness to take time. Thus Buffy deflects a postcrisis apology from a potential boyfriend: "You don't even have to. I'm sure you were pretty freaked out." Clipping would be too casual and seem to make light of the poor guy's natural fear of demons. Buffy is often glib with her demon antagonists: she confronts them with attitude, often indulging in word play as a sort of precombat flourish, a display of her self-possession and confidence. By contrast, though, she can sound menacing when she uses the full phrasal form, slow and deliberate and ostensibly polite: "I'm glad you showed up," she says to a demon she doesn't know well.

Inclined to clip, Cordelia uses the full phrasal forms when she (grudgingly) accepts an inferior social position, much as Willow did in the passage quoted earlier. You can hear, in what follows, Cordelia's reluctance to truckle under, but she needs Buffy's help—it's a matter of life or death—so she speaks more formally, and therefore more respectfully, as she debases herself:

CORDELIA: I knew you'd be here. Buffy, I, ah, I know we've had our differences, with you being so weird and all and hanging out with these total losers. Oooh. Well, anyway, despite all of that, I know that you share this feeling that we have for each other deep down...

WILLOW: Nausea?

CORDELIA: Somebody is after me. They just tried to kill Mrs. Miller—she's helping me with my homework. And Mitch. And Harmony. This is all about me. Me, me, me.

XANDER: Wow, for once she's right.

BUFFY: So you came to me for help.

CORDELIA: Because you're always around when all this weird stuff is happening, and I know you're very strong and you've got all those weapons — I was kind of hoping that you were in a gang. Please! I don't have anyone else to turn to.

Only the desperation apparent in her last plea would move Cordelia to change her demeanor from Queen C to that of supplicant. It isn't easy for her: she can barely sustain the effort, as indicated by the "Oooh" she emits when she realizes that she has slipped back into her familiar, caustic persona. That persona neither needs nor wants Buffy's help, but unless she can put it aside she's unlikely to achieve the result she desires from the conversation.

Clipping can sound casual and assured or glib and somewhat hostile, as in this exchange between Buffy and the new Slayer in town, Faith (Buffy died briefly but was resuscitated, another Slayer was called to replace her, and, when she was killed, Faith was called — it's a Slayer anomaly):

BUFFY: What do you know about Angel?

FAITH: Just what your friends tell me. Big love, big loss, you had to deal and move on but you're not.

BUFFY: I got an idea. How 'bout from now on we don't hear from you on Angel or anything else in my life, which, by the way, is my life.

FAITH: What are you getting so strung up on, B?

Faith's share of the dialogue challenges Buffy, who has reacted to Faith's arrival somewhat defensively; Faith, a warrior, takes full advantage of the social instability she's created. Linguists would call the dialogue here an exchange of "face-threatening acts": each party to a conversation presents a face and hopes it will be respected; you can't accomplish much in conversation if you commit serial FTAs. Of course, "big love, big loss" is dismissive and part of the FTA, but the clipping contributes, too. Faith backs off a bit after Buffy responds in kind (*'bout* neatly matches Faith's tone clipping for clipping) and attempts to reestablish conversational equilibrium; in doing so, she decides not to clip again and push too far, preferring *strung up* to *strung*. She can't help renaming Buffy without Buffy's permission, however, which is nothing if not socially competitive.

Clipping can indicate familiarity and intimacy because it's so casual. It says, "We're the sort of people who don't have to say things the way we're supposed to" and "We're young together and don't talk like our parents" and "We have a code and understand each other, whereas others don't understand us." So Buffy can say to Willow, "Do you wanna hang? We're cafeteria bound." Willow is, at that moment, up to no good, violating their intimacy, but she wants to seem as intimate as usual, so comes up with the unconvincing, "I'm gonna do work in the computer lab, uh, school work that I have, so I cannot hang right now." Most of the sentence is stiff and awkward ("school work that I have"), and styles mix like oil and water: *cannot* and *hang* do not belong together, for where *hang* is clipped from *hang out*, *cannot* is not similarly contracted into informality.

Clipping can establish intimacy, but it can also trade on it; speaking to your group in your group's style of speech engages its loyalty—at least, it should. Buffy clearly has this in mind when her mom's awful boyfriend, Ted, catches her cheating at miniature golf. She tries to convince her friends that, though she clearly misbehaved, he seriously overreacted: "Yeah, I kicked my ball in, put me in jail, and he totally wigged." Like, can you believe him? Cheating was an act of rebellion (Buffy's not naturally a cheater); as she tries to rationalize her behavior and disrespect Ted at the same time, Buffy's slang is still kicking. The language of rebellion can be cool and self-possessed, but it can also be tough. A character named Whistler, a demon guide who sometimes visits Buffy, says to her at a critical moment, "It's all on the line here, kid." Buffy responds, "I can deal. I got nothin' left to lose."

There can only be so many words in any episode of *Buffy the Vampire Slayer*, and they have to accomplish lots of things besides convey the Slayer's slangy style. Thus the choice to clip or not to clip as an expression of style is constrained by an acceptable density of production, in effect, by what the textual market will bear. In *Buffy*, at least, this density is partly a matter of verisimilitude: if the Scooby Gang is supposed to represent youth culture accurately, if the adults are not mere stereotypes, then they all have to speak more or less credibly, more or less as actual people speak. Because the *Buffy* writers were particularly conscious of language and indulged in lots or word play, slang, and other cleverness, they may exceed the slang density of natural speech, but some television is very good at approximating natural rate of speech characteristics, as Sali Tagliamonte and Chris Roberts proved in their study of intensive *so* ("That dress is so you, Monica") in the sitcom *Friends* (2003). Slayer style is not the wholesale fabrication of a new idiom, but the subtle manipulation of elements already present in American English into a variation on an idiomatic theme, a variation both acceptably edgy and, sometimes, but not too often or too aggressively, on the edge of the acceptable.

But the issue isn't how precisely *Buffy* copies natural speech. The examples here are meant to show how speakers negotiate their way through social interactions by forging alliances, taking hostages, raising their flags, and even occasionally surrendering in barely noticeable manipulations of slang. While asserting one's individuality accounts for some of the edginess, fitting in socially requires a good ear for when edgy will work and when it won't and what slang appeals to what social interests of those to whom you speak. Slang, among other vocabulary, and indeed, among other aspects of language (the sounds that make an "accent," structure of sentences, narrative styles) helps to define groups in contrast with one another. But to succeed socially, conversation by conversation, sensitivity to the immediate context guides our choices about how to deploy slang to our advantage.

Conversation is transactional, and language and gesture are the currency with which we preserve or acquire social prestige, with which we affirm our membership in various groups, because, of course, we all belong to more than one. Is slang the paint on the hood of the car, as Labov suggested? Certainly, it is only a small part of the language that constitutes social identity, but it is nonetheless essential, the penny or the nickel you need in order to make change.

IT'S A SMALL WORLD, AFTER ALL

No group is defined solely by slang, but slang participates in defining many a group. Some of the groups in question are very big, what we think of as nations, in fact. According to SlangSite.com, Germans (and perhaps German speakers in other parts of the world) use *delle*, an acronym for *durch einfach liegen lassen erledigt* 'accomplished simply by leaving (something) undone', as shorthand for the best principle for dealing with e-mail. Australians call a 'nobody' a *Neville*, clipped from the older slang phrase *Neville Nobody*. Some Scots note the *lochrity* 'condition of having many lakes' of their fair land; Scotland is also home to the *dance nazi* 'dance critic at a ceilidh'. While *Neville* is well attested, the other items listed here aren't, but that's not to question their authenticity: inevitably, some slang belongs to small groups for short times, after which the group takes up new words, if for no other reason than because identity lies in creativity, creativity means change, and change is good. Supposedly, the graphic design class at Seneca College in Toronto used (still uses?) *printit* as an exclamation announcing that something's done. It's transparent enough and useful enough that it might catch on, moving from one class at one college in one city to all-Canadian currency. No evidence of that yet, but no shame in local slang either.

Indeed, there's probably a lot more slang out there, has been a lot more slang over centuries, than we even begin to realize, just because most of it, most of it by far, never exceeds or exceeded the speech of a few intimate friends. It's ephemeral in a way that makes ephemeral language recorded in dictionaries look standard by comparison. Slang is always changing, and it participates in workaday language change. One can think of socially motivated language change in terms of Labov's speech communities, which are "not defined by any marked agreement in the use of language elements, so much as by participation in a set of shared norms," or in terms of Leslie Milroy's social networks, the personally created, "dense," and "multiplex" associations we maintain in order to get along in life, or in terms of Penelope Eckert's communities of practice: "A community of practice is an aggregate of people who come together around some enterprise," important to change because "linguistic influence is associated with the making of social meaning," and "the co-construction of linguistic change and social meaning will take place in just those interactions in which social identity is at issue." These models aren't mutually exclusive, so one could think of language change in terms of their cooperation. From *cool* to *bad*, from *dude* to *ace boon coon* to *brother*, from *chinchy* to *like, gag me with a spoon*, every slang item begins with a style leader and influences a network of closely aligned speakers, whose interaction is frequent, dense, and socially significant; drawn by work or avocation into various communities of practice, the network's worker bees cross-pollinate the Queen Bee's linguistic innovation until, in some cases, those innovations bloom into a broader speech community's linguistic practice.

The more focused on "practice" the community of practice, that is, the more participants' speech accomplishes work of some kind, the more likely the speech it cultivates is jargon rather than slang. The more focused on "community" the community of practice, that is, the more participants' speech supports the overarching business of being over the specific business of work, the more likely the speech it cultivates is slang rather than jargon. And the likelihood that anyone will belong to more than one network and more than one community of practice is exactly what blurs the territorial boundaries between jargon and slang. Each group is a hive of linguistic activity, but the fields are open to all. When a reconnoitering worker finds pollen fit for a queen, it dances a little dance and the rest fly off to gather as much as they can. But people aren't bees and we can't predict to which hive they'll return or which Queen Bee will validate them. Slang, one might argue, is the honey of group interaction: to some, it all tastes the same;

to the connoisseur, each field has its flavor. Whatever its origin and however it tastes, honey always comes from a hive.

REFERENCES

Obviously, we begin with *Slang Flashcards* (Venice, CA: Who's There, 2003) and *Slang 2 Flashcards* (Venice, CA: Who's There, 2005). We looked so much younger in *The Official Preppy Handbook*, edited by Lisa Birnbach (New York: Workman, 1980). For *hella*'s non–African Americanness, see volume 2 of J. E. Lighter's *Historical Dictionary of American Slang*, described further below; for its regional salience, see Mary Bucholtz, Nancy Bermudez, Victor Fung, Lisa Edwards, and Rosalva Vargas, "Hella Nor Cal or Totally So Cal? The Perceptual Dialectology of California," *Journal of English Linguistics* 35.4 (December 2007): 325–352; though the article is about current perceptions, it is worth noting that *hella* is entered in Pamela Munro's *Slang U.* (New York: Harmony Books, 1989), 106, and *Slang U.* records slang used by students at UCLA, notably in southern California, though the *hella* speakers might be northern Californians who didn't get into Stanford or Berkeley. The sketch "Slang Gang" aired on Fox Television's *Mad TV* on January 4, 1997; it's not possible from published sources to determine who among the show's many writers were responsible for the sketch. "Casino Night," an episode of NBC's *The Office* (that aired on May 11, 2006), was written by Steve Carell and directed by Ken Kwapis. In writing this chapter, I relied on J. E. Lighter's *Historical Dictionary of American Slang*, the first two volumes of which were published by Random House (1994 and 1997), though the project of completing the dictionary has since been taken on by Oxford University Press. I also turned to the online edition of the *Oxford English Dictionary*, edited by J. A. Simpson, E. S. C. Weiner, and others, as well as to the *Middle English Dictionary*, edited by Hans Kurath, Sherman M. Kuhn, Robert E. Lewis, and others (Ann Arbor: University of Michigan Press, 1952–2001). The late Robert L. Chapman's *New Dictionary of American Slang* (New York: Harper and Row, 1986) was superseded by a third edition (New York: HarperCollins, 1995); though far from comprehensive, it is an excellent desk dictionary of American slang. Connie Eble quotes the passage from Chapman (1986) in *Slang and Sociability* (Chapel Hill: University of North Carolina Press, 1996), 80; the subsequent quotations from Eble appear on 81 and 83, respectively. Clarence Major's *Juba to Jive: A Dictionary of African-American Slang* (New York: Viking Penguin, 1994) is an updated and augmented version of *A Dictionary of Afro-American Slang* (New York: International Publishers, 1970).

Randall Kennedy tells the story of David Howard in *Nigger: The Strange History of a Troublesome Word* (New York: Pantheon, 2002), 120–122. Geoffrey Nunberg is quoted from his excellent collection of radio essays, *The Way We Talk Now* (Boston: Houghton Mifflin, 2001), 96. Allen Walker Read noticed that previous historians of American English had forgotten the "Americanism by survival" in "Approaches to Lexicography and Semantics," in *Current Trends in Linguistics* 10, edited by Thomas Sebeok (The Hague: Mouton, 1972), 153. John Russell and Russell John Rickford write about Teresa Labov's research in *Spoken Soul: The Story of Black English* (New York: John Wiley, 2000), 93; Labov published her research as "Social and Language Boundaries among Adolescents" in *American Speech* 67.4 (1992): 339–366. Amy March's comment about "Yankee biddies" appears on 312 of Louisa May Alcott's *Little Women* (New York: Penguin, 1989). SlangSite.com can be found, conveniently, at www.slangsite.com. I listen to *The Tavis Smiley Show* when I can, Friday afternoons at 2, on NPR station WFYI in Indianapolis. Brian Mockenhaupt reports Colonel Scott Henry's comment in "The Army We Have," *Atlantic Monthly*, June 2007, 96. Randy Jackson's "Yo, dawg, check it" is as regular a feature of Fox Television's *American Idol* as Cornel West's tag line is of *The Tavis Smiley Show*—pick your episode! I take Chaucer's text from the third edition of *The Riverside Chaucer*, edited by Larry D. Benson and others (Boston: Houghton Mifflin, 1987), p. 80, lines 4073–4074 of "The Reeve's Tale." I borrowed the quotation from Zora Neale Hurston's *Jonah's Gourd Vine* (1934) from the *OED* sv *man n*[1] and *int.* in sense IV.16.c. Geneva Smitherman's *Black Talk: Words and Phrases from the Hood to the Amen Corner*, was first published in 1994 and then revised (Boston: Houghton Mifflin, 2000); like Major's dictionary, it is an indispensable reference. Scott Kiesling's "Dude" appeared in *American Speech* 79.3 (2004): 281–305; I quote from 284. Penelope Eckert discusses "sociolinguistic icons" in *Linguistic Variation as Social Practice* (Malden, MA: Blackwell, 2000), 216–219. *Fast Times at Ridgemont High* (1982) was written by Cameron Crowe and directed by Amy Heckerling; Sean Penn acted the part of Jeff Spicoli. *Dude, Where's My Car?* (2000) was written by Philip Stark and directed by Danny Leiner; Ashton Kutcher plays Jesse Montgomery III, who asks the famous question. *Scrubs* is a Fox Television comedy that aired first in 2001, and the episode "Her Story," written by Angela Nissel and directed by John Inwood, aired September 28, 2004; Donald Faison plays the role of Dr. Chris Turk, and Sarah Chalke and Heather Graham play the two whitest girls. I quote Geneva Smitherman from *Talkin and Testifyin: The Language of Black America* (Detroit: Wayne State University Press, 1977), 43, and then from *Talkin That Talk: Language, Culture and*

Education in African America (New York: Routledge, 2000), 25 and 126. Walt Wolfram's pithy formulation is from *Dialects and American English* (Englewood Cliffs, NJ: Prentice Hall, 1991), 2. John Baugh discusses *steady* in *Out of the Mouths of Slaves: African American Language and Educational Malpractice* (Austin: University of Texas Press, 1999), 101–110, and *come* on 111–122. Arthur Spears's article is "The Black English Semi-Auxiliary *Come*," *Language* 58 (1982): 850–872. Theresa Perry is quoted from "'I'on Know Why They Be Trippin': Reflections on the Ebonics Debate," in *The Real Ebonics Debate: Power, Language, and Education of African-American Children*, edited by Theresa Perry and Lisa Delpit (Boston: Beacon Press, 1998), 9. I have quoted from Edwin L. Battistella's *Bad Language: Are Some Words Better Than Others?* (New York: Oxford University Press, 2005), 147. William Labov's testimony is quoted from John Baugh's *Beyond Ebonics: Linguistic Pride and Racial Prejudice* (New York: Oxford University Press, 2000), 59. I quote Katherine Connor Martin from her excellent article, "Gendered Aspects of Lexicographic Labeling," *Dictionaries: Journal of the Dictionary Society of North America* 26 (2005): 160. Louisa May Alcott's *Little Women* (1868–1869) is quoted from the Penguin Classics edition (1989), 3, 23, 29, 28, 109, 63, 145, and 15, in that order. Those interested in comparing the slang of *Little Women* and that of *Buffy the Vampire Slayer* can consult my *Slayer Slang: A "Buffy the Vampire Slayer" Lexicon* (New York: Oxford University Press, 2003) for examples; shifts are discussed on 71–77 and *-age* on 62–68; Eble discusses use of *-age* among late twentieth-century college students in *Slang and Sociability*, 33. Elizabeth Grant's *Memoirs of a Highland Lady* (1845) is quoted from the Canongate Press edition by Andrew Tod (1988) at 196, 198, 205, 288, 204, and 191, in series. "The Puppet Show," written by Dean Batali and Rob Des Hotel and directed by Ellen S. Pressman, aired on May 5, 1997. Erin Flaherty's "The Flirt Buddy vs. a Friend with Benefits" is in *Jane*, August 2006, 44; Anna Marrian's "Is It Wrong to Date the Guy You Used to Babysit?" appears on 144–145 of the same issue. I have quoted titles and such at random throughout the issue. Susie Dent's *Fanboys and Overdogs: The Language Report* (Oxford: Oxford University Press, 2005) is the third installment of a delightful series; I refer here to 102–103. Diane Vincent's study is *Pressions et Impressions sur les Sacres au Québec* (Québec: Office de la Langue Française, 1982). Wong Man Tat Parco's thesis is titled *A Sociolinguistic Study of Youth Slanguage of Hong Kong Adolescents,* University of Hong Kong, 2006; I quote from 100. I have summarized some of the information that Anna-Brita Stenström, Gisle Andersen, and Ingrid Kristine Hasund present in *Trends in Teenage Talk: Corpus Compilation, Analysis and Findings*, Studies in Corpus Linguistics 8 (Philadelphia: John

Benjamins, 2002), particularly that on 74, 81, 93, 126, 143, and 187. Harry McGurk and John McDonald published their astonishing discovery of the McGurk effect as "Hearing Lips and Seeing Voices" in *Nature* 264 (December 23, 1976): 746–748. William Labov discusses the "adolescent peak" at several points in *Principles of Linguistic Change: Social Factors* (Malden, MA: Blackwell, 2001), conclusively on 517. Mary Bucholtz writes about "Language and Youth Culture" in *American Speech* 75.3 (2000): 280–283; the quotation here comes from 282. Marcel Danesi is quoted from *Forever Young: The "Teen-Aging" of Modern Culture* (Toronto: University of Toronto Press, 2003), 52 and 54. Lyn Mikel Brown is quoted from *Raising Their Voices: The Politics of Girls' Anger* (Cambridge, MA: Harvard University Press, 1998), 130, and Gerry Bloustien from *Girl Making: A Cross-Cultural Ethnography on the Process of Growing Up Female* (New York: Berghahn Books, 2003), 191. Olivia Allin's "Alcohawk" is in the third issue of *Missbehave* (Summer 2007): 13; Samantha Moeller's "Jeepney Clothing" is in the same issue, on 14. Moeller's characterization of the magazine is quoted from Eric Sass, "Mags Shift from Laddies to Ladies, Target Young Girls," in *Media Daily News*, March 30, 2006, at http://publications.mediapost.com. The *New York Observer* article that reveals Moeller's age, by Gillian Reagan, "They Aren't Sluts — Just Missbehavin': Bad Girl Mag 'Missbehave' Celebrates Its First Anniversary — and Hot Dads, Sex Toys, Sneakers, Lily Allen" (July 24, 2007), can be found at www.observer.com. The quotation from Rosalind Wiseman's *Queen Bees and Wannabes* (New York: Crown, 2002) can be found on 61. Ms. Wiseman is twice misidentified in my book *Slayer Slang: A "Buffy the Vampire Slayer" Lexicon* (2003), as "Rebecca" Wiseman; I'm not sure how it happened, as I had her excellent book in front of me and know perfectly well what her name is. I apologize for the errors. Abe Simpson, voiced unforgettably by Dan Castellaneta, is quoted from "Homerpalooza" (May 19, 1996), written by Brent Forrester, directed by Wesley Archer. *Mean Girls* (2004) was inspired by Wiseman's book, written by Tina Fey, directed by Mark Waters; Rachel McAdams played the role of Regina and Lacey Chabert the role of Gretchen. Quotations from *Buffy the Vampire Slayer* come from the following episodes, *seriatim*: "When She Was Bad," written and directed by Joss Whedon (September 15, 1997); "I Robot, You Jane," written by Ashley Gable and Thomas A. Swyden, directed by Stephen Posey (April 7, 1997); "Reptile Boy," written and directed by David Greenwalt (October 13, 1997); "Lie to Me," written and directed by Joss Whedon (November 3, 1997); "Band Candy," written by Jane Espenson, directed by Michael Lange (November 10, 1998); "Ted," written by David Greenwalt and Joss Whedon, directed by Bruce Seth Green (December

8, 1997); "Passion," written by Ty King, directed by Michael E. Gershman (February 24, 1998); "Welcome to the Hellmouth," written by Joss Whedon, directed by Charles Martin Smith (March 10, 1997); "Becoming, Part 2," written and directed by Joss Whedon (May 19, 1998); "Never Kill a Boy on the First Date," written by Rob Des Hotel and Dean Batali, directed by David Semel (March 31, 1997); "Nightmares," written by Joss Whedon and David Greenwalt, directed by Bruce Seth Green (May 12, 1997); "Out of Sight, Out of Mind," written by Joss Whedon, Ashley Gable, and Thomas A Swyden, directed by Reza Badigi (May 19, 1997); and "Faith, Hope, and Trick," written by David Greenwalt, directed by James A. Contner (October 13, 1998). Throughout the series, Buffy is played by Sarah Michelle Gellar, Cordelia by Charisma Carpenter, Willow by Alyson Hannigan, Faith by Eliza Dushku, Xander by Nicholas Brendan, Giles by Anthony Stewart Head, Joyce by Kristine Sutherland, Angel by David Boreanaz, and Jenny by Robia LaMorte. If the examples here pique your curiosity about slayer slang, you might want to read my *Slayer Slang: A "Buffy the Vampire Slayer" Lexicon*. The material on *Buffy* included here is adapted from my "The Matrix of Motives in Slayer Style," a keynote address at the *Slayage* Conference on the Whedonverses at Gordon College, Barnesville, Georgia, May 25–28, 2006. William Labov discusses Katz and Larzarsfeld's *Personal Influence: The Part Played by People in the Flow of Mass Communication* (Glencoe, IL: Free Press, 1955), leaders, and language change in *Principles of Linguistic Change: Social Factors* (Malden, MA: Blackwell, 2001), 357–360. Sali Tagliamonte and Chris Roberts's article is "So Weird; So Cool; So Innovative: The Use of Intensifiers in the Television Series *Friends*," *American Speech* 80.3 (2003): 280–300. Again, look for the compendious SlangSite.com at www.slangsite.com. William Labov defines the speech community in *Sociolinguistic Patterns* (Philadelphia: University of Pennsylvania Press, 1972), 120–121 and explains its role in linguistic change on 178–179. He expands on his early work significantly in *Principles of Linguistic Change: Social Factors* (Malden, MA: Blackwell, 2001). For an explanation of linguistic networks, see Leslie Milroy, *Language and Social Networks* (Baltimore: University Park Press, 1980). For an explanation of communities of practice, see Penelope Eckert, *Linguistic Variation as Social Practice* (Malden, MA: Blackwell, 2000), 34–41.

STANDING OUT

AESTHETIC DIMENSIONS OF SLANG

You probably remember growing into certain types of slang when you spent more time in the schoolyard than you do now. Of course, there was the broad range of profanity (*fuck* and *shit*), experimentally crude sexual expressions (*suck off* and *carpetmuncher*), romantic metaphors (like *stone cold fox* and *hung*), not to mention all of the *yo*, *like*, and *all* that focused and punctuated the flow of teenage conversation: "Yo, she was all, like, baked and shit at the concert." Some of the slang, though, was a lot cleaner and, unexpectedly, rhymed: "Dude, you show up late in her class and you are cruisin' for a bruisin'," and "I told her I'd wash the car if I could borrow it, and it was, like, slam, bam, thank you ma'am, I had the keys and was out the door," and "[Caprice:] 'Those boots are sick.' [Haley:] 'Hey, whatever floats your boat, chica.' " Kids who spoke like that were too cool for school, and after they rhymed in conversation they'd say, "Hey, I'm a poet and didn't know it." But they did know it, knew it so well that they couldn't help pointing it out, couldn't help stretching it just one rhyme more.

Slang has various social uses, especially on the schoolyard, even when it rhymes. But its value isn't limited to social group identity, social perceptions and attitudes, or social interaction. Some of slang's value is aesthetic, if we interpret the term *aesthetic* broadly. The first definition of the adjective *aesthetic* you'll find in any dictionary will be something like, quoting the *New Oxford American Dictionary* (2005), "concerned with beauty or the appreciation of beauty." Most slang is not "beautiful" in any conventional sense. It's deliberately unconventional language, after all, but the history of art and taste proves that beauty is a very flexible concept.

When we talk of a slang aesthetic, we mean something closer to the *American Heritage Dictionary*'s second sense for the noun *aesthetic*: "An underlying principle, a set of principles, or a view often manifested by outward appearance or style of behavior." I am not proposing that slang is aesthetic in the narrowest senses, such as that beauty is the most exalted of all values, or that beauty is self-sufficient and the best art made for art's sake, though, sometimes, in arts other than slang (some poetry, some music, some painting, some dance) one or more of the narrowest senses apply. It isn't a matter of slang being EITHER aesthetic OR social, but BOTH aesthetically AND socially significant. In slang those two values often operate simultaneously, sometimes without regard for each other, sometimes hand in hand.

As a style, slang certainly operates according to a loose confederation of "principles," which start with the typical attributes of slang discussed in chapter 1: slang is casual, extravagant, facetious, forced, humorous, irreverent, playful, racy, vivid, often superfluous (when slang items are synonyms of standard terms), and often ephemeral. To make this a matter of principle, just turn attributes into statements: "Slang should be casual," "Slang should be irreverent," and so on, and, voilà, principles. Of course, these are rudimentary, and any description of slang aesthetics will have to consider not only what any of the rudiments actually means, but also how the various principles balance against one another, and also whether the desirable state of slang is equilibrium of principles or something more volatile. Several of the attributes and the principles derived from them would, to some degree, apply to poetry as well as to slang. Though slang and poetry aren't the same thing, nevertheless their relationship has long been in the minds of scholars and commentators. At least, slang converges on poetic language and realizes in everyday speech the common, human poetic urge.

The most sophisticated scholars of slang, particularly Connie Eble, in *Slang and Sociability* (1996), and Jonathan Lighter, in his chapter on slang for the *Cambridge History of the English Language* (2001), emphasize the intersection of poetry and slang at metaphor. Eble remarks, "Given the tendency of the general vocabulary toward metaphor, it is not surprising that metaphor abounds in slang," and the more it abounds, one might argue, the more slang resembles poetry. Lighter notes that "slang employs many of the same figurative devices found in poetic language" and itemizes a few examples each of slang antiphrasis and antonomasia, hyperbole and onomatopoeia, metonymy and synecdoche, and others.

No one can deny that metaphor is dead center in slang. If you smoke a lot of *weed* (itself metaphorical), you can get *baked, fried,* or *toasted;* you know those are metaphors for 'very intoxicated', and not just because you don't fit into the baking pan—if you think you can fit into the baking pan, stop smoking. You probably remember the following public service announcement: a hand presents an egg with the script, "This is your brain"; the hand breaks the egg into a frying pan and fries it, while the voiceover intones, "This is your brain on drugs." If your brain were in the frying pan, or if your brain were really an egg, or if the statements and images of the PSA were in any way literal, then it wouldn't be either dramatic or funny or effective.

In early nineteenth-century America a tall, thin person was called a *cornstalk.* From the late nineteenth century well into the twentieth something really worthy was a *peach:* "Gosh, Mom, you're a peach!" In the 1920s a girl good enough to eat (but only metaphorically, not literally) was a *pork chop.* If you were a young black guy falling for a pretty young woman back in the 1950s you might call her a *pepper.* In the 1980s, if she was a *duck* 'snob, stuck-up young woman', you might have to lay out a lot of *lettuce* 'cash in bills'. If you were Italian American she might be a *tomato,* and you'd flash some *escarole* instead. By the 1990s, if you were a *playa,* you might try to *pop her cherry* 'deflower her, or, less metaphorically, take her virginity'. In the twenty-first century, if a room is *popping,* it's in motion like popping corn. It's all metaphor, and you are already thinking up more examples; we could go on like this all day. So let's take slang metaphor as given, and concentrate here on the way sound contributes to slang's aesthetic. Slang often comes closest to poetry in sound.

The slang term *morning glory* means a number of nonstandard things: in racing lingo a *morning glory* is a horse that works out well in the morning but loses in the afternoon race; in sports lingo, probably borrowed from the racetrack, it's the promising but ultimately disappointing competitor; it can refer to morning sex or an early morning erection; in lieu of sexual arousal, it can refer to the first drug injection of the day. The putative "glory" of these things is confined to the mornings or at the outset; there's a pun on the flower, the standard meaning of *morning glory,* but note that the flower doesn't really have anything to do with it—the item looks more metaphorical than it is. As the 1980s folk group Uncle Bonsai famously sang, "Boys want sex in the morning," and all of these meanings for *morning glory* reflect historically masculine preoccupations; they belong to the underworld, a world inhabited, as James Sledd put it, by gentlemen who are not gentlemen and dislike gentility.

Though slang is often characterized as gritty and unshaven, some of it is squeaky clean behind the ears. When *morning glory* forms part of the catchphrase *What's your story, morning glory?* it isn't gritty at all, but pleasant and playful — G-rated slang. As a form of greeting, *What's your story, morning glory?* satisfies the expectation that slang items are synonyms of standard words: they don't have to be, but more often than not, they are. *What's your story, morning glory?* is a synonym for standard *Hello!* or *How are you?* as well as for slang items like *Yo, wassup? What's shakin'?* Or is it *What's shakin', bacon?* Rhymes like *cruisin' for a bruisin'* are synonyms, too: *cruisin' for a bruisin'* means 'asking for trouble'; *slam, bam, thank you ma'am* means something like 'suddenly as a consequence'; *whatever floats your boat* means 'serve your own taste' (unrhymed slang alternatives include *whatever turns you on*); and *too cool for school* means 'supercool', where cool wears tattoos of truancy and flips the bird of detention or suspension.

Trustworthy slang dictionaries, like Lighter's *Historical Dictionary of American Slang* (1997), include *What's your* (or *the*) *story, morning glory?* so there's reason at least to entertain the possibility that it counts as slang. Rhymes like *cruisin' for a bruisin'* also appear in major slang dictionaries, like Dalzell and Victor's *New Partridge Dictionary of Slang and Unconventional English* (2006) and Jonathon Green's *Cassell's Dictionary of Slang* (2005), but Green's dictionary is notable for also including *slam, bam, thank you ma'am* and *whatever floats your boat*: Dalzell and Victor include *whatever turns you on*, and having provided it, they may have decided to save space and not list all of the available synonyms (even a big slang dictionary can't include every item of slang). Lighter does not include *cruisin' for a bruisin'*, and we'll have to wait for future volumes of his dictionary to see whether he includes rhyming phrases from late in the alphabet. Add classic rhyming slang to these examples, and altogether they confirm Eble's assertion that "rhyming is the favorite sound effect of slang."

Of course, there are lots of rhyming salutations, farewells, and queries; some of them are generic and familiar, slang clichés. The most famous of these is *See you later, alligator*; the usual response is the equally all-purpose *In a while, crocodile*. Contriving rhymes like these is a favorite pastime in the Adams household, one of quite a few parlor games in which Jenny daily proves she's more verbally proficient than I. Some of her rhymes are borrowed, and so are some of mine: I'll say, "See you later, alligator," and she'll answer, "Not too soon, you big baboon," which I think she picked up on her Catholic school playground.

If I want to know what's on Jenny's mind, I ask, *Whatcha doin' pruin, stewin'?*[1]
Rainy weekend days can be dull, and a little connubial rhyming goes a long way
to lighten the mood. As Henry Bradley, one of the *OED*'s editors, suggested, our
"desire to secure increased vivacity" mingles with our "desire to secure [an]
increased sense of intimacy," or something like that. The rhymes, you see, are
adjunct to our desire.

My rhyming repertoire isn't all borrowed, though. Here are three of my
favorite inventions: *How's it goin', protozoan? Why so glum, sugarplum?* and *Don't
be silly, tiger lily.* Others may have invented the very same rhymes, but if they are
new to you feel free to use them whenever you like. *How's it goin', protozoan?* is
obviously of the general, *What's your story, morning glory?* and *See you later, alligator* kind. The other two apply more narrowly, as the person to whom they're
addressed needs to be glum or, in some measure, silly, though in either case
rhyme alleviates any criticism. Rhymes like these are fun to invent, and anyone can do it. The *Historical Dictionary of American Slang* first records *What's
your story, morning glory?* from 1944, in Chester Himes's novel *Black on Black.* By
1985, according to *HDAS*, someone had extended the earlier, shorter version to
"Tell the truth, snaggle tooth / What's your story, morning glory?"

Jenny and I figure that, eventually, we'll make up rhymes like these with our
(currently notional) children. This opens up an interesting problem: Are these
rhymes slang, or are they closer to nursery rhymes, part of what the folklorists
Peter and Iona Opie called "the language and lore of schoolchildren"? A family
can function as an in-group, but if everyone who reads this book starts asking,
"How's it goin', protozoan?" it won't be exclusive to our family for long. Instead,
I suppose, it and similar greetings, farewells, and queries will mark all of the cool
people who rhyme for fun. But that still begs the question: we might all be making up silly verse rather than slang. I'm unlikely to "teach" my children slang;
they could more easily learn Street from the Knock Knock flash cards. Perhaps,
then, when we're versifying we're not doing slang after all.

---

1   For a decade I spent summers working at Camp Rota-Kiwan, a Boy Scout camp outside
    of Kalamazoo, Michigan. Nic Clement, who was program director during my first couple
    of years there, used to lead "The Prune Song," which at one point runs, "Little seed in-
    side a pruin / Is it night, or is it nooin? / Whatcha doin' pruin, stewin'?" The spelling here
    indicates that *prune* and *noon* were pronounced in two syllables when singing the song.
    Rota-Kiwan, though meant to sound vaguely Native American, is actually a blend of *Ro-
    tary* and *Kiwanis*, because the Rotary and Kiwanis Clubs generously donated the land that
    established the camp.

Yet rhymes like these more or less satisfy all the dictionary definitions of *slang*: they are casual, vivid, humorous, and playful; they aren't racy, but they can be irreverent. If I want to be cheeky with someone who's full of himself, I might say, sarcastically, "Don't make me laugh, you big giraffe." No one who takes himself too seriously likes to be called a giraffe, but it's perfectly reasonable, in the interests of sarcasm, to use an animal with a small head to make fun of someone with a big head: both rhyme and metaphor tend to diminish the target. I can drop the phrase into conversation so casually that casualness itself is part of the insult; playfulness can be insulting because you aren't allowed to play with anybody and everybody. But sometimes I just can't resist the slang impulse: I am one of those "ingenious individuals" who H. L. Mencken said would employ slang "to make the language more pungent and picturesque."

In her short novel *The Ballad of Peckham Rye* (1960) Muriel Spark indulges in some period slang for pungency; her characters use it playfully and insultingly and sometimes, at the point of rhyme, almost violently. Young people in the novel meet at a local dance hall. "Findlater's Rooms," we're told, "were not given to rowdy rock but concentrated instead upon a more cultivated jive." Findlater's is a hip, happening place. The slang attitude is evident in the hipsters' speech: they stretch metaphors to the snapping point, but do so without moving their mouths — they're that cool. "Come and wriggle, snake," one invites another. "Come and leap, leopard," insists yet another, embellishing metaphor with alliteration. The temperature rises between two of the men, though, for the usual reasons: "Got a pain, panda?" Said in the right tone, that can be a provoking question: alliteration on /p/ is just the right plosive touch. But the response in this case throws down: "Feeling frail, nightingale?" On the playground, flippant rhymes are fighting words.

At home, I assure you, I don't dare to be cheeky — I wouldn't get away with it. Or maybe rhymes like these mark the outer boundary of domestic cheekiness. Sure, rhyming is fun, and rhymes have a pleasurable phonetic feel in the mouth, but there's also the excitement of finding out how far I can go, what unlikely rhyme I can pull off, and, at times, what I can get away with. And, of course, there's self-admiration for the result: I have mad rhyming skillz. Once I'm in the groove, though, even I'm not sure exactly what I mean when I widen my eyes and say *Don't rock the boat, you billy goat!* or furrow my brow and say *Please don't pout, my sauerkraut.* Who do I think I am, rhyming around with family and friends, when I could speak a straight and standard line?

As Lighter argues of the relationship between poetry and slang, "A central purpose of poetic language is to prompt introspective reflection; a central function of slang is to short-circuit reflection and to exalt snap judgments and habitual attitudes among social peers." When I make my cleverest rhymes, I am mediating these two extremes: if the rhyme is deftly made, and specific to the occasion, I may prompt some reflection, but I am certainly playing the game from habit to consolidate a group identity as well. Someday, when Jenny and I make up new rhymes with our children, we'll trade them as a game, one in which the children discover and practice certain tricks of the English language, and I glimpse just how much they take after their mother.

Earlier, in chapter 1, I was somewhat critical of the *Merriam-Webster Collegiate Dictionary*'s entry for *slang*, but in cases like these, it proves relevant: Merriam-Webster emphasizes that slang items are "extravagant, forced, facetious figures of speech," and these adjectives aptly describe the rhymes in question. Certainly, the *baboon* in *Not too soon, you big baboon* is extravagant; *Slap my femur, little lemur* is undoubtedly forced, not just because it's hard to think of sentences where both *femur* and *lemur* belong, but because it's even more artificial to rhyme them; and *Don't make me laugh, you big giraffe* is facetious, at least in the context described above. Perhaps most important, such rhymes are extravagant, forced, and facetious merely for the sake of being extravagant, forced, and facetious, which makes them all the more extravagant, forced, and facetious.

Along with all of these slangy things, rhymes like *What's your story, morning glory?* or *How's it goin', protozoan?* are poetry, or at least verse; they are, in some elements, poetic. Each of these rhymes is really a couplet or pair of couplets (or, I suppose, one could interpret each as an internally rhymed single line of verse):

How's it goin',	See you later,
Protozoan?	Alligator.
	Not too soon,
	You big baboon.

Granted, if these are miniature poems, they aren't very sophisticated, not villanelles or complexly idiosyncratic free verse poems. They aren't meaningfully vivid in the way of a very short poem like William Carlos Williams's "The Red Wheelbarrow" (which, with sixteen words, is four times as long as *How's it goin' protozoan?*), not metaphorically suggestive: they can be specific characterizations, as when *Don't make me laugh, you big giraffe* is a put-down, or very generally metaphorical, as when *morning glory* refers to someone who is fresh, pretty, even glorious as a flower. But unlike T. S. Eliot's peach in "The Love Song of J. Alfred Prufrock" or Williams's red wheelbarrow, they don't attempt any more universal significance.

In most cases *What's your story, morning glory?* doesn't propose any meaningful metaphorical relationship between the person addressed and morning glories or any species of flower. The appeal of such slangy rhyme is that it's verse any of us can make, just because it doesn't have to be very meaningful: the meaning is in the discourse, in the rhyme's conversational role, or in the off-the-cuff art of coining such a rhyme. The rhyme puts less meaning into *morning glory* than the other slang uses do, the ones where there's early glory. Thus rhymes like *Don't be silly, tiger lily* are very different from rhyming slang, which is item-for-item meaningful: *Sweeney Todd* means *Flying Squad* means *police*. Like rhyming slang, couplet rhymes are a form of play: some rules of the game are linguistic rules, rules embedded in the very structure of language, like those for what makes a rhyme.

Some rhymed couplets serve irreverent purposes, but the purpose isn't the sum of their irreverence: we aren't supposed to rhyme in speech. Rhyming is artificial and obtrusive: it challenges social rules of language use, just as slang does, and so it is irreverent about language itself. In some cases it's impossible to tell verse and slang apart. If you walked down the street speaking in rhymed couplets instead of conversational English, you would be engaged in an act of cultural rebellion; either that or you'd be dissociated from "normal" behavior. In Frank Perry's film *David and Lisa* (1962) conversational rhyme is evidence of psychosis. Slang is marginally unacceptable, too, but we can use it without people thinking we're crazy; indeed, it's as though slang is poetic speech we can get away with using in conversation, rebellion we can minimize or amplify as the context allows. The difference between slang and poetry is partly a matter of kind, but perhaps as much a matter of degree.

Slangy irreverence is not limited to rhyme, nor the poetics of slang confined to the nursery. Eble moves from rhyme as a sound of slang to alliteration, and the many alliterative euphemisms for masturbation prove how paradoxically reproductive alliteration can be: *bash the bishop, grip the gorilla, jerk your jewels, paddle the pickle, pound your pork, pull your pud, punish Percy in the palm, punish the pope, rub your radish, stir your stew, wave the wand*, and the slightly more complex alliteration of *unstable the stallion* for the men; for women, we have *beat the beaver, cunt cuddling, finger fun, grope the grotto*, and *polish the pearl*. Do women masturbate less than men? Do they have fewer words for their masturbation?

Perhaps, as Katherine Martin suggests, we have overlooked women's sexual euphemism because we prefer to believe that only men use fancy words for self-gratification.

Of course, there are rhyming euphemisms for masturbation, too, like *jerk the gherkin, tickle the pickle,* and *yank the plank* for the men; *flit your clit* and *itch the ditch* for the women. And there's the unexpectedly masculine, metaphorically graceful *gallop the antelope*. No one would question that *bash the bishop* is slang, not merely because it's a sexual term, and not merely because it's a euphemism for (of all things) a clinical, standard sexual term (that is, one that should need no euphemism), but also because no one is confused by the euphemism, which is coy, self-conscious, and just as evidently about masturbation as the word *masturbation*. The playfulness of such items implies the strength of the taboo against self-pleasuring. Anyone hearing *bash the bishop* or *punish Percy in the palm* will detect synonyms for something other than violence against bishops or people named Percy, just as surely as bobbies heard criminal inclinations in the East End of London from behind the curtain of rhyming slang.

Rhyme, alliteration, and metaphor are all poetic devices. When everyday speakers turn mundane experience into poetry by means of these devices, sometimes going so far as to speak in verse, they straddle the domains of poetry and slang. Both challenge the social and structural norms of language but also improve on ordinary speech—at least, slang speakers are convinced that ordinary speech expresses less than they mean, perhaps attitudes they prefer to express indirectly. Remember Walt Whitman's capsule explanation of slang:

> Slang, or indirection, [is] an attempt of common humanity to escape from bald literalism, and express itself illimitably, which in the highest walks produces poets and poems, and doubtless in pre-historic times gave the start to, and perfected, the whole immense tangle of the old mythologies. . . . Slang, too, is the wholesome fermentation or eructation of those processes eternally active in language, by which froth and specks are thrown up, mostly to pass away, though occasionally to settle permanently and chrystallize.

We have more to say than the literal conveys and new mythologies of self to propagate; we want to sparkle in conversation so that we can think well of ourselves, so that others occasionally think well of us, too. Once upon a time *See you later, alligator* may have sounded effervescent; now it sounds flat through overuse, which drives us to invent rhymes like *How's it goin', protozoan?* according to ancient patterns, to pour new wine into old bottles, so to speak. It doesn't have to be wine of depth or vintage; froth is good enough for living in the moment. If we want to see what settles and crystallizes, we can always look in a dictionary.

INDIDDLYFIXING IS THE SHIZNIT

Everybody knows about prefixing and suffixing from school: *fix* is the base, *pre-* or *suf-* the prefix, and *-ing* the suffix. You can suffix to inflect a word, that is, to indicate its grammatical use. So, you can fly like a bat outta hell, or all y'all can fly like bats outta hell, where the suffix *-s* makes singular *bat* into a plural; you can bash the bishop like there's no tomorrow, even though you bashed the bishop yesterday, where the suffix *-ed* puts *bash* in the past tense; my speech may be slangy, but yours is slangier, though probably not the slangiest ever, where *-er* and *-est*, respectively, indicate comparative and superlative uses of *slangy*.

Prefixing and suffixing can be derivational as well as inflectional; that is, we can derive new words from old bases: your boss can be really bossy (*boss* + *-y*) or she can be the uberboss (*uber* + *boss*) who leaves bossiness (*bossy* + *-ness*) to an underling (believe it or not, *under* + the diminutive suffix *-l-* + another diminutive suffix *-ing*—the double diminutive is what makes the underling so demeaningly under). From your perspective, you work as hard as you can, but they overwork (*over-* + *work*) you and undercompensate (*under-* + *compensate*) you, so you reconsider (*re-* + *consider*) your commitment (*commit* + *-ment*). By analogy with prefixing and suffixing, infixing is just what you'd think, the derivational process of inserting something into the "middle" of a word in order to make a new one. Other languages infix as readily as English suffixes and prefixes. Some, like Ulwa (a language of Nicaragua) and Malagasy (a language of Madagascar), inflect with infixes; others, like Tagalog (a language of the Philippines), infix to derive new words.

In America, though, we don't teach about infixing in school, at least, not until college. Most English infixings are slang, and some of the most familiar are the worst kind of slang: fifth graders who toss them around during recess are likely to end up in the principal's office. A short list of such words includes *absofuckinglutely*, *fanfuckingtastic*, *guaranfuckingtee*, and *rigoddamndiculous*. In fact, though, and in spite of these familiar examples, many infixings don't insert "bad" words into their bases, but are morally neutral extended forms, like Homer Simpson's *edumacation*. There are at least two interesting things about such words: first, they add little or no lexical meaning to the unextended form; second, they are spoken with pleasure, for the sake of the way they sound, rather than for what they mean.[2]

The sound of infixing is partly rhythmic. Of course, all speech is rhythmic, and each language (indeed, each dialect of a language) has a prosody, a set of rules by which its rhythms work. Infixing calls attention to speech rhythm, so is more nearly poetic. If you use an infixed form like *absofuckinglutely* in conversation, you may not register its essentially trochaic structure. A trochee is a "foot" of verse that contains two syllables, a stressed syllable followed by an unstressed one: ab' so fuck' ing lute' ly. *Absolutely* also follows a trochaic pattern, and the first syllable of *fucking* is stressed, too, so you can't insert *fucking* into *absolutely* just anywhere: **abfuckingsolutely* and **absolutefuckingly* aren't plausible English infixings because they contort the stress patterns of words from which they're made. Not surprisingly, *prosody* is the term literary types use for the metrical and rhythmic elements of verse. There's a conceptual relationship between everyday speech and poetry, and slang prosody merely intensifies that relationship.

When Mark Peters checked in 2005, a search for *edumacation* generated "a whopping 19,000 Google hits." Even if we adjust that result for references to *The Simpsons* and duplicate hits, we end up with a pretty impressive number for such a wacky word. It's a particularly humorous infixing, since *edumacation* doesn't sound very educated. In his article "The Simpsons: Embiggening Our Language with Cromulent Words" (2005), Peters observes, "Since education is an institution much-maligned by the undereducated, overeducated, and educated alike, it's not surprising that such a note-perfect mockery of the word could catch on." While -*ma*- doesn't contribute any lexical meaning to *education*, it's far from meaningless, because it expresses attitude, a bad attitude in this case, the antiestablishment rebellion characteristic of much slang: when you say *edumacation*, you're poking fun at the principal, sticking it to The Man.

---

2 From a linguistic point of view, this is imprecise: meaning is more complex than adding up a string of definitions, and often we mean more than we say. If Jenny asks me whether the drying is done, she really means that I should fold the clothes. When I say *absofuckinglutely* I mean it with emotional intensity, not just *very* + *absolutely*, and in English some infixing serves an intensifying purpose. Rather than lexical meaning, or the meaning of words, this is pragmatic meaning, the meaning of speech acts. Words like *edumacation* aren't superfluous in context, even if they seem superfluous to those who think each word should have only one meaning in all contexts. Given an infinite number of contextual meanings there would be too many "words" for us to manage! But we manage without overexerting ourselves. Much of this chapter is devoted to the pragmatics of slang.

Mockery is just one use to which the quick, prosodic infix can be put. There are lots of *Simpsons* infixings with *-ma-*, such as *metabomalism, pantomamime, macamadamia,* and *saxamaphone*.[3] Homer, who isn't the brightest bulb and seems to have absorbed little enough from his edumacation, may have trouble pronouncing words like *metabolism;* they're all nonsense syllables to him, so how does he know when to stop?[4] Homer's befuddled forms resemble one in Eric Linklater's novel *Magnus Merriman* (1934): Magnus is arrested after he and a friend, Meiklejohn, have brawled in a tony restaurant about which was the better poet, Shakespeare or Racine. He explains to the police, "We're drunk. . . . Irremededially drunk. Irremededially." Too much whiskey, too much Duff beer, university educated, intellectually challenged. When it comes to infixing and other novel language, Homer is a sort of idiot savant; Magnus Merriman, on the other hand, is a former soldier, a poet and a politician, that is, a gentleman who is not a gentleman and dislikes gentility.

Saxamaphone, though, is Homer's loving wordplay with his daughter, Lisa, and *pantomamime* and *macamadamia* are examples of fun words made more fun to say because the infix also duplicates the preceding syllable (*-toma-*, where the *o* and *a* represent the same sound, the vowel called "schwa" and *-cama-*), which is to say that it constructs a sort of rhyme within those words. In these cases, too, the *m* in *-ma-* alliterates with other *m*'s. And *-ma-* is unstressed like the syllable it duplicates, which is rhythmically especially effective in *maca-madamia*. There's plenty of phonetic pleasure in saying these words, and the pleasure is in the poetry. Homer doesn't know what some of his infixings mean and he's no linguist; he's never thought about whether placement of an infix is governed by segments, syllables, or morphemes, or according to stress, or in what combination of those phonological and morphological features.

3 In *A Natural History of Infixation* (2007) Alan C. L. Yu refers to such infixings as "Homeric," in honor of Mr. Simpson. Yu considers infixings of this type in English to be the only examples of "true" infixing in the language, given patterns and uses of infixing in other languages around the world. The argument is technical, but fascinating.

4 Accidental infixing isn't new with Homer Simpson. " 'My only comfort,' " Amy March explains to her sister Meg, "with tears in her eyes, 'is, that my mother don't take tucks in my dresses whenever I'm naughty, as Maria Parks' mother does. My dear, it's really dreadful; for sometimes she is so bad, her frock is up to her knees, and she can't come to school. When I think of this *degerredation,* I feel that I can bear even my flat nose and purple gown, with yellow skyrockets on it.' " This is one of Amy's many "lapses of lingy," as her teacher, Mr. Davis, calls them.

Nevertheless he always knows where to stick the infix — not a linguist, then, but a poet of sorts.

The type of extension illustrated by *pantomamime* is not exactly new to English. In some very old slang words, *-ma-* originated in *my*: *figmajig* 'toy that bobs around', is a nonsense-sounding version of *fig my jig*, of which Anatoly Liberman writes, "Its obscene meaning stands out a mile, as the idiom goes." But *my* is not clearly the source of *-ma-* in *thingamajig*, which, like *saxamaphone*, exhibits reduplication, though in *thingamajig* there are two inserts, *-a-* and *-ma-*, as there are in a recent, more specialized word, *resetamabob* 'thingy that resets something automated', which is modeled on the earlier, more generic word. Most dictionaries suggest that *razzmatazz* (which dates from the 1940s) is a version of *razzle-dazzle* (which dates from the late 1880s). If it is, then *-ma-* is probably independent of *my*; its sole purpose is to extend *razz-tazz* so that it sounds more like what it means.

Similarly *-de-* started out meaningful and became a nonsense extension in time. *Dandelion* was originally French *dent de lion*, best glossed 'lion's tooth' but literally 'tooth of lion'. A word like *hobbledehoy* 'gawky youth' contains the same *de*: as Liberman explains it, *Robert* was a familiar name for the Devil in the Middle Ages, when French *de* and *le* 'the' were still used in the construction of names; *Hob* was a nickname for *Rob*, and *Hobbard* for *Robert*, and over time *Hobbard de Hoy* became the all but unrecognizable *hobbledehoy*. Modern words, like *gobbledegook*, which dates from the 1940s, and even accidental forms like *irremededially*, are formed on the same pattern, but without any meaning behind *-de-*.[5]

Words like *macamadamia* and *hobbledehoy* are similar to words found in classic nursery rhymes, such as the following:

Hush-a-bye, baby, on the tree top;
When the wind blows the cradle will rock.

and

Rock-a-bye, baby,
Thy cradle is green,

5 Anatoly Liberman gives exhaustive (but exhilarating, not exhausting) accounts of *hobble-dehoy* and similarly infixed *ragamuffin* in the recently published first volume of his *Analytic Dictionary of English Etymology* (2008).

> Father's a nobleman,
> Mother's a queen.

and

> Cock a doodle doo!
> My dame has lost her shoe,
> My master's lost his fiddlestick,
> And knows not what to do.

In such cases, the insert -*a*- serves a poetic function, the syllable that fulfills the line's metrical destiny, something especially important in the first two cases, which are lullabies and usually sung. Not all nursery rhymes are so innocent:

> Hickety, pickety, my black hen,
> She lays eggs for gentlemen;
> Gentlemen come every day
> To see what my black hen doth lay.
> Sometimes nine and sometimes ten,
> Hickety, pickety, my black hen.

This last rhyme may be a euphemistic description of illicit behavior. (Why do the gentlemen come each day? To count eggs? Really? That's some hen!) The differences between nursery rhyme and slang occasionally are not so great after all. The infix -*et*- usefully extends *hicky* and *picky*, for metrical reasons. At its best, though, -*et*- is onomatopoetic: when you speak the lines, you can hear the hen's *hickety pickety* pecking for corn, or feel the bum-numbing discomfort of

> A farmer went trotting upon his grey mare,
> Bumpety, bumpety, bump!
> With his daughter behind him so rosy and fair,
> Lumpety, lumpety, lump!

or the rhythm of feline exertion in

> Diddlety, diddlety, dumpty,
> The cat ran up the plum tree;
> Half a crown
> To fetch her down,
> Diddlety, diddlety, dumpty.

Onomatopoeia is a variety of metaphor: the sound of the word represents the word's meaning. In an infix like -et-, slang sound effects merge seamlessly with slang metaphor.

In *The Simpsons* Ned Flanders's infixing rivals Homer's, but -*diddly*- is his favorite insert. As Mark Peters writes, Flanders is "hyper-holy," and his infixes sanctify a typically profane process. He is also gratingly cheerful, absatively posilutely looking on the bright side of things, and *diddly* perfectly conveys his sunny attitude: *murder* and *dilemma* sound a lot less forbidding when infixed as *murdiddlyurder* and *dididdlyemma*, if not quite as effusively good natured as *dediddlyighted* and *buenos ding dong diddly dias*, which is technically an interposing rather than an infixing because the insert is placed in the middle of a phrase rather than a word. After a session with Flanders most of us need something like polamarized sunglasses for our ears.

Fans of *The Simpsons*, and probably others who have never seen an episode of the show (it's nearly impossible to avoid its cultural influence completely), have adopted -*diddly*- and placed it alongside profanity, which works surprisingly well in lighthearted contexts, as in the interposings *hi diddly fucking ho, ho diddly fucking hum, jack diddly fucking shit, nice diddly fucking day*, and *yee diddly fucking ha* (because *yeefuckin'haw* isn't emotively intensified enough). *Yee diddly fucking ha* in itself may not be poetry, but it is the germ of poetry and expresses the human impulse to poetic invention, which comes from recognizing in the language we speak the possibility of play and the reconstitution of what we find, what's given, into the unexpected.

If you think that identifying slang as poetic demeans poetry or attributes linguistic canniness to the hoi polloi at the expense of Genius, there is no competition here: we are able to enjoy poetry because it practices and perfects the linguistic playfulness with which we are all familiar, and more schoolchildren would enjoy poetry if it were presented to them not as something beyond them, but as something for which they have a natural capacity. A poem can be more significant culturally than any single item of slang. Poems are structurally, metaphorically, and thematically multidimensional; as a linguistic artifact, a good poem accomplishes more than a single word. But surely slang processes like infixing, taken in the aggregate, are also culturally significant. How much you value slang depends on what cultural credit you give to nursery rhymes, advertising, and language play that isn't anthologized but that affirms daily and all over the world the occasional linguistic genius of people who are poets and didn't know it.

But young people know they are poetic when they take the -*z*- of *razzle-dazzle* and *razzmatazz* and make something of it, fo' shizzle. One recently popular infix is variously -*z*-, -*iz*-, -*izn*-, in forms like *fuznuck*, *hizouse*, and *shiznit*. This set of infixes serves a few purposes: *biznitch*, *fuznuck*, *hizo*, and *shiznit* are transparent euphemisms (or, if they aren't so transparent, read *bitch*, *fuck*, *ho* 'whore', with stress on the second syllable of *hizo*, and *shit*), the kind that give you time to run before the nearest authority figure catches on. Speakers take these euphemisms in strange directions. If you want to emphasize (albeit playfully) that someone is a bitch, you can say that he or she is a *biyatch* or *biyotch*, usually pronounced "bee atch" or "bee otch"; when you do, you are putting yourself out there — it's theatrical speech. It's not clear why you'd try to dress pejoratives up with infixes, but *bizatch* and *biznatch* are available if you need them.

Some of my students insist that this infix intensifies, that it's one thing to be *the shit* and another, better thing to be *the shiznit*, the *ubershit*, so to speak; it's one thing to be a bitch, but anyone you called a *biznitch* would be one serious bitch, and a *biznatch*, stress on the second syllable, would be a bitch on wheels. Their claim makes some sense, since -*fucking*- and euphemisms like -*freaking*-, -*blooming*-, -*bloody*- intensify the base or matrix into which they are inserted. The supposed intensifying effect isn't restricted to profanity because something even better than the *bomb* can be the *bizzomb*. It isn't even restricted to the inserts -*z*-, -*iz*-, and -*izn*-: SlangSite.com records *adorabubble* (I think it should be *adorabable*) and defines it as 'super adorable'. In a form like *bizounce* 'bail, leave', however, we simply see language at play, speech sounds enjoyed for their own sakes.

The -*z*-, -*iz*-, -*izn*- set of infixes is closely associated with African American slang, extended to a larger population of English speakers worldwide through hip-hop culture. Nowadays, if you want to, you can operate a translation program on your blog or Web page at Gizzoogle.com and convert the text into something Streetish, with plenty of infixes. The rapper Snoop Dogg claims to have coined the suffix -*izzle* and the set of infixes in the 1990s, leading to his song, "The Shiznit" (1993); but, though he's taken that claim to the bank, the infix was already in use, at least from UTFO's "Roxanne, Roxanne" (1985) and perhaps earlier, depending on what you count as a bona fide example of the pattern. Why does Snoop Dogg want credit for "inventing" the infix? Inventive language is a way to stand out against the background of American culture; successfully endorsing and promoting a recognizable idiom makes a style leader, affirms his status and his cultural or subcultural authority. The -*iz*- set of infixes, then, is an instrument of fitting in and of standing out, the confluence of slang's social and aesthetic dimensions.[6]

LEXIFABRICOGRAPHY AND THE LEXICALLY MEANINGFUL INFIX

Infixing, like poetry, attracts the ear. From *rock-a-bye* and *cock-a-doodle-doo* to *metabomalism* and *hizouse*, it's just common enough, embedded enough in folk speech, like nursery rhymes, and popular song to be marginally acceptable in some (by no means all) conversation. And, like poetry, infixing surprises us: it's unorthodox enough to count as slang, if not poetry itself, especially when it's used deliberately to tweak our orthodox sensibilities. The poetics of infixing goes well beyond sound, however. In the past few decades, say, from 1980 forward, infixing has occasionally imitated extreme poetic diction, resurrecting a classical tradition of which many contemporary poets are unaware and on which, as a result, they rarely if ever draw. If the relation between infixing and poetry is unexpected, it's also undeniable; certain features of ancient poetry may be preserved better in speech today than in today's poetry.[7]

James B. McMillan, whose classic account of English infixing and interposing was published in 1980, argued that infixing yields a word like *absofuckinglutely*

---

6   Against the background of prosodic infixing, it's difficult to place a very new development described by Jeff Prucher in *Brave New Words: The Oxford Dictionary of Science Fiction* (2007), the graphic infix, in forms like *bheer*, *Ghod*, and *ghood*. As Prucher explains, "adding -h- to a word does not change the word's meaning, but instead indicates that it is being used humorously or in a fannish context." Obviously, this sort of infixing doesn't work well in speech; it's an innovation of Internet communication meant to provide unspoken speech with something like the pragmatic opportunities provided by infixing in spoken speech. Graphic infixing shares important characteristics with prosodic infixing: it's a humorous way of standing out, but because it's "fannish" it's also useful in fitting in.

7   This is an altogether historical comment, not a criticism of contemporary poetry, as though it would be "better" if it were more like ancient Greek or Latin or Renaissance poetry. Putting aside the dubious question of "progress," poetic conventions change over time as they must, thus another resemblance between poets and speakers of slang: while critics and readers sometimes wish poetry would "stay the same" over time, younger poetic generations must distinguish themselves from older ones. Successive poetic generations develop different poetries, much as successive generations of speakers develop different slangs. In any event, one cannot believe that continuity is the only property of poetic development unless one believes that poetry transcends, or ought to transcend, the social sphere of language use. If you believe that, then we must agree to disagree.

or *absobloominglutely* fabricated from "a polysyllabic word as the matrix and an emotive intensifier (an expletive or a euphemism) as the insert." In these examples, polysyllabic *absolutely* is the matrix, expletive *-fucking-* and euphemistic *-blooming-*, respectively, the inserts or infixes. Interposing is pretty much the same process, but a fixed phrase rather than a word, serves as the matrix: interposed, *No way!* becomes *No fucking way!* or, euphemistically, *No freakin' way!* The distinction between a lexical item like *absolutely* and one like *no way* is shadowy; some phrases behave like words, and the difference between words and phrases, in some contexts, is a technicality.

McMillan insisted that an insert, whether in infixing or interposing, "is typically an expletory intensifier, its function that of an emotive stress amplifier." By implication, then, there's no lexical meaning to the inserts: there's no sexual meaning, no actual 'fucking,' meant by *-fucking-*, nor anything like 'blooming' in *-blooming-*, nor, since it's a euphemism for *-fucking-*, any 'fucking' in *-blooming-* either. Meaning in such infixings is partly lexical, of course, because *absolutely* means 'absolutely', but it's also partly pragmatic; that is, its meaning depends on social context beyond the easy reach of dictionary definitions. The insert intensifies the matrix, if not explosively then at least emphatically; an infixing carries emotional or attitudinal meaning greater than the sum of its parts.

McMillan's Rule aptly and durably describes the phenomenon of infixing and interposing in English: it allows us to predict and interpret scads of forms like *fanbloodytastic, guaranfuckingtee, rigoddamndiculous*, and *unfuckingbelievable*. When speakers are bottles of emotion all shook up, infixing blows the cap and slang shoots into the air, froth and specks of language, as Whitman put it. Expletives often relieve anger or frustration, but infixings and interposings complicate the emotion and convey frustrated amazement and amazed anger in speech. They can convey other complex emotions, too, such as anxiety and exhilaration, as when a novice skydiver yells "Five thousand, five hundred feet! Haven't I got to do something here? Oh yes, the para-FUCKING-CHUTE!" or shit-eating satisfaction: "'Yee-fuckin'-haw,' whoops Natalie Maines at the end of the Dixie Chicks' taped message to Top of the Pops 2." If she'd been even more enthusiastic, she'd have let go with *Yee-diddly-fuckin'-haw*. All of these are everyday English infixings, some of them well established and frequently used, some invented for their special contexts and occasions.

As with so many slang phenomena, infixing pops up in *Buffy the Vampire Slayer*. In the episode "Shadow" (2000) the exiled god Glorificus, bent on nothing less than catastrophe, rants against inconvenient terrestrial constraints:

"Everything takes time. What about my time? Does anyone appreciate that I'm on a schedule here? Tick tock, Dreg—tick frickin' tock." Linguistically, there's nothing remarkable here. Indeed, the item simply reminds us of the conventions for infixing and interposing in English as described in McMillan's classic article on the subject. The matrix *tick tock* is recorded in every standard dictionary; *-frickin'-* is just the sort of insert that McMillan describes as an "emotive stress amplifier." Where there's frustration there's an expletive. Or maybe it's the other way around. Anyway, inserts in conventional infixing are semantically empty; *-frickin'-* doesn't mean anything more than the emotional baggage it carries.

Fuck, in its myriad manifestations, is the expletive that satisfies, and euphemisms like *frickin'* aren't far behind. Nevertheless, SlangSite.com introduces an upbeat knockoff of the classic infixing, *fabflippintastic*, which it defines as "something that is incredibly good, so saying it's fantastic isn't enough. You have to combine three words to express your joy." Joy is an emotion, but not a stressful one; it is amplified by the combination of *fabulous* and *fantastic*, not to mention *-flippin-*. This insert sounds pleasanter than *-fuckin'-*: it is at least emphatic and carries no taboo. But it also carries no lexical meaning: there's no flipping of anything. Or, on closer inspection, perhaps there is lexical meaning after all. Is *-flippin-* here not merely an f-euphemism for the f-word (from *flipping*, recorded as a euphemism for *fucking* in all the big slang dictionaries) but also related to *flipping out*, which, among other things, means 'delighted' and sounds delighted, too?

According to McMillan's Rule, inserts in infixings and interposings should be expletive (or emphatic) emotive stress amplifiers, pragmatically meaningful for that reason, but not lexically meaningful, even if, without the surrounding hyphens, you'd find them in dictionaries, defined like any other word. By contrast, McMillan insisted that "some inserts which are not expletives and which add lexical meaning to their matrices rather than emotive intensity should not be classified as infixes." He illustrated the point with literary coinages, such as Gerard Manly Hopkins's *wind-lilylocks-laced* and e. e. cummings's *democra(caveat emptor)cy*, which, he suggested, were examples of tmesis, or perhaps diacope, rather than infixing. For McMillan, lots of ancient Greeks, and some modern scholars, tmesis and diacope were exclusively poetic language. You can bet that American soldiers in World War I weren't reading books on Ancient Greek poetic technique in the trenches (though some of the British officers probably were); we can reasonably assume, therefore, that infixing and tmesis are, just as McMillan asserted, distinct linguistic phenomena.

Recent evidence, though, proves that genuine infixes and interposings can take meaningful inserts on occasion, whenever an infixing or interposing with such an insert best serves a complex, probably humorous rhetorical situation. When it does, arguably, slang approximates poetry. For instance, in 1997 "Peppermint Pat-Eye" wrote the following about a recent snowboarding adventure:

> The idea behind Camp Snoopy was born in a swirling Xanax/booze haze somewhere over the Atlantic Ocean en route to the Arctic Circle. The camp staff, [snowboard] riders from all over the world . . . all agreed to meet at Rijksgransen, Sweden. . . . I was tentative about the idea at first — going to a camp in Rijksgransen seemed a bit blown out: "Oooh, Jaffrie, we've been bloody nailing it 'ere mate! The world's best unknowns spinning 900s over me bloomin' head! *Absoschmuckinglutely* paradise."

Peppermint may have had in mind any number of model infixes when coining *absoschmuckinglutely*, but the Cockney pastiche and the phrase "over me bloomin' head" suggest that he or she hears, in the recesses of memory, Eliza Doolittle in Lerner and Loewe's *My Fair Lady* singing the line, "Oh, so loverly sittin' absobloominlutely still."

Fuck and its derivatives, including euphemisms, are so procreative that an addition to their family hardly warrants a gala christening, but we should celebrate *absoschmuckinglutely* because (1) it's an unrecorded euphemism of *absofuckinglutely*, (2) it's an instance of the previously unrecorded infix *-schmucking-*, (3) it's an early example (though not the earliest) of a clearly lexically meaningful insert in an English infixing or interposing, and (4) it's a weird example of what Keith Allan and Kate Burridge call "euphemistic dysphemism," the category of words meant dysphemistically but uttered euphemistically. *Schmuck* is a negative word, a dysphemism for 'fool', which, in this instance, the speaker uses to take himself or herself down a peg. Lexically, however, *schmucking* is a euphemism for *fucking*, because it flies under the taboo, as, pragmatically, does *-schmucking-*, a euphemism for *-fucking-*. That's a lot of work for a single word to do.

According to Lighter's *Historical Dictionary of American Slang*, *absofuckinglutely* may have originated during World War I, in soldier slang, and first appeared in print in 1921. It has had a worldwide currency in English slang since and is well illustrated in Jesse Sheidlower's *The F-Word* (1995), which has a lot to say about it and many other *-fucking-* infixings and interposings. That's not a surprise: Lighter records many parallel infixes (1) with *absolutely* as the matrix, such as *absobloodylutely* and *absogoddamlutely*; (2) with *fucking* as the infixed element, or insert, such as *fanfuckingtastic*, *guaranfuckingtee*, *disafuckin'pear*, and *afuckin'way*, evidence that infixed *-fucking-* can intensify nearly any part of speech; and (3) with a euphemism for *fucking* as the insert, such as *absofrickinlutely* and *ofriggenkay*; not to mention (4) syntactic interposings with *fucking* or one of its euphemisms as the interposed element, such as *no fucking way*, *where in the effin hell*, and *so friggin what*. Ostensibly, *absoschmuckinglutely* is merely one more example of category 3, though it is an interesting addition because relatively few euphemisms are recorded as inserts. McMillan listed only eight, and *HDAS* has added a handful more.

True to our expectations, infixed and interposed *fucking* and its euphemisms are assigned more or less arbitrarily and are meaningful only as intensifiers and euphemisms. Significantly, though, context suggests that *absoschmuckinglutely* means differently than the many parallel forms, because *-schmucking-* from *schmuck* 'fool, oaf, jerk' reflects Peppermint Pat-Eye's initial concern that the Camp Snoopy enterprise and his or her participation in it was foolish or would make him or her look foolish. Thus the insert unusually adds a stratum of lexical meaning to the word. When McMillan suggested that "some inserts which are not expletives and which add lexical meaning to their matrices rather than emotive intensity should not be classified as infixes," he did not anticipate an infixing like *absoschmuckinglutely*, in which the insert is an expletive AND adds lexical meaning, not rather than, but IN ADDITION TO emotional intensity.

-Schmucking- is one of very few euphemisms for *-fucking-* with independent meaning. *-Frigging-*, *-fugging-*, and *-effing-*, though admirably expletive, are lexically meaningless; *-freaking-* may be the only other euphemism in this family that COULD add lexical meaning to the infixed word, though one rarely, if ever, encounters a context where it does. *-Schmucking-* is the only recorded etymologically "appropriate" euphemism for *-fucking-*. *Schmuck* 'fool, oaf, jerk' descends from Yiddish *schmuck* 'male sexual part' (literally it means 'pendant'), parallel to English *dick*, *dork*, and so on. Therefore, *-schmucking-* is not only an unusually meaningful euphemism for *-fucking-* but also the only independently dysphemistic one.

Although *-schmucking-*'s lexical and dysphemistic meanings were originally separate from *-fucking-*'s, sound closely associates the two inserts: obviously, they rhyme, and, as Roy Blount Jr. puts it, "The most pervasive sound, by far, in words relating to sex is the *k* or hard *c*." No other recorded euphemism for *-fucking-* rhymes with it (*-fugging-* comes closest; the two constitute a minimal pair), and though some preserve the /k/ as well as the initial /f/ (*-freaking-*, for instance), *-schmucking-* may best preserve *-fucking-*'s expletive excellence.

In other words, although context indicates that -*schmucking*- adds lexical meaning even as it euphemizes, the sound of -*schmucking*- nevertheless better recalls -*fucking*-'s dysphemistic meaning. Whether euphemisms function better as expletives by emphasizing the /f/ or /k/ often depends on sound pattern and a speaker's illocutionary situation and is probably a matter of taste. Undoubtedly *absoschmuckinglutely* is the most dysphemistic euphemistic dysphemism in the whole -*fucking*- famdamn'ly.

How long has infixing and interposing with meaningful inserts been going on? Not very long, though some earlier forms without strictly meaningful inserts may have contributed to the very possibility of such things. With models in mind, speakers may feel licensed to innovate. *Jesus Christ* (in Greek, 'Jesus, the Anointed One') is a phrase, but it's also idiomatically a name that counts as a single lexical item, so it's difficult to decide whether *Jesus H. Christ* is an infixing or an interposing. It probably doesn't make any difference. In his *Autobiography* (1910) Mark Twain claimed that *Jesus H. Christ* had been around since the mid-nineteenth century, though its first recorded use is from 1892. It may well be an Americanism, given the evidence. Certainly the *H.* in *Jesus H. Christ* is expletive: as Roger Smith put it in "The *H* of *Jesus H. Christ*" (1994), "Rhetorically, the interpolations have the same emphatic effect as infixing, like the affirmative absogoddamnlutely favored by Marine drill instructors."

But is the *H.* also lexically meaningful? With good reason Smith thinks not, at least not in a strict etymological sense. The *H.* most likely comes from the Greek abbreviation for *Jesus*, *IHΣ*, or iota-eta-sigma, the first three letters of Jesus' name. For reasons that aren't clear, Medieval Latin often represented the Greek abbreviation as *IHC*. In other words, the *H.* is neither an initial nor independently an abbreviation. Most Americans know as much about the Greek alphabet as they do about tmesis and diacope, but they see *IHS* and *IHC* on stained-glass windows, vestments, publications, and the like and inevitably provide folk etymologies for them. If they believe that the *I* stands for *Iesus* 'Jesus' and the *S* for Latin *Salvator* 'savior', then they interpret the intervening *H* as an abbreviation for Latin *hominum: Iesus Hominum Salvator* or 'Jesus, Savior of Mankind.' In a sense, if people believe in this expansion, then *H.* is meaningful, whether or not it was meaningful a thousand years ago. Folk make it meaningful when they concoct the folk etymology.

The *Iesus Hominum Salvator* interpretation, however fanciful, is seriously meant, but others are jocular, vulgar, and blasphemous, as Smith illustrates with *Jesus H. Particular Christ, Jesus Henry Christ, Jesus Harold Christ, Jesus Hebrew*

Christ, and *Jesus Hebe Christ*. Of these, all are emphatic, but only the last two, identifying Jesus as Jewish, arguably have meaningful inserts. The pragmatic force is complex, as in *absoschmuckinglutely*: the inserts *Henry* and *Harold* diminish Jesus, as though *Jesus Christ* 'Jesus the Anointed One' (that is, 'Messiah') were a name like any other and Jesus just a guy with a middle name. But neither name has any lexical meaning; like all personal names, they're a type of pointing when they actually refer to someone. *Jesus Hebe Christ* identifies Jesus as Jewish in a transparently anti-Semitic way, though the expansion of *Jesus H. Christ* closest to having a meaningful insert is probably *Jesus Holy Christ*. But all of these are after-the-fact explanations of a typically "expletory intensifier, its function that of an emotive stress amplifier," some of them no less expletory than the original.

Infixing and interposing take a new direction in the film *The Blues Brothers* (1980), written by James Landis and Dan Ackroyd. "Joliet" Jake Blues (played by John Belushi), recently released from the joint, in search of redemption, ends up at the Triple Rock Baptist Church, where the Reverend Cleophus (played by James Brown) asks, "Have you seen the light?" and Jake cries out, "Yes! Yes! Jesus H. tap-dancing Christ, I have seen the light!" Landis and Ackroyd seized an opportunity to make an old expletory intensifier new. The question, though, is whether *-tap-dancing-* counts as a meaningful insert. It isn't lexically meaningful in quite the way *-schmuck-* in *absoschmuckinglutely* is meaningful, but after a series of handsprings, Jake dances ecstatically, and some of what he dances could be called tap. In the film's context, then, *-tap-dancing-* serves well as an "emotive stress amplifier," and *Jesus H. tap-dancing Christ* is either a sort of expletory tmesis or a meaningful infixing.

With *Jesus H. tap-dancing Christ* pointing the way, slang steps out in a newly poetic direction. In the film *Heathers* (1988), for instance, when Veronica (played by Winona Ryder) finds one of the Heathers in the school restroom about to commit suicide, she complains, "Heather, you're throwing your life away to become a statistic in *US-fucking-A Today*," and she means that Heather will become common by doing what others do, the obvious thing, as published in a newspaper that, in some people's estimate at the time, tended to simplify or trivialize news compared to newspapers of record. In its early years, the story goes, *USA Today* had front-page photographs of flowers announcing "Spring Is Here!" while the *New York Times* and the *Wall Street Journal* documented war, recession, and all of the depressing business of news as usual. Of course, this version of history is hyperbolic and unfair, but anyone who has seen *Heathers* knows just how mean-spirited a film can be — I mean, mean-spirited in a good way.

Fuckin'-A is well attested in *HDAS* and *The F Word*, but not as meaning 'obviously, undoubtedly, absolutely' (where 'obviously' can be mildly derisive, roughly equivalent to 'No shit!'). However, consider the following bit of dialogue from the film *Office Space* (1999):

> LAWRENCE: When a boss wants you to work on Saturday, he generally asks you at the end of the day, right? . . . So all you've got to do is avoid him . . . the last few hours on Friday, duck out early, turn off your answering machine; you should be home free, man.
>
> PETER: That's a really good idea.
>
> LAWRENCE: Fuckin'-A, buddy.

That's the *fuckin'-A* we're talking about. Following the emerging trend, the infixing or interposing *US-fucking-A Today* (it suffers from the same problem of classification as *Jesus H. Christ*) dismissively attributes a meaningful quality, conveyed by the insert, to *USA Today*. According to McMillan's Rule, infixed and interposed inserts aren't supposed to carry lexical meaning, but *fucking-A*, a form both expletive and meaningful, has it both ways.

The examples accumulating here suggest that McMillan's Rule extends not only to infixing, but also to syntactic interposing, "the insertion of emotive intensifiers into collocations that are normally not interruptible or are interruptible under restrictions that exclude intensifiers." As with infixing, the insert in syntactic interposing should not carry lexical meaning: "In the insert position *bloody* cannot have its ordinary meaning; the survivor and the knights in *born bloody survivor* and *white bloody knights* are not gory." The point can be made colloquially: when Jack Walsh, Robert De Niro's character in the film *Midnight Run* (1989), explodes with "Here come two words for you: Shut the fuck up!" he proves that inserts generally lack meaning, that they don't "count." So McMillan's Rule applies to interposing as well as infixing. Does the exception regarding meaningful inserts apply as well?

In some contexts infixes and interposings are rhetorically tricky, attempting to mean more than any one word should mean, so they enlist unexpected lexical resources, such as the lexically meaningful insert. Consider the following infamous monologue from the film *Cruel Intentions* (1998):

> KATHRYN: It's all right for guys like you and Court to fuck everyone, but when I do it I get dumped for innocent little twits like Cecile. God forbid I exude confidence and enjoy sex. Do you think I relish the fact that I have to act like Mary

Sunshine 24/7, so I can be considered a lady? I'm the Marcia fucking Brady of the Upper East Side and sometimes I want to kill myself.

There is perhaps no similarly efficient means for Kathryn to convey her duality: Marcia Brady (simply a television alternative to Mary Sunshine) by day, and Marcia Brady fucking, that is, *Marcia fucking Brady*, by night. In this case, the insert actually carries its "ordinary meaning," a type of lexical meaning that inserts are supposed to relinquish for the privilege of being infixed or interposed.

A very similar interposing occurs in an episode of *Buffy the Vampire Slayer*, "Becoming, Part 2" (1998). For those who need catching up, Angel, a vampire who once had a soul (as a result of a gypsy curse) and lost it again (as a result of sexual relations with Buffy because the curse stipulated that he would lose his soul when he experienced true happiness), has apocalyptic plans. Buffy must stop him, and Spike, another archvampire, volunteers his help, for reasons including those expressed in the following monologue:

> SPIKE: I want to save Angel. I want to save the world.... We like to talk big, vampires do. "I'm going to destroy the world"—it's just tough guy talk. Struttin' around with your friends over a pint of blood. The truth is, I like this world. You've got dog-racing, Manchester United. And you've got people, billions of people walking around like Happy Meals with legs. It's all right here. But then someone comes along with a vision and a real passion for destruction. Angel could pull it off. Goodbye Piccadilly, farewell Leicester bloody Square, know what I'm saying?

Leicester Square WOULD be bloody if Spike had his way. Here the insert *-bloody-* is a little more than merely emotional stress amplifier; though only obliquely, humorously, and contextually, *-bloody-* actually means 'bloody,' meaning of a sort McMillan specifically excluded.

Spike's *Leicester bloody Square* parallels Kathryn's *Marcia fucking Brady* in *Cruel Intentions*: both are obliquely, humorously, contextually meaningful (it is unproductive, if not impossible, to untangle these three conditions). Both interrupt names rather than idiomatic phrases and both appear in monologues, suggesting that parameters of discourse may influence production of this type of meaningful interposing. In one respect, they are different: *bloody* is an adjective, whereas *fucking* is a verb reassigned to the status of insert. Although *-fucking-* is not a transitive verb (a person named *Marcia* is not fucking another person named *Brady*), it humorously invokes intransitive *fucking*, as Kathryn (by her own account) is Little Mary Sunshine by day, but Marcia Brady of the Upper East Side fucking by night.[8]

One suspects from such examples, from *absoschmuckinglutely* to *Marcia fucking Brady*, that the new variety of infixings and interposings occurs in fairly complex rhetorical situations. A rhetorical problem arises for which one solution is a particularly meaningful infix or interposing; occasionally, an opportunistic writer or speaker will break the supposed rules and solve that problem by means of that infix or interposing. Usually the problem involves humor: the writer or speaker feels the simultaneous pressure of dual rhetorical forces, both the need for an "emotive stress amplifier," a need that infixing and interposing serve exceptionally well, and the need to elicit humor, which often requires the intersection of lexical meaning involved in an immediate verbal context and the transgressive sense that a rule is being violated.

Arnold Zwicky and Geoffrey Pullum (1987) view infixing and interposing, even in their classic manifestations, as a type of wordplay, like "secret languages, riddling, punning, insult games, and the like." The clever blend of *USA Today* and *fucking-A* certainly supports their view, as does the punning use of *fucking* in the quotation from *Cruel Intentions*, or of *bloody* in Spike's rant. Wordplay of this kind is closely aligned with slang: its products are sometimes forced, artificial in the sense that they are limited to the game and fabricated for an audience invested in the game. But they are essentially playful, in the nature of games, and transgressive, because they break the rules of speech outside of the game. The more casual they seem (they can't be casual, really), the more they affirm the speaker's aesthetic proficiency.

These infixings and interposings, with their blends, puns, and meaningful inserts, are very clever; they are also, following the Merriam-Webster definition of *slang*, forced and facetious and too good to be true of natural speech. Here is an example of a super-meaningful interposing formed from a typically expletive one by accident; it wasn't meant to be clever but somehow managed to end up that way. In the film *Jawbreaker* (1998), written and directed by Darren Stein,

<hr/>

8   This syntactic maneuver is not unique to the film: the online retailer Blowfish offers its customers a "symbolic silicone dildo" called "Jackhammer Jesus," which it describes as "Jesus fucking Christ. Literally." These purveyors of religious-themed sex toys do not mean to suggest that "Jesus [is] fucking Christ," but that "Jesus Christ [is] fucking" whoever is on the receiving end. Naturally, such elision and transformation lead to misunderstanding. Such forms are not preferred in most contexts.

the character Courtney Shane, played by Rose McGowan, several times uses the phrase *peachy fucking keen*, as in "Remember, everything is peachy keen — peachy fucking keen." Courtney's characteristic interposing adheres to McMillan's Rule: although *fucking* here is not exactly an "emotional stress amplifier," it is an attitude amplifier, because it's transgressive and used to establish Courtney as the sort of girl who transgresses. Frankly, it's a cross between assertive and menacing.

On June 3, 2002, the USA television network aired *Jawbreaker* and, unable to preserve the original script's profanity, overdubbed Courtney's phrase as *peachy fuzzy keen*, transforming a conventional interposing into one with a meaningful insert. Undoubtedly, the motive behind the replacement of *fuzzy* for *fucking* was primarily phonetic: to supply a plausible alternative to *fucking*, the facially obvious initial fricative /f/ would need to be reproduced, but the mouth's position for /k/ is nearly indistinguishable from that for /z/ (it's the tongue's position that distinguishes them), and the ultimate nasal /n/ or /ŋ/ is easily lost, so *fuzzy* would adequately mask McGowan's original *fucking* in all but a vestigial sneer. Producers and engineers at the USA Network chose to overdub one of very few words phonetically close to the script's unacceptable form.

Fuddy, fungi, funky, funny, fussy are also phonetically satisfactory alternatives, but those responsible for the replacement encountered an unusual problem: all of these are so obviously meaningful that they cannot replace *fucking* as an emotive stress amplifier and also cannot interrupt *peachy keen* without producing, for various reasons, risible forms (*peachy fuddy keen, peachy fungi keen, peachy funky keen, peachy funny keen, peachy fussy keen*). In other words, the writers, directors, and producers were backed into finding a phonetically credible meaningful form, and *fuzzy* was the only possibility. The choice, however, probably had nothing to do with the relative meaningfulness of the euphemistic insert chosen. *Peachy fuzzy keen* is a particularly interesting form: *absoschmuckinglutely, US-fucking-A Today*, and *Marcia fucking Brady* all depend on context for their meaningfulness, but *fuzzy* is meaningful in *peachy fuzzy keen* because peach skin is fuzzy, so the meaning depends not on a broader context, but on the semantic relationship between insert and matrix.

Though it's an accident, *peachy fuzzy keen* reminds us that television is worth watching: it generates new words, not always in spite of, but sometimes because of, the medium and its constraints. And it really makes no difference whether the meaningfulness of the insert is accidental or not: for anyone who watches the overdubbed version, *peachy fuzzy keen*, not the original, rule-abiding interposing, is the relevant form, the one that might incite imitation or serve as a model for future interposers. Few adolescents borrow a word or phrase from a film and propose it to their eight best friends as a form to use.

That is, if Gretchen from *Mean Girls* had tried to introduce *peachy fuzzy keen* instead of *fetch*, it wouldn't have caught on. Gretchen, bless her heart, is attracted to slang for aesthetic reasons; maybe she hasn't thought it out in terms of an aesthetic program, but she likes *fetch* because it sounds cool, and *peachy fuzzy keen* would catch her ear, too. The aesthetics would be partly semantic, though. You can just hear her say, enthusiastically and expectantly, because she's the type of person who always thinks she's got it right this time, "Peaches are fuzzy, get it?" Regina, who is interested in slang's social value, isn't interested in aesthetics; she would make Gretchen pay, sting her with an insult or a look that says it all, for lacking the adult lexical experience that makes euphemisms like *peachy fuzzy keen* transparent.

Besides the accidentally meaningful interposing, there's also the faux infixing to consider. Infixings and interposings can be so artfully fabricated, so rhetorically complex, that imitations can pass as the real thing, which, I suppose, is in itself a type of wordplay, a transgression upon a transgression. As the exemplary Christian character on television's *The Simpsons*, Ned Flanders avoids infixing because it is a species of swearing; even if an insert isn't profane, or a euphemism for something profane, it amplifies only negative emotions (anger, frustration, dismissiveness, disbelief), those that swearing usually conveys. Always cheerful in his faith, Flanders amplifies his positive emotion in reduplicative forms such as *okelly dokelly* and inversions such as *absatively posilutely*.

On February 13, 2000, however, Flanders, in an emphatic moment, deployed *absonotly* 'absolutely not' in lieu of the infix *absofuckinglutely not*. *Absonotly* is not an infix: it replaces *-lute-* with *-not-*, rather than inserts *-not-* at a stress / syllable appropriate point in the matrix *absolutely*. (**absoly*, not a word, is not a matrix.) But the form clearly imitates infixing, and, interestingly, the humor depends on inserting the lexically meaningful *-not-* in place of the independently meaningless *-lute-*, both as an emotional stress amplifier and to convey the sense 'absolutely not.' The humor derives partly from the audience's immediate grasp of the word's meaning, which depends both on the insert's meaning and the audience's willingness to accept the grammatical pattern behind the item, however unusual, as legitimate.

One still might object to classifying any of the forms catalogued here as infixings or interposings. "Sixteenth-century scholars," McMillan wrote, "imported the terms TMESIS and DIACOPE to describe the interruption of a compound by another word." So, where an infixing or interposing is not an "emotional stress amplifier," he insisted, we observe tmesis or diacope instead, a simple enough distinction and the fundamental one, it would seem, yet neither McMillan nor anyone else imagined that an insert could simultaneously be expletive AND add lexical meaning, not rather than, but IN ADDITION TO emotional intensity.

Neither of the classical rhetorical terms quite captures the phenomenon described here. According to Richard A. Lanham's *Handlist of Rhetorical Terms* (1991), *diacope* is "repetition of a word with one or a few words in between: 'My heart is fixed, O God, my heart is fixed' (Peacham)," whereas *tmesis* is "separation of the elements of a compound word by another word or words: 'West—by God—Virginia'; 'how dearly ever parted' (*Troilus and Cressida* III, iii) for 'however dearly parted'." Diacope is clearly not the relevant rhetorical figure, and tmesis, too, is implausibly applied to forms like those described here, where interruptions follow the stress / syllabic rules that apply to infixing, whereas cummings's *democra(caveat emptor)cy* clearly does not and more nearly approximates tmesis.

It would be unusual to find a speaker of current American English aware of either diacope or tmesis. While Lanham and other glossaries of literary terms define both terms, the *Princeton Encyclopedia of Poetry and Poetics* (1974) bothers only with tmesis. One could argue that a current American lexical item exhibits diacope or tmesis whether it wants to or not, but it seems worth noting that even college students studying rhetoric and poetics might not encounter diacope, and only serious students of poetry, certainly not even all poets, would know tmesis when they see it. Diacope and tmesis are all Greek to most of us. Current speakers model their speech on what they know, and they know a lot more about infixing and interposing than they do about musty rhetorical figures. Everyone underestimated the pragmatic opportunities that infixing and interposing enable, and, one suspects, it was only a matter of time until someone seized those opportunities. Evidence suggests that the time has come. A twenty-first-century speaker of American English would identify the type of lexical interruption that looks like tmesis as infixing or interposing instead. In accepting the both / and of emotive stress amplifier and meaningful insert, in resisting an either / or decision in the case of *Tmesis v. Infixing*, speakers (and readers and listeners) demonstrate a very poetic understanding of English.

McMillan's position on infixing and interposing is a bit confused: *West—by God—Virginia* includes an expletive insert, after all, one that's only marginally lexically meaningful. Perhaps the issue is less whether inserts can be lexically meaningful than that they MUST be expletive. All examples of infixing and inter-posing presented so far have been expletive, at least to some degree: each insert has been 100 percent bona fide expletive, a euphemistic expletive, or a pun one side of which is expletive. Is the nonexpletive infix or interposing possible? For that would be the one most clearly approximating tmesis. Perhaps it is, tucked away in an overlooked corner of American speech. In "Slay the Critics," the let-ters to the editor section of Dark Horse Comics' series of *Buffy the Vampire Slayer* comic books, a correspondent named Brandon wrote in 2002, "Fassbender & Pascoe, in my *unprofessional* opinion, need to take a leap of faith, and really *do* something to the Buffy-comicverse." In order to take the form as an infixing, one must take *-comic-* as the insert and recognize *Buffyverse* 'world of all things relat-ing to Buffy the Vampire Slayer or the television show, *Buffy the Vampire Slayer*,' a quotidian blend of *Buffy* and *universe*, as the matrix.

As recorded in *Slayer Slang: A "Buffy the Vampire Slayer" Lexicon* (2003), *Buffy-verse* is fully lexicalized, illustrated in the glossary by twelve quotations spanning 1999 to 2002, from sources as diverse as The Bronze and Bronze: Beta (official *Buffy* posting boards), a *Buffy*-related Web site, a book about the television series, articles in *American Libraries* and *Entertainment Weekly*, and essays from two scholarly collections about the show. The glossary also includes three quotations that illustrate the term's attributive use. *Buffy-comicverse* subscribes to a mor-phological, rather than a rhetorical, model; thus the item under consideration here is probably an attempted infixing rather than an accomplished tmesis.

As is so often the case with infixing and interposings that stretch conven-tions, there are reasons to question whether *Buffy-comicverse* is an infixing at all. For instance, the *Buffy* in every other *Buffyverse* refers to the character, not to the show, and does not appear in italics, as it does in the form under scrutiny here. Also, it isn't clear why *Buffy* is separated from *comicverse* with a hyphen: one might interpret this as evidence of attributive compounding rather than infixing, with *comicverse* a novel blend; certainly, in "I'm hoping, wishing, you can get some fresh blood to pick up the *Buffy*-pencil," the sentence immediately preceding that with *Buffy-comicverse*, *Buffy* serves just such a formative purpose. Yet earlier in the paragraph Brandon laments that he misses "the teens and the twenties of the *Buffy* comics," in which the attribution is accomplished without any hyphen. Or perhaps Brandon blends *Buffy-comic* and *universe*. Or perhaps the hyphen attempts to ensure that we understand the form as an infixing, by indicating that *Buffy* is not used merely attributively but as one component of a complex item. But the Buffyverse (broadly construed) provides other examples of nonexpletive meaningful infixing and interposing. In a late episode of the spin-off series, *Angel*, titled "Just Rewards," Spike, who has become a ghost, is explaining how a necromancer will help him to occupy Angel's body: "Necro here is gonna give me my body back, after I take yours for a test drive, fix his little problems, and here's the kicker — I go in, and you go pfft . . . off to never never come back land." So viewing Brandon's form as infixing is at least plausible.

Buffy the Vampire Slayer, so often in the vanguard of innovation, provides an even more surprising interposing than those recorded previously, a semantically subtler form. Indulge the fantastic for a moment or two. In the episode "Doomed" (2000) an earthquake hits Sunnydale, California, and Buffy, the Slayer, sees the event as a portent: "There's gonna be lots of red faces when the world comes to an end," she claims, and she's right. The earthquake is one stage in the world's collapse, motivated by demons not easily conquered. The broader context is significant. When Buffy and her associates recognize the demons' signature, Rupert Giles, the Watcher, exclaims, "It's the end of the world." "Again?!" shout Buffy, Willow, and Xander simultaneously.

To achieve the destruction of the world, the demons require the Word of Valios. When Giles discovers that the Word of Valios is actually represented by an amulet among his collection of magical artifacts, he says, "Oh as usual dear." It's big, this Word-of-Valios, end-of-the-world thing. Yet the deflationary interposing corresponds exactly, though humorously, to the catastrophic situation. The Buffyverse is filled with unexpected challenges, so many that the unusual is all too usual.

The insert *-as usual-*, in its meaningfulness, is unusual, too, all the more interesting because the insert is not expletive but "impletive," at the opposite pletive pole from the expected one: it adds lexical meaning to its matrix, not IN ADDITION TO but RATHER THAN emotive intensity. A form like *Buffy-comicverse* is SIMPLY nonexpletive and thus quite different from *oh as usual dear*. For one thing, the latter could be *oh frickin' dear*, if the speaker were expletively inclined — expletive and impletive are opposite values. In other words, there is a difference between "nonexpletive" (a category that includes both *Buffy-comicverse* and *oh as usual dear*) and "anti-expletive" (a category that includes only *oh as usual dear*); and there is a difference between, on one hand, expletive inserts (such as *Jesus H. tap-dancing Christ*) and impletive inserts (such as *oh as usual dear*) and, on the other hand, "nonpletive" ones (such as *Buffy-comicverse*).

In what circumstances will the impletive supersede the expletive, avoiding a turn into the nonpletive? Probably only those in which the speaker, wearied by potential apocalypse season after season, is an Oxford-educated English librarian, inclined toward stereotypical restraint. Infixes and interposings are formed with meaningful inserts in particular rhetorical situations. Anyone, in a fit of pique, might shout *unfuckinbelievable;* few indeed would resort to *Oh as usual dear.* Giles's unique interposing nonetheless challenges McMillan's Rule and invites us to keep our ears clean and our minds open as the youngest word-formative process in English gains maturity.

Whereas the impletive interposing with meaningful infix is a marginal variety of a marginal feature even of slang, let alone English at large, nonpletive infixes and interposings may be trendy. Certainly, many recent ones are more interesting and cleverer than *Buffy-comicverse.* For instance, Rebecca Onion, in an article in *Bitch* (2004), comments, "Among the supposedly liberal and elite women who come in for a drubbing are Hillary Clinton (of course), Katie Couric, Susan Sarandon, Rosie O'Donnell, *Good Housekeeping* editor Ellen Levine, Barbara Walters, Diane Sawyer, Tina Brown, et Botoxed cetera." Had Gerard Manly Hopkins or e. e. cummings written for *Bitch*, we might view this as an instance of tmesis or diacope, poetic tropes that resemble infixing and interposing; Ms. Onion, however, like most current speakers of American English, probably has interposing, albeit the nonpletive variety, in mind. So has Alexander Masters in *Stuart: A Life Backwards* (2005), though his interposing retains vestiges of expletive: "I nod. Is there any point in saying that if I have ever been close to punching him, it has been during the last yapping half-yapping-hour?"

Advertising is drawn to the sort of shocking cleverness typical of such forms: they are memorable, not so much because you'll remember the infixing or interposing in every case, but because you will have experienced a sort of linguistic event, which makes the advertised product or service memorable. While changing planes in Newark on my way to Oakland for the American Dialect Society meeting in January 2005, a Jetway advertisement assured me that my satisfaction is *guaranclickin'teed* by Continental Airlines when I book my flights online at the Continental Web site. This form's meaningful insert retains some of *-fucking-*'s expletive quality, however, and most closely resembles *absoschmuckinglutely* among especially meaningful infixes and interposings accumulated during the past few years.

Advertisers are cleverest for sophisticated audiences, like my fellow University of Michigan alumni, to whom Apple once pitched iTunes as *techKNOWLEDGEy.* I prefer to think that *knowledge* was capitalized so dramatically because knowledge is more important than technology, that knowing is more important than the techy means to knowing. In hindsight, though, Apple may not have taken the sophistication of Michigan alumni for granted: arguably, the capitals are patronizing, a cunning device to ensure that we noticed their fancy word and recognized it as an infixing, or a pun, or both — to be honest, I still can't say. God forgive me, I'm still in thrall to Microsoft.

All of the forms illustrated here, whether expletive, impletive, or nonpletive, are meant to stand out in context, and the speakers (journalists, advertisers, those whose products or services are advertised, really clever people who like to play around with language so people sit up and take notice) in each case hope, through their inventiveness, to stand out as well. The words are stunts, the poets who invent them exhibitionists. At the very edge of credibility, then, an exhibitionist like Stephen Colbert will come up with something like *metafreephorall* (which made its *Colbert Report* debut on April 19, 2007), a contwisticated double infixed blend: (1) *-free-* interrupts *metaphor*, but it can't be meaningful without the *-forall* in *free-for-all*; (2) *-phor-* replaces *-for-* in *free-for-all*, but unlike *for* doesn't mean anything independently (like *schmuck, bloody, fucking-A*, or *clickin'*), so isn't really a meaningful insert; and (3) interpreting this as an infix depends entirely on the obstinately meaningless and also nonpletive word fragment *-phor-*. Words like *metafreephorall* are invented only when Stephen Colbert challenges Sean Penn to a metaphor throw-down: the word is as absurd as the event, and one rarely encounters a similarly absurd event.

Journalists and advertisers, scriptwriters and satirists aren't the only ones to test linguistic acuity and aesthetic sensibility by pushing words to the limit. Slang Site.com records a number of nonpletive infixings, examples of slangy tmesis:

- *accipurpodentally* 'accidentally on purpose, deliberately while pretending innocence'
- *e-anticiparcellation* 'anticipation of electronic mail'
- *e-appreparcelhensive* 'worried that electronic mail may carry a virus'
- *intelphakenlectual* 'know-it-all who puts on intellectual airs'

not to mention two particularly helpful words given the current discussion:

- *interexplijective* 'word or phrase with an expletive injected into the middle of it', a good word for McMillan's infixings and interposings, though itself an example of the tmetic variety

- *lexifabricography*, which SlangSite defines as 'art of desperately inventing a word to substitute for one you can't think of right now', but which I prefer to think of as an infixed synonym for *coin* and as a word whose form perfectly illustrates its meaning

"They're making these up!" you say. "These are all stunt words, and no one would use them in everyday speech." And you have a point: Who thinks fast enough and well enough to produce such contrived forms on the conversational fly? But in "extreme" situations, one might argue, where people see the opportunity to develop or refine the possibilities inherent in infixing and interposing, they do. They are practicing slang, not merely at its poetic, but at its most poetic. Just because the words are stunts doesn't mean they're ONLY stunts: many of the forms discussed here, from *absoschmuckinglutely* to *accipurpodentally* are more expressive or more precise than any alternatives, and in stretching just a bit too far, they probe the limits of an important slang category.

THE RAUNCH AND THE HIP: TWO SLANG AESTHETICS

English slang is almost as diverse as the English vocabulary altogether, so trying to define a slang aesthetic is a bit like trying to define an "English" one: it isn't really possible. You can distinguish slang from other types of speech on general terms, but aesthetics purposefully organize the disordered mass of slang in the interests of style self-consciously promoted by speakers and easily identified by others. Some of these styles last long enough, spread far enough, and are raised high enough in public consciousness that they become iconic. Slang aesthetics are defined against the background noise of mainstream English, but they also distinguish among possibilities latent within slang. Speakers draw on the slang we have and fabricate new slang, too, in order to promote one aesthetic, however temporarily, at the expense of others.

In this behavior, slang speakers strongly resemble other artists, most especially poets, some of whom are quite explicit about the aesthetic foundations on which they build their own styles. In "Of Modern Poetry," not an essay about poetry but itself a poem, Wallace Stevens urges, "It has to be living, to learn the speech of the place." Stevens was often a rarefied poet, yet the sentiment expressed here intersects with Whitman's description of slang, since slang is a most vital part of the living language. For Stevens, modern poetry has to be and do several things, and, he concludes, "It must be the finding of a satisfaction," though he doesn't go into what would be satisfying, or to whom. As much as it's meant to require something of a modern poem, that tenet of Stevens's aesthetic also describes successful slang: the slang speaker occasionally achieves a Zen moment of lexical rightness when, without any apparent effort, a word or a phrase achieves perfectly, if only momentarily, a desired social or aesthetic effect.

Stevens isn't the only poet to write an aesthetic manifesto. In "The Kind of Poetry I Want" Hugh MacDiarmid argues for "A poetry the quality of which / Is a stand made against intellectual apathy," so, as Lighter points out, rather different from some slang, as it resists comfortable social habits. But MacDiarmid is just as committed to "A poetry that can put all its chips on the table / And back it to the limit," that is, poetry played by a poet who may be a gentleman but finds that gentility gets in the way of his art. Stevens and MacDiarmid wrote poetry meant to last, and they wrote at some length. The slangster speaks for the moment, composes poetry on the fly; conversation moves so quickly that slang is noticed for its immediate, almost atmospheric effect. But no one can return to it, as to a poem, and assess its significance, certainly not the speaker. Slang is not itself the medium in which to argue a slang aesthetic; the best argument for a slang aesthetic is not a matter of the slang idea, but of the very act of slang.

Nevertheless, were one to write a poem titled "On Modern Slang" or "The Kind of Slang I Want," one would proclaim fundamental truths about slang such as "It must be extravagant and racy" or "It must be casual and extravagant" or "It must be playful and facetious" or "It must be playful and forced." Such canons of the slang aesthetic are often paradoxical and need further elaboration; at least they must be activated in a word or phrase in which two or three competitive (if not incompatible) qualities are somehow, temporarily, contextually brought into equilibrium. In fact, the full-on slang aesthetic is unlikely to be achieved in any one act of slang: it encompasses continua and polarities on which any more particularly defined slang aesthetic draws, the arrangement of which constitutes that slang's distinctive character.

As an illustration of these principles, consider two classic slang aesthetics: the Raunch and the Hip. The Raunch lexicon is replete with words for vomiting, defecation, urination, masturbation, drink and drugs, penises, vaginas, and buttocks — much the same vocabulary Jonathon Green counted up and Susie Dent later reported in *Fanboys and Overdogs* (2005), as mentioned in the previous chapter. Think Spring Break, Girls Gone Wild, drunken women baring their breasts, drunken men drooling at naked breasts, movies like *Road Trip*

(2000) and *National Lampoon's Van Wilder* (2002), and you have a good idea of what Raunch is all about. By contrast, Hip is smooth like jazz, free like the Beats, relaxed as the aftermath of a junkie's morning glory. Hip is about being in the know, which might imply a community of knowing hipsters, yet there is no such "community" because Hip is against the grain and individual. Hip belongs in a small room of small tables cramped in front of a small stage. Raunch belongs in a big frat house filled with people who (thankfully) you don't know.

Raunch is playful, extravagant, racy, and vivid. If you're self-consciously mature, it's also disgusting; whether it's humorous depends on your sense of humor. It's forced only in the sense that its speakers are well aware that their speech may offend others; awareness diminishes the casualness somewhat, because, out of the corner of its eye, Raunch is sly. What binds the raunchy together is their shared sense that anyone who is offended misses the point, needs to lighten up, has a stick up her ass. When Ariel Levy talked to women who like Raunch, they told her "it was all in fun, all tongue-in-cheek, and for me to regard this bacchanal as problematic would be old-school and uncool." Levy doesn't agree. In *Female Chauvinist Pigs: Women and the Rise of Raunch Culture* (2005), she sees Raunch as an offense to feminism: " 'Raunchy' and 'liberated' are not synonyms," she writes. "It is worth asking ourselves if this bawdy world of boobs and gams we have resurrected reflects how far we've come, or how far we have left to go."

Sly Records, based in Salem, Oregon, began in 1996, according to Eric B.'s "history of sly records (to the best of my memory)," which opens the label's Web site, www.slyrecords.com. It is undoubtedly one of Raunch's natural habitats. One of the site's features is "This Week's Hip New Slang Word or Phrase." The aesthetic may not be Hip, but you'll certainly be hip to Raunch if you visit the site often, so in one sense, however unlikely it seems, *hip* bears on Raunch. It's an interesting development that slang is a side attraction to a commercial venture, the act that draws 'em in to whatever else the site has to offer because it gestures knowingly toward a Raunch-friendly audience. This wouldn't surprise Levy, who notes that "Raunch culture is not essentially progressive, it is essentially commercial."

In the following lexicon culled from the Web site (with labels for parts of speech and definitions provided by me, on the basis of information in the entries), American English is "constantly exploding in little blasts of exhibitionism," as Levy might put it. She may not approve, but she knows what Raunch is all about.

bagpiping *v or n* Penile stimulation in the armpit

ballsackian *adj* Stupid

box out dealin' *v* Of a woman, showing genitalia, usually because she's unclothed or mostly unclothed from the waist down

brotisserie *n* Three-way with two men (who put the *bro* in *brotisserie*), one at each end of the woman

brumsky *n* Fart expelled between a woman's breasts

cherryoke *n* What one breaks in one's first karaoke performance

chrome labia *n* Unsatisfied sexual arousal; female alternative for masculine *blue balls*

clitorically speaking *adv* "A funny way to sound smart"

cock holster *n* Mouth of one you don't like, *pie hole*

diamond turd cutter *n* Buttocks so well formed that excrement passing between them is cut like a diamond

doing laundry *v phr* Heterosexual sexual intercourse that resembles a wash cycle

double eye blinky *n* Party prank played on someone passed out from alcohol or drug intoxication, in which the (male) prankster places one of his testicles on each of the victim's eyes, with the penis running along the bridge of the nose

going bananas *v phr* Significant breast movement unrestrained by a bra

groin grabbingly good *adj phr* Really great

ham-hocked *adj* Very drunk

helm of the bobsled *n* Dominant male sexual position when "workin' a fine young lady from behind and . . . holdin' on tight"

I wanna bite that chick's ass *interj*

lobbin' *v* Of male genitalia, arrested in a state between erect and flaccid

mandruff *n* Flakes of dried semen shed from a woman's pubic hair

maple bar *n* Area between genitalia and anus

NIBM *n* Nicotine-induced bowel movement

pulling root *v phr* Masturbating (male)

pull it out of your ass like anal beads *v* Know something "really random"

road cunny *n* Cunnilingus supplied in a moving vehicle; see ROAD HEAD

road head *n* Vehicle-borne fellation; see ROAD CUNNY

slap five on her *v phr* Congratulate each other on participating in a BROTISSERIE or similar three-way sexual arrangement

smile like a donut *v phr* Make an O-shape with the mouth, as during orgasm

sprung like a slinky *adj* Of a male, sexually aroused; see LOBBIN'

taint *n* MAPLE BAR

taintalingus *n* Oral stimulation of the MAPLE BAR, or TAINT

tittoo *n* Tattoo on a woman's breast
traf *n* or *v* "A polite way to say fart"
tramp stamp *n* Tattoo on the small of a woman's back
unload the groceries *v phr* Vomit

This lexicon of Raunch has a little bit of everything, though not necessarily something for everyone. It ranges from the concrete (*mandruff*, *tittoo*) to the metaphorical (*cock holster*, *maple bar*), from the clever (*cherryoke*) to wishful thinking (*brotisserie*) to the imaginary (*double eye blinky*), or perhaps it's my wishful thinking that it's imaginary. Some of the terms are astonishingly vivid and in some cases (not all) effectively obscure their nasty referents: thus *bagpiping*, *brumsky*, *diamond turd cutter* (*turd* gives the nasty away), NIBM (an item of a secret language that most of us don't want to learn), *taintalingus* (the *taint* will be unfamiliar to many, but *-alingus* will alert the least alert among us).

Some items in Eric B.'s raunchy lexicon are incredibly clever and not a little poetic. Perhaps the most poetic is *cock holster*, a metaphorical compound meaning 'mouth', what in the context of Germanic epic, *Beowulf*, for instance, is called a "kenning," like *whale road* for 'sea' and *word hoard* for 'language; folklore'. I suspect that many, from professors to undergraduates, assume that kennings are a thing of the past, like epic, but kennings are alive and kicking in slang. In his explanation of *cock holster* Eric B. points out that it's a synonym for *pie hole*, another slang kenning for 'mouth.' Of course, I'm not suggesting that Eric B. and other slangsters model their slang on Anglo-Saxon poetic forms, any more than modern-day infixers model their creations on tmesis or diacope. Compounds, metaphor, and metaphorical compounds are in a sense natural to English, elements of the language available to speakers when aesthetic circumstances encourage their use.

And the poetry of Raunch doesn't stop there. It's a nasty image, the buttocks so diamond-perfect that they cut diamond turds, but a glorious one, too: the juxtaposition of *diamond* and *turd* is astonishing before it's offensive, the slang technique so deft as to ameliorate what, in principle, seems beyond amelioration. *Sprung like a slinky* is so vivid and fun that it's impossible to resist as slang or poetry, even if you don't like thinking about penises. And *lobbin'* actually pretty effectively fills a lexical gap: *semitumescent* and *partially erect* are too stiff by far to describe the phenomenon. *Lobbin'* is perfect in slang sound as well as in slang meaning; it's as close as the Raunch lexicon comes to Hip, at least on the terms developed below.

Blue balls has little to recommend it poetically, just everyday alliteration to emphasize the color of genital agony. But *chrome labia* is genius: Why is the woman who has chrome labia unsatisfied if not because she is smooth, shiny, cold, metallic? Otherwise, she'd have no trouble finding sexual satisfaction out there, among all of those raunchy guys. Weirdly, though, chrome labia are like the chrome of classic cars: the guy who likes cars likes to touch the chrome, but hesitatingly, to avoid smudges. Unsmudged, though, he can see himself in the chrome: it's all about him. Thus where Raunch sometimes seems cool and almost hip, sometimes it's offensively male adolescent and refuses to grow up: items in the list describe instinctual simian behavior (*groin grabbingly good*) or male sexual preoccupations based (I suspect) more often on lad magazine fantasy than experience (*road head, road cunny*) or disparaging views of women (*tramp stamp*; surely they're not all tramps, but our sisters, wives, mothers, and bosses, too), while *unload the groceries* can pass without comment.

I mean, clitorically speaking, how old does a guy have to be to resist grabbing his groin when he sees a hot chick? But he's not a bad guy. He's a guy from your neighborhood, with good parents, charming around his parents' friends, and the girls next door stick up for him, whether they've gone wild or not. He's the kind of guy who thinks that *traf* is a polite way to say *fart*—just in case you need one. Sure, sometimes he's *ballsackian*, but that's accidentally clever, still obsessed with genitalia but formed from the highly intellectual *Balzac*, so you can't say the little stoner didn't learn anything in college, even if that's all he remembers from Great Books 201, MWF 10:00–11:00. The Raunch vocabulary is the perfect intersection of what is nearly taboo and poetry. Just because some of Raunch is unmistakably masculine doesn't mean that Raunch is a masculine slang aesthetic. Women enjoy Raunch, too, as the writing in *Missbehave* proves, and they are just as likely to wake and bake before Great Books as the guys.

Though the title of the site's slang page is "This Week's Hip New Slang Word or Phrase," much of Eric B.'s slang isn't new. *Bagpiping* is entered in both Green and Dalzell and Victor (sv *bagpipe v* in the latter), but both remark that bagpiping is usually a homosexual practice, which might come as a surprise to the genius behind Sly Records. Lighter does not enter it, but because there's no standard equivalent he would view *bagpiping* as the standard term rather than as slang, which also might come as a surprise to the genius behind Sly Records. As a sense of *box*, 'vagina' is well attested and certainly current; as Ariel Levy describes, "Mia Leist was suddenly very excited. The bartender had just told her about a 'girl-on-girl box-eating' contest in Fort Lauderdale later in the week." Girls Gone Wild, Fort Lauderdale, box-eating contest — that's Raunch, yo.

Our *lobbin'* seems to be a functional shift to a verb from the noun *lob*, which means exactly this type of penis. The transparent *road head* is entered in Dalzell and Victor but not *road cunny* (which suggests that the genius behind Sly Records believes you should give to receive); *taint* is recorded in both dictionaries (in Green, sv *t'aint*, with additional forms *taint*, *taintmeat*, and *tent*) and defined politely as the 'perineum', but neither includes *taintalingus* (raunchy but generous; women may be objects, but they're objects with rights). The New Partridge records *traf* 'fart' but restricts it to Australia. Clearly, Americans are also capable of back slang, as long as the words in question have one syllable.

For Green, *unload* means getting rid of everything BUT the groceries; both Green and the New Partridge include lots of *pull* + NOUN forms for male masturbation, but not this one. The point behind the simile *smile like a donut* may be more familiar to readers as *O-face*, popularized by Drew, the permanently adolescent character in Mike Judge's film *Office Space* (1999). Popularity may rest more in recognition than in use, however, as *O-face* has yet to appear in any of the slang dictionaries. Both dictionaries have entries based on *ham-hock*, but the meanings are quite different, associating *ham-hock* with African American cuisine rather than drunkenness. The genius behind Sly Records says he got the term from Glasgow, Scotland, in which the African American association is minimal.

While, from the Green / Dent perspective, Raunch seems an inevitable, natural stylistic interpretation of the English slang lexicon, Hip is even more closely aligned to the fundamental values of slang. I don't think I realized this fully, or with the requisite precision, until I read John Leland's *Hip: The History* (2004). For instance, Leland points out, "Hip permeates mainstream daily life at the level of language, music, literature, sex, fashion, ego, and commerce." Of course, it does so partly because slang permeates mainstream daily life and Hip is part of slang, yet slang permeates mainstream daily life partly because it includes Hip among its iconic varieties. Slang in general may not identify with sympathetic varieties of "music, literature, sex, fashion, ego, and commerce," but, like Raunch or any other distinctive brand of slang, Hip certainly does.

It's the very slangy aspect of Hip that, "by bringing constant change and obsolescence, it creates ever new needs to buy." But neither slang nor Hip as a subset of slang is all about buying and selling. As Leland puts it, "Hip brings the intelligence of troublemakers and outsiders into the loop, saving the mainstream from its own limits," so as Hip circulates through the American culture, it clears the way for ideas, attitudes, and styles that convention impedes or excludes. In this, Hip is really no different from other slang: Raunch, too, has its saving qualities, but we are reluctant to admit them; at least, confronted with two resistance aesthetics, Raunch and Hip, many of us choose the latter to avoid the former.

As Leland argues, Hip "requires an audience. Even at its most subterranean, it exists in public view, its parameters defined by the people watching it. You decide what is hip and what is not. Hip requires a transaction, an acknowledgment," a point I made toward the end of chapter 2 about slang of every description. The sociology and social history of Hip (the things that concern Leland most) parallel the sociolinguistics of Hip speech; on another axis of relationship, because Hip speech is slang, the social dynamics of slang govern Hip. Thus it comes as no surprise that, in Leland's words, "Hip is an ethos of individualism, but it tends to grow in cliques," nor that, "as an aesthetic of the hybrid, hip embraces difference and loves experiment. Where divisions exist, as between black and white or gay and straight, it crosses them."

Leland may be a bit more confident about such crossing than the evidence warrants. At least the groups involved may resist either of two suggestions: first, that Hip is somehow a free agent and transcends the cultures in which it moves; second, that as Hip moves, it somehow universalizes it manifestations, whether in language, fashion, music, or anything else. Leland's argument is well informed and thoughtful, a little daring, perhaps a little wrong. He identifies Ralph Waldo Emerson and Walt Whitman as "original hipsters," and he makes a good case for them and others who might not have come to mind immediately as hip—though anyone who has seen W. T. Cranch's caricature of Emerson as the "naked eyeball" from Emerson's *Nature* will find it difficult to reconcile that image with Leland's. Yet Whitman and Emerson, too, are early American theorists of slang and its place in language and culture, as I argued in chapter 1; the correspondences between slang and Hip noted here more or less confirm Leland's unexpected recognition of those original hipsters.

Importantly, though, some who have thought about the nature of Hip for a long time and are especially expert regarding its language do not agree entirely with Leland about the nature of its fluid circulation throughout American culture, though they generally agree about the essential definition of *hip* and its etymology. Like Leland, who relies on Clarence Major's *Juba to Jive* (1994), Geneva Smitherman claims that American *hip* derives from Wolof *hepi* 'open one's eyes', and that it means 'aware, informed, "with it" '. Everyone agrees about the definition, which is affirmed by historical usage. The etymology may leap beyond the evidence, however; Lighter insists that the origin of *hip* and its variant *hep* is unknown.

As discussed in chapter 2, Smitherman very reasonably objects to careless relegation of African American English to slang. "When blacks use calques [loan translations, among which *hip* from *hepi* would figure]," she writes in *Talkin and Testifyin* (1977), "the lingo is negatively assigned the status of 'street' or 'hip' talk—in other words, slang. Yet in the native African languages these are not considered slang expressions. This would suggest that many of the terms in Black Semantics have been or are improperly labeled and misperceived by blacks as well as whites as not hip to the source of soul talk." In other words, the affiliation between Hip and African American identity is stronger than Leland supposes, Hip less an American phenomenon and more an African American one.

So Smitherman agrees that, "given the pervasiveness of the mass communications network and the explosion of soul, the process of borrowing general, casual white talk from the black vocabulary is inevitable." Nevertheless, to Smitherman's mind, there's no doubt about whence Hip comes: it "moved out of the black community via white musicians and others of the artsy Hip Set (whom [Norman] Mailer referred to as 'white Negroes')." John Russell and Russell John Rickford in *Spoken Soul* (2000) concur. They note "Spoken Soul's aptness for expressing the exotic in the plainest of terms, for expressing the unremarkable with the greatest flamboyance," and suggest that "Duke Ellington might have meant this, in part, when he observed in 1932 that 'it don't mean a thing if it ain't got that swing.' With that pronouncement, Ellington lent the era its jingle and proclaimed mainstream America square. And she *was* square when compared with the dancing, jazzing culture then emerging from New York and other cities, a culture in which black vernacular was the parlance of the hip." The issue is whether Hip crosses back and forth from white to black and black to white (Leland's take on things), or whether Hip represents an African American aesthetic of profound importance to the history of American style (as Smitherman and the Rickfords argue). How you interpret the sound and affect of Hip within slang depends on whether you identify them with jazz and blues or with some broader cultural knowingness.[9]

9 Smitherman writes about words from the African American lexicon appropriated into other registers of American English: "An interesting example of such a term is the word *hip* (which was always represented as *hep* in the *Archie* comic book days of my youth—and

It's difficult to know whether, in all of its social and aesthetic tendencies, Hip follows slang or leads it. Aficionados of Hip may want Hip to take the lead, if for no other reason than to protect us all from Raunch. But surely Hip would be a reluctant leader: taking the lead isn't hip. The aficionados may admire Hip, but they may not be hip. Snoop Dogg isn't hip when he grabs credit for *-izzle*. Hip can't exactly lead slang because leadership requires a sense of the future and, as with all slang, "the payoff for hip is not in the future, but in the present."[10] Of all varieties of slang, Hip is by far the most obviously a language of being: it's not the language of looking forward or getting the job done; it's not the language of playing well with others or fitting in; it's not the language of standing out, though, paradoxically, Hip stands out like someone walking through a busy intersection in slow motion.

"Hip has a lexicon of surrogates: cool, down, beat, fresh, rad, phat, tight, dope (but under no circumstances, gnarly, bodacious or neat). But really, hip is hip, enduring through all permutations. Anyone who leaves the house with bed head has an idea of where its light shines." In chapter 1 I had some trouble deciding whether *bed head* is slang. Words and what they describe aren't the same things, but if bed head is hip, then it stands to reason, doesn't it, that *bed head* is slang? But even if *bed head* is slang, it isn't Hip. The lexicon of Hip departs radically from that of Raunch, and contrasting the two varieties demonstrates just how many different aesthetics American slang can comprehend, indeed MUST comprehend, because "difference" is fundamental to both the social and the aesthetic value of slang—difference not just from the mainstream, but also from other slang aesthetics.

---

interestingly enough, a number of blacks who went to schools with whites were constantly 'corrected' for this pronunciation, I among them). In the black community the term has always been rendered as *hip* and used widely in the community, not just among the teeny-bopper set. Well, nowadays, everybody and they momma is talking bout bein hip and rendering the word with Black America's 'mispronunciation.' " Lighter's entries for *hep* and *hip* suggest that the forms are almost simultaneous, but for the former reasonably notes that movement from the vowel of *hep* to that of *hip* is more likely than movement in the other direction. In a situation like this, one naturally asks, "What would Dr. Mambuca do?"

10 This suggests that, in an important sense, the best leaders of slang, not necessarily the best speakers of slang, are not hip. Thus Gretchen may be an effective slangster and hipster, but not a Queen Bee, whereas Regina is a classic Queen Bee and gets to lead, in spite of the fact that she's not so terribly hip. Gretchen, one might argue, hangs with the wrong people.

The language of Hip, like all slang, has attitude, and Hip's attitude is especially "loose," in sound and structure and semantics. Perhaps not all Hip is African American in origin, but some certainly is, and some of that is used mostly by African American speakers and those whites who live, work, jazz, and jive among them. If that's the way it *bees*, for instance, you've got a word in *bees* that sounds slow and long because of its vowel and its voiced bilabial (the / b /) and alveolar fricatives (the /z/) and forms minimal pairs with *buzz*, *biz*, and *booze*, all of them hip. (One has to admit, though, that *bees* is a homophone of *bees* and *bee's*, respectively plural and possessive of *bee*, and forms minimal pairs with *geez, keys, knees*, including *the bee's knees, seize, tease*, and *wheeze*, none of which is particularly hip.) In *Black Talk* (2000) Smitherman defines *bees* as "that's how it is, that's the way it goes, that's life; an existential reference to the human condition," in other words, an excellent example of slang as the language (of the essence) of being.

Similarly "loose," at least referentially, is *it ain no thang*, "meaning that whatever 'it' is, it's not a problem or obstacle, it can be dealt with" (sv *ain a thang*), but notice, too, that the vowels get longer as words move from the official dictionary into Hip. In the 1970s, if you were *bout* something, you were "involved in doing something, especially something meaningful." Now, if you're *bout it*, "a variation of older term BE BOUT resurfacing in HIP HOP," you are either "agreeable with something" or *down with* whatever it is, or you are describing a person (maybe yourself) as "very good, excellent; up on contemporary culture, in the know" — that is, hip. *What it is* is what it is. Yet all of these are phonetically relaxed ways of not being very committed to anything; again, the language of Hip, like the core of slang generally, is a language of being, not a language of purpose.

Hip slang is full of items that paradoxically emphasize the unstressed syllable of uncommitment. You look in the mirror and you're *boomin'* or *slammin'* and you say either of those words in self-approval. You leave your *crib* well pleased with the world and your place in it, *stridin'* 'walking rhythmically, with soul', *skinnin' and grinnin'* 'smiling and giving everyone you meet a high five', on the way to *chillin', hangin', rollin'* with the people who matter to you. In the sound structure of such words, the first, stressed syllable puts it out there, and the second, unstressed one takes it back. In a way, for the young among us, this retracted stress, this syllabic lack of commitment, is the slang of aspiration: Who doesn't want to hang or chill or roll, or whatever, where *whatever* stressed a dozen different ways represents the lexical apogee, the slang Mount Everest, of uncommitment? *Lobbin'* fits into this pattern, a word for a penis that can't make up its mind. Slang speakers borrow many of these terms from the African American lexicon, on which Hip depends, but not everyone who uses them is hip, and some African Americans may wish that some words had not "crossed" culturally. I have in mind those African Americans, and there are many, who have never uttered slangy *whatever* in their lives.

Because Hip is unobtrusive it's harder to identify its slang than the in-your-face slang of Raunch. It was easy to come up with a long list of Raunchy words, not just because they were available on one Web site, but because Raunch is too vivid to blend in and doesn't want to blend in but to shock, and because, in Raunch, size matters. Hip, you'll notice, is not as funny as Raunch. Or perhaps it's a limitation of mine that I can't write about it humorously. Part of what's funny about Raunch is individual items of the slang, which, in fact, can glitter like diamond turds or pop like your cherryoke. Another funny part is that people actually utter the Raunch lexicon, and sometimes we're laughing at them as much as we're laughing with them, maybe sometimes laughing at ourselves when we cross the line into Raunch territory. The humor, then, is a matter of irony. But Hip admits no irony of a similar kind. Because Hip is knowing, it views the rest of experience with the utmost irony, but no one who's Hip is left to view Hip ironically.

In the end, there are no two slang aesthetics more distinct in relation to each other than Raunch and Hip. But the aesthetic behind *How's it goin', protozoan?* is different from Raunch and Hip, and that underlying *Yee-fucking-diddly-haw* different from all three of those, and that underlying *lexifabricography* different still. The poetic manifestos about the kind of slang that speakers of any of these subslangs want would vary significantly. Like poetry, slang is the aesthetic exercise of linguistic ingenuity. Like poetry, too, slang is a robust linguistic category as long as it allows, even promotes, the widest possible aesthetic diversity.

SLANG AS A NEGATIVE CAPABILITY

Regarding the resemblance between slang and poetry, Lighter writes, "In comparison with ordinary English, it might well be said that slang works at a heightened intensity, like a kind of negative poetry." Even if it's great poetry's dark side, great slang may observe some of poetry's fundamental values. In a famous letter to his brothers, Tom and George, on December 27, 1817, John Keats redefined a fundamental aesthetic problem:

> Brown & Dilke walked with me & back from the Christmas pantomime. I had not a dispute but a disquisition with Dilke, on various subjects; several things dovetailed

in my mind, & at once it struck me, what quality went to form a Man of Achievement especially in Literature & which Shakespeare posessed so enormously—I mean *Negative Capability*, that is when man is capable of being in uncertainties, Mysteries, doubts, without any reaching after fact & reason.

Slang, I propose, is negative poetry suffused with negative capability, or a capability closely aligned with it, anyway.

Slang always combines affective qualities (casual, vivid, hip, rebellious, playful), which, if not always paradoxical, are at least competitive. Using slang, as speaker or listener, requires that one NOT attempt to bring it down to something. *Diamond turd cutter* is not merely gross, but it's also not merely an unusually sharp metaphor jutting into everyday conversation; it's offensively and beautifully vivid, casually rebellious (because all offense is rebellion), racily playful, and to appreciate the slang object one must take it whole, as a holistic lexical experience, without judging one of its qualities without regard for the others.

As with poetry, we can "read" slang, that is, explain it, analyze it, or criticize it. Also as with poetry, if we reduce it to any "mere" thing in the course of that reading, explanation, analysis, or criticism, we misunderstand slang at the most elemental level. The insistently rational, those who resist paradox and feel the need to resolve it, tend not to read much poetry, and I suspect that they don't appreciate slang much either. As Leland says, "Taking the long view, hip is exactly what it has always been: an undercurrent of enlightenment, organized around contradictions and anxieties." He quotes the awesome iconic seventies rock group Tower of Power, whose "What Is Hip?" (1975) says what needs to be said:

Hipness is—What it is!
And sometimes hipness is
What it ain't!

If you respond, "Hey, how can hipness be what it ain't, and how can it be what it ain't sometimes and what it is at other times?" you are, dear reader, missing the point.

In 1528 Baldassare Castiglione published *The Book of the Courtier*, a set of dialogues between Italian aristocrats about what qualities combined to make the ideal courtier. They conclude that the courtier should be a warrior, poet, philosopher, diplomat, patron—that is, just about everything. He should be supremely accomplished at all of these complicated things, but no matter how difficult the task, he would perform with ease and grace, without, as we might say today, breaking a sweat. As an equestrian, the courtier practices for war by guiding his warhorse through paces and figures that simulate their movement in battle. Nowadays, we call that exercise "dressage," a sport in which observers (Olympic judges, for instance) should not see the rider instruct the horse: rider and horse must move seamlessly, as one. This capacity to do the hard thing without letting on that it's hard had no word in Italian, so Castiglione invented one, *sprezzatura*, not slang but an addition to the jargon of gentility, back when gentility was a serious, full-time occupation.

At first glance, *sprezzatura* doesn't appear relevant to the slangster, since it's a quality of gentlemen who really are gentlemen and define themselves according to their gentility. This paradox, of the challenge performed easily, is fundamental to poetry: try to write about metaphysical truth in haiku or the power of art to defy death in a sonnet. It also often operates in slang: *US-fucking-A Today* (the culturally referential, rhetorically apt, casually rebellious, interposing blend) comes from Veronica's mouth as though it were natural speech, from which, paradoxically, we conclude that it's forced. It's important to slang that something so forced is uttered as though anyone could say it: it may come off as a "stunt word," not plausibly slang as we speak it, but as metalinguistic commentary it suggests what ideal slang should be. Is it a metaphor? Is it a free-for-all? Is it a metafreephorall?

Some of those complicated infixings and interposings, not to mention the lexical antics of Raunch, may be trying too hard as they prove their metalinguistic point. But consider the slang that really, really works: *bad, cool, chill, down*. This stuff works so well that you have to be reminded it's slang, and you couldn't really explain how someone borrowed them from standard English and slanged them. It's easier with Raunch: *cock + holster* (with a little kenning influence from the model *pie hole*), and you've got *cock holster*, produced when someone with a particular aesthetic attitude requires an insult. But what possessed someone to respond to someone else's "You wanna get something to eat?" with "You wanna get baked?" or "Let's get it on" with "I'm down." How effing cool is that? No fancy verbal art. Just the sudden, perfect appropriation of an everyday adverb, of all things, as slang. Nothing so easy could be harder, and the appropriation is a work of art after all.

At some level, the level of rebellion, resistance, or whatever, slang is really serious. All slang resists at least a little; even rhyming greetings and farewells question the legitimacy of "normal." From playground taunts to expressing cultural disaffection, slang is a political act, language in which social behavior and the individual collide. There's something unsettled about slang, and it's always just a little unsettling. In other words, slang is frivolous, ephemeral language that addresses something seriously, permanently wrong, the unsettledness of the human condition. How is the everyday speaker of English going to get at that problem without accepting, let alone operating, the paradox of slang?

REFERENCES

As in earlier chapters, throughout this one I have consulted the *Oxford English Dictionary* online, as well as the two published volumes of J. L. Lighter's *Historical Dictionary of American Slang* (New York: Random House, 1994 and 1997); Tom Dalzell and Terry Victor's *The New Partridge Dictionary of Slang and Unconventional English*, 2 volumes (London: Routledge, 2006); and Jonathon Green's *Cassell's Dictionary of Slang*, 2nd edition (London: Weidenfeld & Nicolson, 2005). I also refer to both *The New Oxford American Dictionary*, 2nd edition, edited by Erin McKean and others (New York: Oxford University Press, 2005), and *The American Heritage Dictionary of the English Language*, 4th edition, edited by Joseph P. Pickett and others (Boston: Houghton Mifflin, 2000), regarding *aesthetic*. Connie Eble's comment on slang and metaphor is quoted from *Slang and Sociability: In-Group Language among College Students* (Chapel Hill: University of North Carolina Press, 1996), 69; Lighter is quoted from "Slang," in *The Cambridge History of the English Language*, Volume 6: *English in North America*, edited by John Algeo (Cambridge, UK: Cambridge University Press, 2001), 224. I recommend "Boys Want Sex in the Morning" and all of the songs on *The Essential Uncle Bonsai* (Yellow Tail Records, 1992). I refer indirectly to James Sledd, "On Not Teaching English Usage," *English Journal* 54 (1965): 699, throughout the chapter. I quote Eble again, this time on rhyme, from *Slang and Sociability*, 42. Henry Bradley is quoted from Eric Partridge, *Slang To-day and Yesterday* (New York: Bonanza Books, n.d.), 4. *The Language and Lore of Schoolchildren* (Oxford: Oxford University Press, 1959) is one of many excellent books by Peter and Iona Opie. I quote Muriel Spark's *The Ballad of Peckham Rye* (1960) from *A Muriel Spark Trio* (Philadelphia: Lippincott, 1962), 291, 294, and 296, in series. H. L. Mencken is quoted from *The American Language* (New York: Knopf, 1936), 563. I quote Lighter on the relationship between poetry and slang from his chapter in *The Cambridge History of the English Language*, Volume 6: *English in North America*, 226. Prufrock's peach can be found in "The Love Song of J. Alfred Prufrock," in T. S. Eliot's *Complete Poems and Plays* (New York: Harcourt, Brace & World, 1971),

7; William Carlos Williams's red wheelbarrow can be found in *Selected Poems* (New York: New Directions, 1985), 56. Frank Perry directed *David and Lisa* (1962), and Eleanor Perry wrote the script, based on a novel by Theodore Isaac Rubin. The masturbation euphemisms listed here are borrowed from Tom Dalzell's much more comprehensive collection in *The Slang of Sin* (Springfield, MA: Merriam-Webster, 1998), 174–176. Whitman is quoted from *The English Language: Essays by Linguists and Men of Letters, 1858–1964*, edited by W. F. Bolton and David Crystal (Cambridge, UK: Cambridge University Press, 1969), 58. *The Simpsons*, source of so many wonderful words, needs no citation. Mark Peters's essay about those words is *"The Simpsons*: Embiggening Our Language with Cromulent Words," *Verbatim: The Language Quarterly* 30.2 (Summer 2005): 1–5. Alan C. L. Yu's account of "Homeric infixation" can be found in *A Natural History of Infixation* (Oxford: Oxford University Press, 2007), especially 174–177 and 181–190. Amy March's degerredation is noted by Louisa May Alcott in *Little Women*, edited by Elaine Showalter (New York: Penguin, 1989), 40. Eric Linklater's excellent and too little read novel *Magnus Merriman* (1936) is quoted from the Canongate Press edition (1990), 132. Anatoly Liberman discusses *figmajig* in *Word Origins* (New York: Oxford University Press, 2005), 65, and the infix *-de-* on 69–71. His articles on the etymologies of *hobbledehoy* and *ragamuffin* can be found in *An Analytic Dictionary of English Etymology* (Minneapolis: University of Minnesota Press, 2008), brief versions on xxxix–xl and xliii, respectively, and the long versions on 111–114 and 181–184, the same. The nursery rhyme texts are all quoted from Peter and Iona Opie, *The Oxford Dictionary of Nursery Rhymes* (Oxford: Oxford University Press, 1951), 61, 62, 128, 201–202, 162, and 113–114, in series. Mark Peters is quoted from the earlier cited article, in this case from 3; I have also benefited here from a paper Peters presented at the annual meeting of the American Dialect Society, January 5–8, 2006, in Albuquerque, New Mexico, titled "In-diddly-fixing Innovations: The Ned Flanders Effect." SlangSite.com is easy to find, at www.SlangSite.com. I have relied on Kathleen E. Miller's account of *-iz-* and *-izzle* in "On Language: Izzle," *New York Times Magazine* (September 12, 2004): 22. Jeff Prucher discusses the graphic infix *-h-* in *Brave New Words: The Oxford Dictionary of Science Fiction* (New York: Oxford University Press, 2007), 87. James B. McMillan's "Infixing and Interposing in English," cited variously throughout the section, appeared in *American Speech* 55 (1980): 163–183. The skydiver is Will Storr, quoted from "Noooooooaaaarrgh: Loaded Soils Its Undercarriage at 13,000 ft Skydiving over Spain," *Loaded* 73 (2000): 115; Natalie Maines whoops it up in Dorian Lynskey's "Dixie Chicks," *Q* (1999): 36. The *Buffy* episode

"Shadow," written by David Fury and directed by Daniel Attias, aired on November 21, 2000; Glorificus / Glory was acted by Clare Kramer. "Peppermint Pat-Eye" coined *absoschmuckinglutely* in "Camp Snoopy," *Transworld Snowboarding*, October 1997, 99. Eliza Doolittle is quoted from "Wouldn't It Be Loverly?" in Alan Jay Lerner and Frederick Loewe's *My Fair Lady*, film version directed by George Cukor (1964), with Audrey Hepburn playing Eliza Doolittle, though the line in question is sung by Marnie Nixon, whose versions of the songs replaced Hepburn's in the soundtrack. Keith Allan and Kate Burridge discuss euphemistic dysphemisms in their book *Euphemism and Dysphemism: Language Used as Shield and Weapon* (New York: Oxford University Press, 1991). Jesse Sheidlower's *The F-Word* (New York: Random House, 1995), includes an introductory essay by Roy Blount Jr., quoted here from xiv. Roger Smith's "The H of *Jesus H. Christ*" appeared in *American Speech* 69 (1994): 331–335; I have the information about Twain at secondhand from this source; I quote from 332. *The Blues Brothers* (1980) was written by James Landis and Dan Ackroyd and directed by John Landis. *Heathers* (1988) was written by Daniel Waters and directed by Michael Lehmann. Though it may be hard for readers to believe that *USA Today* has not always been held in highest esteem, see Peter Prichard's *The Making of McPaper: The Inside Story of USA Today* (Kansas City, MO: Andrews, McMeel & Parker, 1987), especially 196. *Office Space* (1999) was directed and written by Mike Judge; the role of Lawrence is acted by Diedrich Bader, that of Peter by Ron Livingston. *Midnight Run* (1989) was written by George Gallo and directed by Martin Brest. *Cruel Intentions* (1998) was written and directed by Roger Kumble; Kathryn was played, unforgettably, by Sarah Michelle Gellar, who listened to James Marsters deliver Spike's monologue in *Becoming, Part 2*; written and directed, unforgettably, by Joss Whedon, it aired on May 19, 1998. I quote from A. M. Zwicky and G. K. Pullum's "Plain Morphology and Expressive Morphology," in *Proceedings of the Thirteenth Annual Meeting of the Berkeley Linguistics Society, February 14–16, 1987: General Session and Parasession on Grammar and Cognition*, edited by Jon Aske and others (Berkeley: Berkeley Linguistics Society, 1987), 332. Blowfish, online retailer of sex-related things, can be found on the Web at www.blowfish.com. *Jawbreaker* (1998) was written and directed by Darren Stein; Rose McGowan's portrayal of Courtney Shane was peachy fucking keen. Gretchen and Regina, played by Lacey Chabert and Rachel McAdams, respectively, are characters in *Mean Girls* (2004), written by Tina Fey and directed by Mark Waters. Ned Flanders, as voiced by Harry Shearer, expletes *absonotly* on *The Simpsons* in the episode "Alone Again Natura-diddly" (February 13, 2000), written by Ian Maxtone- Graham and directed by Jim Reardon. In the discussion of tmesis and diacope, I refer to the second edition of Richard A. Lanham's *A Handlist of Rhetorical Terms* (Berkeley: University of California Press, 1991), and Alex Preminger, Frank J. Warnke, and O. B. Hardison's *Princeton Encyclopedia of Poetry and Poetics* (Princeton, NJ: Princeton University Press, 1974). Brandon coined *Buffy-comicverse* in his letter to "Slay the Critics," in *Buffy the Vampire Slayer #43* (Milwaukie, OR: Dark Horse Comics, 2002), [27]. Information on *Buffyverse* is from my *Slayer Slang: A "Buffy the Vampire Slayer" Lexicon* (New York: Oxford University Press, 2003), 158–159. The *Angel* episode "Just Rewards" aired on October 8, 2003; it was written by David Fury and Ben Edlund, directed by James A. Contner; Spike was played by James Marsters. The *Buffy* episode "Doomed," written by Marti Noxon, David Fury, and Jane Espenson, and directed by James A. Contner, aired January 18, 2000; the characteristically impletive Rupert Giles was played by Anthony Stewart Head. Rebecca Onion is quoted from "Sisters of No Mercy: Dubious Logic and Knee-Jerk Defensiveness in Women's Magazines," *Bitch: Feminist Response to Pop-Culture* 25 (2004): 13. Alexander Masters is quoted from *Stuart: A Life Backwards* (New York: Delacorte Press, 2005), 92. Poet Laureate Robert Pinsky moderated the *metafreephorall* between Stephen Colbert and Sean Penn on Comedy Central's *The Colbert Report* on April 19, 2007. SlangSite.com is chock-full of words you never imagined; for the word lover, it's definitely worth a visit. The section titled "Lexifabricography and the Meaningful Infix" draws freely on a series of short articles of mine: "Another Effing Euphemism," *American Speech* 74.1 (Spring 1999): 110–112; "Infixing and Interposing in English: A New Direction," *American Speech* 76.3 (Fall 2001): 327–331; "Meaningful Interposing: An Accidental Form," *American Speech* 77.4 (Winter 2002): 441–442; "Meaningful Infixing: A Nonexpletive Form," *American Speech* 79.1 (Spring 2004): 110–112; and "Meaningful Interposing: A Countervalent Form," *American Speech* 80.4 (Winter 2005): 437–441. I am grateful to Connie Eble, the editor of *American Speech*, who accepted all of these for publication, and to the American Dialect Society and Duke University Press for permission to include material from them here. Wallace Stevens's "Of Modern Poetry" can be found in *The Collected Poems of Wallace Stevens* (New York: Knopf, 1982), 239–240. Hugh MacDiarmid's "The Kind of Poetry I Want" is quoted from his *Selected Poetry*, edited by Alan Riach and Michael Grieve (New York: New Directions, 1992), 212 and 219. Susie Dent reports on Jonathon Green's slang statistics in *Fanboys and Overdogs: The Language Report* (Oxford: Oxford University Press, 2005), 102–103. *Road Trip* (2000) was directed by Todd Phillips and written by Phillips and

Scot Armstrong; *National Lampoon's Van Wilder* (2002) was directed by Walt Becker and written by Brent Goldberg and David Wagner. I quote from Ariel Levy's *Female Chauvinist Pigs: Women and the Rise of Raunch Culture* (New York: Free Press, 2005), 4, 5, 29, and 17, in series. Drew, in *Office Space*, is perfectly permanently adolescent partly because Greg Pitts plays him that way. You can see all of the raunchy words and phrases listed here and many, many more at www.slyrecords.com. I quote from John Leland's *Hip: The History* (New York: HarperCollins, 2005), 7, 8, 8 again, and 8 again, 69, 51, 274, and 11, in series. Quotations from Leland are interrupted by some from Geneva Smitherman's *Talkin and Testifyin: The Language of Black America* (Boston: Houghton Mifflin, 1977), 45 and 69 (the note also quotes from 69), and John Russell Rickford and Russell John Rickford's *Spoken Soul: The Story of Black English* (New York: John Wiley, 2000), 73–74. Lighter on slang as negative poetry is quoted from "Slang," 224. Keats is quoted from *The Letters of John Keats*, edited by Hyder Edward Rollins (Cambridge, MA: Harvard University Press, 1958), 1:193. Leland's *Hip* is quoted again, this time from 14–15 and 4, in that order.

IT'S ALL IN YOUR HEAD

COGNITIVE ASPECTS OF SLANG

Recently a group of researchers, principally Philip Davis (a professor of English at the University of Liverpool), Neil Roberts (a professor in Liverpool's Magnetic Resonance and Image Analysis Research Centre), and Guillaume Thierry (at the University of Wales, Bangor), measured the brain activity of human subjects while those subjects read Shakespeare's play *Coriolanus*.[1] They discovered that when Shakespeare used words in odd ways, for instance, when he put a word typically recognized as a noun to use as a verb—"He godded me," for instance—the subjects' brains were suddenly very active. Apparently the

---

1 Less read and even less performed, Shakespeare's *Coriolanus* was probably his last tragedy; scholars believe that it was written in 1608, though it wasn't published until the First Folio of 1623. Caius Marcius Coriolanus, a victorious Roman general who, when offered the consulship upon his return to the city, refuses it with contempt for the mob and is banished for his arrogance, attempts revenge against Rome by leading his former enemies, the Voluscians, against it, almost captures the city, but is talked out of it by his mother, and is then killed by the Voluscians. It was a good choice for the experiment because listeners were unlikely to recognize the lines they were hearing, their excitement clearly the result of the unfamiliar linguistic turns taken in the text. At times the story might have set them on edge, I suppose. When Guy Palladis, a central character in Eric Linklater's novel *A Man over Forty* (1963), is adrift after university, his mother suggests a career in politics. "That's out of the question," he replies. "I read *Coriolanus* when I was young—perhaps children shouldn't be allowed to read Shakespeare?—and it shocked me profoundly. And politics haven't changed much have they? They're far more stable than science."

activity was positive: it wasn't as if the brains were confused, exactly, but rather as if they had been awakened from linguistic boredom. The conclusion was obvious: reading Shakespeare, or any author who pushes the linguistic envelope a bit, is good for your brain. Even if you were bored reading *Coriolanus*, it's a good bet that your brain thoroughly enjoyed it.

That maneuver, "He godded me," is what linguists call a functional shift or lexical conversion. Many English words are born in such shifts: *swim* or *use* as nouns from verbs, for instance, or *surface* or *text* (clipped from *text message* and then shifted) as verbs from nouns. Eve V. Clark and Herbert H. Clark describe the phenomenon comprehensively in their classic article "When Nouns Surface as Verbs" (1979). It's unlikely that more than 10 percent of "new words" at any time result from functional shifts (and that's a VERY generous estimate), so though we may accept words shifted centuries ago without much electrochemical excitement, relative to other ways of making up words shifts are unexpected, so they take us by surprise. *Text* still surprises many speakers of English, but by the time today's young are old, EEGs and MEGs and MFIs won't register any surprise when human subjects read or hear it: the *text* of today is the standard *use* of tomorrow.

If this works for shifts, imagine how it works for infixings and blends, which are less frequent among the new words we make and among the core of our vocabulary. Then think about how much more excited the brain gets when, rather than the expected expletive, an infix is lexically meaningful, or an infixing with a meaningful insert is also a blend (*US-fucking-A Today*), or when the apparent expletive in an interposing is actually descriptive (*Marcia fucking Brady* or *Leicester bloody Square*), or when we have to unpack *cherryoke* or *chrome labia*, which are more than blends or compounds but depend on a simultaneous interpretation of the word's structure and its metaphorical impulse. The brain activity triggered by a functional shift is measurable. As we measure the effects of linguistic invention throughout language, that is, from the poetic ether down to the grittiest Street, we'll find our brains challenged far beyond the reach of mere functional shifts. This is your brain on slang.

Language can take us by surprise in the office, during a sermon, while we listen to sports commentary on television or, even better, on the radio. Invention is not confined to slang or poetry, and that complicates our understanding of slang, since the line between what it accomplishes and what other language accomplishes is neither bright nor a barrier. The occasional novelty that pops up in conversation on a date, the witticism that attracts or repels but won't be ignored or forgotten might be slangy or poetic without counting, exactly, as slang or poetry: it's language with style that resembles slang, or poetry, or, given the previous chapter, both. Actually, any language that strikes us as sufficiently different from whatever we're used to is likely to stimulate our brains, including dialectal differences and supposed usage errors. The average English teacher's brain must be overly stimulated indeed.

Nevertheless, language along the axis of slang and poetry is likely to stimulate our interest more than the language spoken every day in our part of town or neck of the woods, because slang and poetry set out to push buttons and pull levers in the brain. It's impossible to prove, of course, but one suspects that poets and speakers of slang alike have always understood, intuitively, that they were manipulating the linguistic reactions of those in the vicinity of their speech, pushing even the most obdurately normal among us into momentary abnormality. Those who won't budge probably don't read poetry and probably detest slang. Alas, it's true: even if they don't have criminal tendencies (though some surely do), at the base of it poets and slang speakers disrupt the comfortable lives of ticky-tacky neighbors.

This issue of whether slang jazzes or bugs us is not "merely" cognitive, of course, but also social. We aggregate on the basis of what feels comfortable to us: maybe it means nothing to others, maybe it inflames them; members of the in-group respond to the group's slang, but quite differently when unfamiliar slang marks them as the out-group. The newer the slang, the more excited all of us get. As slang conventionalizes and marks a broad in-group (youth today, for instance) in the minds of many in the out-group (middle-aged parents, teachers, journalists, politicians), it bothers those in the out-group who suffer unexpected brain activity.

What ignites the circuitry in our brains isn't just lexical, and neither is slang. We think of slang as words: as the conventional wisdom has it, slang items are socially deviant, clever or colorful, forced or facetious synonyms for standard words. In fact, though, processes of word formation can be slangy: it's not the individual word per se but the formative pattern, under certain conditions, that's slang. These patterns are intimately connected to the phonology, or sound structure, of a language, and its syntax, or phrase and clause structure, as well, not to mention the complex semantics borne of the interactions among lexis, syntax, and discourse. Remember the tendency of snowboarders and skateboarders to describe a series of tricks as something like, "She just did backside tweak to fakie," to which the speaker can add as many tricks with *to* as the boarder performs. The jargon isn't just in *backside tweak* and *fakie* but in the endlessly additive, mildly nonstandard structure of the sentence.

Nowhere is the slanginess of word formative processes more evident than with infixing and interposing. These aren't historically inflectional processes in English, and as derivational processes they are among the least productive; thus, results of these processes inevitably surprise our brains. That is, when *edumacation, irremededially* (both of which observe rules about which sounds can occur among what others, and more rules about stress patterns in word structure), *guaranclickin'teed* (which proves that infixes can have lexical meaning, effectively doubling the semantic content of any infixed form), *absonotly* (which isn't an infix but sounds like one, so is interpreted as though it were one on the basis of formal parallels), and *shut the fuck up* (a four-word phrase with two words that don't count lexically, are hard to account for syntactically, but add a lot of pragmatic value) — when any or all of these take us by surprise, the individual items aren't the culprits so much as the deeper processes of which the items are superficial, but delightful, manifestations.

Infixing and interposing aren't the only word-formative processes implicated in slang. In *Slayer Slang* (2003), I focused on two suffixes, *-age* and *-y*, as central to slang in *Buffy the Vampire Slayer* (1997–2003), slang that belonged to Buffy and her associates, the Scooby Gang. Their speech defined them as an in-group, and one aspect of that speech was its cleverness, sometimes self-conscious, sometimes not. Often innovative, it was also patterned and to some degree predictable: phrasal verbs used by female speakers were usually clipped (as described in chapter 2); the *-y* suffix occurred whenever possible but historically unlikely; and quippage, especially Buffy's, had its peculiar rhythm. For the first three seasons or so the show's language was thick with *-age* suffixed forms, from *agreeage* to *slayage* to *wiggage*, and the Buffyverse at large, especially on Internet posting boards, imitated that tendency. Then, perhaps, having exhausted the social and pragmatic values of *-age*, the show and fans alike were *-age*d out and started to explore how far they could push *-y*.

As lexical items, the suffixes play a role in slang aesthetics and in the construction of social meaning: the *-age* in *foodage* or *fundage* indicates masses of snacks or cash; *-age* is superfluous (*food* or *funds* will do), so is playful and resists "the rules" laid down by teachers and such. *-Age* is also accepted by certain groups as an in-group marker: if you can use it plausibly, you may belong to the group in question. Neither *-age* nor *-y*, however, is inherently slangy: there's nothing slangy about *sewage* or *vicarage*, *blustery* or *sugary*. When a suffix like *-age* or *-y* (or other really old suffixes like *-dom* as in *Buffdom*, *-kin* as in *Buffkin*, and *-ness* as in *Buffyness*) is used to slangy effect, it works not only because of the specific lexical content, but because suffixing as a process plays a role in slang, especially suffixing at unlikely frequencies or suffixing in unlikely contexts.

Buffy the Vampire Slayer provided an unlikely fictional context for *-y* suffixing and gave us items like *stiff upper lippy*, *stay iny* (as opposed to coming out of one closet or another), and *crayon-breaky*. (For accounts of these and many other *-y*-suffixed items, see my *Slayer Slang* [2003].) Other odd *-y* suffixed forms popped up on television, far away from the Buffyverse: so, in the HBO series *Six Feet Under*, Robbie can insist to Ruth that she's being too *co-y* (that is, **codependenty*). All of these examples do, in fact, push *-y* pretty far, farther than most speakers throughout most of the history of the English language could imagine: far from *rain*, *wind*, and *snow*, one-syllable nouns all early suffixed into the adjectives *rainy*, *windy*, and *snowy*. *Stiff upper lip* is a four-syllable phrase, an unlikely candidate for suffixing of any kind; *stay iny* makes sense only by association with *come out*, a reversal of metaphor that requires both cultural knowledge and quick synthesis to comprehend; and, though *codependent* is really the base just clipped out of hearing, *co-y* is, on the face of it, an impossible PREFIX + SUFFIX compound. Some people's brains are up to television, and others' are not. But if brain activity constitutes some sort of pleasure, then this sort of unorthodox lexifabricology affirms (some of) television's aesthetic value.

It's not accurate to locate such developments only in the very late twentieth century or very early twenty-first. Lynda Mugglestone has recently examined the *Oxford English Dictionary*'s proofs in order to understand editorial decisions that shaped the dictionary's published text: "Since English in practice has no limits and is endlessly created anew by its users who coin words such as *gymcrockery* or *bite-beast*, *ironworky* or *jog-trotty* according to the whim of the moment, the lexicographer must exclude some words that he knows to be in existence but of which the claims can, for one reason or another, be judged to be less pertinent than those of other words." The forms listed above are recorded in the *OED*, but many other *-y* suffixed forms were excluded, one presumes. It's difficult to assess, then, how far *-y* had developed toward its current, slangier applications. Very clearly, though, time and use have eroded many of the earlier constraints on suffixing with *-y*, so that nowadays almost anything goes.

Over some weeks in 2004 and 2005 I tested *-y*'s apparently infinite productivity by searching for unlikely *-y* suffixed forms on the Internet. I would sit at the keyboard for exactly one hour, typing conjectural forms into the search field; that is, I made stuff up. Often whatever appeared in the first few hits would suggest later searches. After a while I realized that I couldn't make much up: as hard as I tried, most of my attempts at lexifabricography proved that I wasn't fabricating anything. For example, at 11:00 a.m. on January 22, 2005, I started with *truthy*, but then went on to discover the following:

- *beliefy*, as in "Frankly, I don't understand the topic, but I got the gist that it's about bashing beliefy things"
- *faithy*, as in "Orthodox Christianity 101 — Studies in the Faithy"
- *fingery*, as in "desperate fingery climbing in the edges low down"
- *climby-thing*, as in "on the climby-thing";
- *journaly*, as in "Most will post journaly stuff here"
- *magaziney*, as in "Most of my old British mates are, sadly, still magaziney people"
- *officey*, as in "I follow him into our new $40,000 office space and he reveals a nice new area with computer, desk, chair, and all that other officey crap"
- *sitcomy*, as in "Murphy Brown's baby? I think I switched off about that stage, it was starting to get too sitcomy for my liking"
- *slackery*, as in "I hate it when I get all slackery with my AP classes"
- *virusy*, as in "virusy computers"
- *shamey*, as in "The Shamey Indiscretion of Flan"
- *rulesy*, as in "I also enlist the help of the players and make them do some of the rulesy legwork"
- *Jesusy*, as in "I needed to say this in case my posts become more Jesusy"
- *saviory*, as in "Dawn will either show up in the last episode and do something really 'saviory,' or . . ."
- *campaigny*, as in "It sounds campaigny and political"
- *malfunctiony*, as in "Everything gets a little transporter-malfunctiony after that," or "It was really only big enough for one person, and rickety and malfunctiony"
- *bartendery*, as in "Do I sense a little bartendery bitterness?"
- *auctiony*, as in "There were two auctiony spaces next to each other"
- *airwavey*, as in "Sounds great, especially the break! Very airwavey"
- *super-protecty*, as in "The Slayer would get all super-protecty"
- *markety*, as in "The titles didn't help — they sounded too markety"
- *zebraey*, as in "Zebraey — resembling a zebra"
- *chefy*, as in "owing to conflicts with his very chefy schedule"

- *mixed signally*, as in "Damn him and his mixed signally ways!"
- *four-lettery*, as in "But the language gets four-lettery at one point"[2]

Session after session produced more or less the same results: roughly twenty-five items from about twice as many attempts (not all words I tried, in other words, had been invented yet). Some of the results weren't very adventurous (*officey*, *chefy*) but some were challenging, whether because the base just seemed radically the wrong sort of word to suffix in a slangy direction (*Jesusy*, *saviory*), or because it was a multisyllabled phrase (*mixed signally*), or because it was a multi-syllabled phrase clipped from a longer phrase used metaphorically (*four-lettery*; as Buffy would say, it's all "metaphory"). Imagine the electrochemical firestorm that last item would ignite in the average brain.

And, as they say on late-night television, there's more! Slayer slang includes a *much* that deviates from general American English adverbial *much*. The form is relatively frequent in slayer slang and is a hallmark of slayer style, though it didn't originate with *Buffy the Vampire Slayer*. If you trip while walking with a sarcastic friend, the friend might ask, "Walk much?" This VERB + *much* pattern is familiar in colloquial English, but it's not the pattern mainly at issue in slayer slang; rather, ADJECTIVE + *much* as in "Pathetic much?" and NOUN + *much* as in "Broken record much" are the emerging slang forms. The earliest instance of ADJECTIVE + *much* discovered so far is "Underdeveloped much?" from a sketch on *Saturday Night Live*, October 7, 1978. The next recorded instance is in the film *Heathers* (1989); it was used occasionally between that film and the first season of *Buffy* (1997), at least in some Google user groups.

No one has yet found NOUN + *much* before 1998, when it appeared in *Mademoiselle* ("Meanwhile, *My Best Friend's Wedding/Friends* much?") and the film *Jawbreaker* ("Tuna much?"; it's about whether Queen Bees and their wannabes eat tuna salad sandwiches in the cafeteria, and you really need to watch the movie to get it). These unexpected *much* forms aren't used frequently, but they are current in American slang:

---

2   Unfortunately, in some cases, I was moving so quickly through the material that I copied into my notes too little context for some of these items. As a result, the meanings of those items, or the motives for coining them, are a little unclear. I can only apologize for this sloppiness: I was getting a little self-competitive, I'm afraid, trying to find more, and more aberrant, -*y* suffixed forms within my allotted hour. Though it's not particularly important to the present argument, it is interesting that, in the case of this session and pretty much all of the others, roughly 10 percent of the results were clearly associated with *Buffy the Vampire Slayer*.

- On *Grey's Anatomy* (February 15, 2007) Alex asks, "Dramatic much?"—an example of the increasingly common ADJECTIVE + *much* variety.
- In the film *Juno* (2007), Juno objects to the name proposed for her unborn child by its prospective adoptive parents. The prospective father, Mark, reports that "Vanessa likes Madison for a girl," to which Juno replies, "Madison? Hold on, isn't that a little, um, gay?" Mark replies, "Wow. Pretentious much?" *Pretentious much* also gets play in a variety of contexts on the Web. It's the sort of slang that confirms your membership in the chat room even as you call someone out, a subtle negotiation of social power like those illustrated in chapter 2.
- On *Heroes* (November 19, 2007), Elle (superpowered assassin) objects to her father (who is also her control), "Overprotective much?"
- On the *Missbehave* Web site, Emilia Perez blogs "Bitter Much?" (May 1, 2008), an entry about "Ask *Missbehave*," a new feature in the magazine that provides those who "never will (nor will ever bother to) understand dudes' uber-complicated psyches" with an opportunity to discuss "their boy-related problems."
- On The Superficial, an entertainment gossip Web site, someone asks of some celeb's current appearance, "Tan much?" (11:02 a.m., March 5, 2007), and someone else speculates, "Fake tan much?" (11:10 a.m., March 5, 2007). Whereas both *tan* and *fake tan* might be verbs, *fake tan* is more likely a noun, which casts some doubt on *tan*, too.
- Again on The Superficial, someone comments on an article titled "Rose McGowan Forgets Her Bra" (March 21, 2007), "Wow. Cocaine much?" where *cocaine* is certainly a noun.

When you consider where these *much*es occur (teenish films, twenty-something mags, magazine Web sites, teenish TV, slightly older TV catering to viewers who saw the films and read the mags, gossipy Web sites devoted to celebrities who starred in the films and TV shows), not to mention their casual transgression of basic grammatical rules, rules you learned in eighth grade (whether you remember them or not), such as "Adverbs don't modify nouns," it's easy to accept ADJECTIVE + *much* and NOUN + *much* as slang.

Significantly, these *much* phenomena are not merely lexical; though, I hasten to add, there's no shame in being merely lexical. The electrochemical shock to our brains isn't just a matter of *much* but a matter of with what *much* combines, and also the ellipsis that does or doesn't occur depending on the grammatical pattern. For instance, when you say "Walk much?" you are really saying "(Do you) walk much?" In the case of VERB + *much*, the relationship between ellipsis and the sentence expressed is natural and clear. The ellipsis in ADJECTIVE + *much* is also predictable: "Pathetic much?" would be "(Are you) pathetic much?" If we supply the material missing from the slangy sentence, however, we encounter two problems. First, we sense that use of *much* in the elaborated sentence is unidiomatic, so we try to improve the sentence some, for instance, by looking for further ellipsis at the end of the sentence: "Are you pathetic much (of the time)?" Or we try to solve the problem by moving the adverb: "Are you much pathetic?" — no, that would have to be "Are you often pathetic?" But then we encounter the second problem: does *much* in ADJECTIVE + *much* mean 'often' or 'intensively'? Doesn't "Pathetic much?" translate easily into "You are so pathetic," which isn't really about frequency of patheticness? In the truncated sentence, we don't have to choose meanings; slang use of *much* has it both ways.

Obviously, NOUN + *much* sentences are even more problematic. Take the earlier example, *broken record much*: Buffy has disappointed her sister, Dawn, too often: "I'm sorry, okay?" Buffy offers. "Broken record much," is Dawn's reply. That's not obviously elliptical, or at least, HOW it's elliptical isn't obvious, even if it is somehow elliptical. It's certainly not an elliptical question (in the episode, Dawn's intonation doesn't raise interrogatively but lowers at the end of her reply), not "(Are you a) broken record much?" As in most cases of ADJECTIVE + *much*, it's not clear either whether Dawn thinks Buffy is often a broken record or very a broken record; of course, frequency and intensity can overlap, as they probably do in Dawn's critique of the situation. Also, "broken record" is metaphorical, so the translation should be something like "You are so (very much) like a broken record." In fact, a lot of meaning is packed into that nonsentence, *Broken record much*, pragmatic meaning that far exceeds the sum of the lexical parts: "Why do you make the same mistakes over and over and, like a broken record, offer the same excuses?" is what Dawn really means. It's not a question meant as a statement (as are many ADJECTIVE + *much* forms), but a statement meant as a question, and a complicated one at that.

"Walk much?" is less challenging than "Overidentify much?" let alone "Hey, respect the narrative flow much?" And none of those compares to "Off message much?" or "Control-freak much?" or "Curb much?" (asked of someone who needed practice at parallel parking), or "Bait and switch much?" or "Déjà vu much?" or "A fine example of maturity to the pupils of Sunnydale High much?" The obvious problem with these *much*es is their combination with adjectives (sounds odd, though grammatically correct) and nouns (definitely grammatically incorrect); the subtler problems have to do with whether what precedes *much* is multisyllabic, phrasal, metaphorical, and so on, and the degree of ellipsis and its effects among the various *much* combinations. Combining with *much* in the manner described here is a slang process, in other words, and as much syntactic as it is lexical, as much a matter of process as of result.

I don't text, but I've spent some time lurking in chat rooms and posting boards, so I have gradually become aware of initialisms like *BTW* 'by the way', *IMHO*, 'in my humble opinion', *LOL* 'laugh(ing) out loud', and *ROTFLMAO* 'rolling on the floor laughing my ass off'. I've heard the first and third in casual conversation, and, admittedly, the first and second are a bit like *RSVP*. Any of these, used in conversation or in Web texts, functions partly as a discourse marker, like *so* in "So, I went to the Irish Pub last night and there were all these cute guys there." The second is a little different, a response to something shared by two or more people who constitute an in-group. They're *so* an in-group that they speak in code, or, because all slang is coded, serious code.

Consider *ROTFLMAO*: this is an excessive (read "forced") string of initials that implies (1) a lack of interest, effort, or time to speak the whole phrase (read "casual") or (2) precise, playful extravagance. In either case, though, it's the process of initialism that's slangy, especially when pushed to an in-your-face limit, as in *ROTFLMAO*. Either you get this sort of language or you don't: not the items, but the process and constraints (or lack of them) on that process are what mark in-groups from the out- ones. I remember well my own uncharacteristic sense of in-ness the day I deciphered *ROTFLMAO*. After several years of lurking on posting boards I had figured out *BTW*, *IMHO*, *LOL*, and other initialisms from the context of posts in which they appeared. I managed, after having seen it repeatedly, to figure out *ROTFLMAO* as well. Then I rolled on the floor laughing my ass off at my own cleverness. A few months later I discovered the FAQ page of the site on which my epiphany had occurred. After some consideration, I reckoned that *FAQ* means 'frequently asked questions', and, of course, new users of the posting board frequently asked questions about the initialisms used there; indeed, all of the initialisms I had worked out on my own were defined there. I receded, rather quickly, back into the out-group, where I belonged.

Those hip to such linguistic stylin' are likely to experience increased brain activity when they encounter less usual *much* patterns. Such forms are wholly experimental and belong wholly to their contexts; they aren't abstracted from those contexts into general use, and they won't end up in dictionaries. The same is true of infixings, interposings, and many *-y* suffixed forms, though such suffixing may be less jarring to the linguistically savvy brain because the opportunities for novel -*y* suffixing have developed over centuries. Texting has established many initialisms as newly permanent fixtures in the vocabulary, but you've got to be in the in-group of texters to recognize them without alarm. (Many "speakers," including Microsoft Word, are in the out-group. I can't help but think that, for Microsoft, that's embarrassing, though no surprise to Apple partisans.)

In other words, in all of these cases, shifting, infixing and interposing, -*y* suffixing, collocations with *much*, and initialisms — and, of course, many other cases not considered here — slang is less a matter of words stored in our cranial dictionaries, more a matter of structure. As mentioned in chapter 1, William Labov suggests that, in the context of language change, "slang is merely the paint on the hood of the car." Were slang items just synonyms for other words, he might be right; in fact, some slang items serve just this synonymic purpose and no more. But slang is also implicated in the processes by which words and sentences are formed, and this structural implication isn't characteristic of English alone: all languages have at least a little slang. All right, slang isn't the engine of language, nor a piston, nor the timing belt. But slang may be the springs that allow the hood to open and shut, or the latch that holds it shut. Slang, in fact, may be important to language without being quite fundamental. You don't need paint on the hood of your car, nor a hood, nor a body at all, but cars as we know them today, as they've developed, in some cases necessarily, in some cases contingently, generally have bodies, hoods, springs, latches, paint, and much more. It's unwise to be reductive about cars or, for that matter, language.

William J. Frawley, one of America's preeminent cognitive linguists, argued recently in a lecture at the Modern Language Association's annual convention that, if we accept that the brain is the origin of all language phenomena, then all questions about language ultimately will be answered by understanding the brain. We might learn more about language by studying the brain more and language less. Some linguists are less cognitive than others and locate linguistic phenomena in social behavior rather than the brain. We know that development of the human brain occurred not in a vat, but in response to social engagement; we know, too, that any individual neural network develops in response to worldly experience, some of which is social. All of this leads us to an obvious, but not often asked question: If slang is in the brain, isn't it likely there for a reason?

SLANG AND LANGUAGE PLAY

Slang's role in cognition isn't limited to giving our brains lexical thrills. That it does so endows slang with value in social interaction: I can use slang to get your attention, to stimulate your interest in me, and to establish a relationship with you by means of a code or style we recognize as mutually stimulating. But lots of behaviors excite the brain, pleasurable means to social ends, like touching and kissing, for instance. Slang is more than just a means to an end, though, because it plays a role in language learning: as a type of language play, slang is an instrument of language acquisition in the very broadest sense.

This is a somewhat adventurous claim, and I don't want to claim more than I can argue plausibly. I stop short of saying that slang figures in what Noam Chomsky and his followers call "linguistic competence" because that term has a fairly narrow meaning among linguists. We acquire language, the theory goes, because we have language in our cognitive makeup.[3] We have more linguistic knowledge, in fact, than experience of language behavior around us justifies. Chomsky's view of language depends on this "poverty of stimulus paradox": we couldn't exhibit the common, human linguistic expertise we do at the ripe age of five or six unless something other than experience accounted for it.

True, experience of language triggers linguistic competence or the language instinct or organ or program, or whatever you want to call it. But *language*, as

---

3 There is no way to characterize, in a paragraph or two, the subtlety of Chomsky's theory or the subtle disagreements among Chomsky's followers about details of the program called variously and at different historical stages Generative Grammar, Universal Grammar, Minimalism, and other names, "the system of principles, conditions, and rules that are elements or properties of all human languages," as Chomsky put it. Steven Pinker's *The Language Instinct: How the Mind Creates Language* (1994) is a readable (indeed, entertaining) account in the Chomskyan tradition; Stephen R. Anderson and David W. Lightfoot's *The Language Organ: Linguistics as Cognitive Physiology* (2002), though an excellent book, requires more concentration; unless you go to the beach to study, it's not beach reading. As Pinker writes, "The story I tell in this book has, of course, been deeply influenced by Chomsky. But it is not his story exactly, and I will not tell it as he would." Some linguists and many social scientists interested in cognition from other perspectives (such as child psychology) disagree that Chomsky's theory explains all language phenomena, all aspects of child language acquisition, the status of linguistic competence among other cognitive abilities, and the list goes on. For some examples of dissent from Chomsky's Standard Theory (yet another among many nicknames), see Louise M. Antony and Norbert Hornstein, *Chomsky and His Critics* (2003).

Chomsky and so many other linguists mean the term, isn't the language we encounter in the social world; rather, *language* is the language within us, and social experience of language triggers *language*. Thus Steven Pinker points out in *The Language Instinct* (1994) that because "language is so tightly woven into human experience that it is scarcely possible to imagine life without it," we mistakenly attribute language to experience: "Thinking of language as an instinct inverts the popular wisdom, especially as it has been passed down in the canon of the humanities and social sciences," from one or more of which you, like the author of this book, probably graduated. "The real engine of verbal communication," Pinker writes (though "writing is clearly an optional accessory" of language), "is the spoken language we acquired as children." If you think that language is a product of culture, well, Pinker advises, think again: "Language is no more a cultural invention than is upright posture."

One may accept the bulk of the Chomskyan view of language and still have reservations. As Guy Cook argues in *Language Play and Language Learning* (2000), "Chomsky's narrow definition of 'language' . . . effectively confines acquisition studies to the development of the formal linguistic system in a first language between the ages of roughly two and six." By "formal linguistic system" Cook means phonology, the sound system of a language, and syntax, or the rules for phrase, clause, and sentence structure in that language. Cook questions the "assumption" that "acquisition is only about the independent development of grammatical and phonological competence considered in isolation, rather than in interaction with the child's physical, social, and personal development."

Cook also notes a second assumption relevant to the question of slang's role in language learning: "that this acquisition of grammar and phonology comes to an end in or around the sixth year, and that at that point in a child's development there is some kind of qualitative break when the process of acquisition is, as it were, complete." As a result, "on the one hand, there is little attention in the literature of this [the Chomskyan] tradition to the environment of very young 'prelinguistic' children. On the other hand, there is an equivalent lack of attention to the language of older children: to literacy, vocabulary, and discourse skills, or to the relation between language acquisition and the development of imagination and ideas." Prelinguistic children are so cute, but let's put them aside for the sake of argument; here, we're interested in older children and their slangier tendencies.

The process of acquisition breaks qualitatively much as Chomsky suggests: acquisition after the critical stage is qualitatively different from acquisition in that stage. In our teens, we aren't learning how to speak a meaningful stream of sound; we're not even figuring out how to structure arguments or narratives. By then, we've been arguing with authority and entertaining our friends with stories for years. In those later years, acquisition also slows: there's just less of it as we get older, fewer instances of discovering something about the structure of language. Acquisition also becomes less and less efficient as we age: what we learn from later experiment with language is less valuable in purely linguistic terms than anything we learn in the critical stage. If teens worried about how much new stuff they were learning about language, they'd totally wig at the diminishing returns. But teens don't typically focus on linguistic competence and the role it plays in their ongoing development: they have their first jobs, first loves, snowboarding, arguing with authority figures, and lots of just hanging out with friends, or whatever.

None of this means that acquisition doesn't continue beyond the critical stage: we spend a lifetime refining the abilities we've acquired by the time we start school. It doesn't mean that later, super-competent acquisition is unimportant, that it doesn't count — it just doesn't count in Chomsky's linguistics. As Joel Sherzer asserts in *Speech Play and Verbal Art* (2002), "Play and art are both inherent and potential in linguistic structure; they are an important part of what language is all about." Some language play occurs in the crib and is fundamentally important, arguably essential, to the development of linguistic skills, but language play and the art that comes from the linguistic and conceptual abilities it fosters aren't restricted to the nursery or even to preschool experience. Cook's point is just that language play continues well past that stage and that it's a productive activity, even if the results are different in linguistic kind and effect from those of earlier language play.

Throughout this book I have considered varieties of slang that are clearly also language play: "playful" is a characteristic of slang recognized in most of the dictionary definitions and scholarly accounts discussed in chapter 1. Rhymes like *How's it goin', protozoan?* are doubly playful, not only in the rhyme, but also in the exaggerated metaphor. Rhyming and back slang started out as subterfuge but soon became language games you could play for fun, like anagrams or Scrabble. In Argentina's version of back slang, called *al vesre* (a reversed form of *al revés* 'backward, inside out'), *kilombo* 'whorehouse' becomes *bolonki*. You can use *al vesre* to cover your tracks in conversation with the hip among the unhip, but *al vesre* isn't all about concealing illicit activity. A simple enough word, like *pibe* 'guy' becomes *bepi*. So this *bepi* goes into this *bolonki* and . . . Never mind, it gets all fucked up—which is appropriate, because *bolonki* is a slang euphemism for 'fucked-up situation.' Sherzer explains that similarly

> French offers a particularly interesting set of play languages. *Parler à l'envers* 'Speak backwards' reverses the order of the first two consonants or consonant clusters of a word or pair of words: *Passe moi la bouteille* 'Pass me the bottle' –> *Sap moi la toubeille Verlan* (*l'envers* 'backwards' said backwards), the most contemporary of French play languages, reverses syllables, pronounces words backwards, and/or reverses the order of the first two consonants or consonant clusters of a word or pair of words.

An Indonesian slang spoken predominantly in Jakarta operates in part along similar principles, but it also includes a peculiar infix: *bapak* 'father' becomes *bokap*, *begitu* 'so, how very' becomes *begokit*. In these cases the final vowel or combination of vowel and consonant (the "rhyme," as linguists would say) is removed from the base and the infix *-ok-* inserted in what remains: "My *bokap* is *begokit* not hip." (Of course, in Indonesian, the whole sentence would be in Indonesian.) The slang is called Prokem, infixed from *preman* 'gangster' (drop *-an*, insert *-ok-*, a slanged borrowing from Indonesian Dutch *vrijman* 'free man'). Like *al vesre* and *l'envers*, Prokem is itself an item of itself, a playful fact that is part of the language game.

Slang, in other words, is a veritable canasta of language play, and speakers play it in nearly all of the world's languages. Spanish and French are closely related Indo-European languages, and we might expect that language play in one would resemble language play in the other. Indonesian, however, is an Austronesian language and, though hypothetically related to French and Spanish in linguistic prehistory, is structurally very different from them and from another Indo-European language, English. It is significant that language play, indeed language play of the same types, occurs around the globe and through time. It isn't mere coincidence: playful infixing, the possibility of it, figures, not just in the language of *The Simpsons*, nor just in American slang, nor just in slang of English and related languages, but in the very structure of language as encoded within us, as a feature (albeit an infinitesimally minor one) of human cognition.

Infixing is often brought up in the context of language play. Recently Alan Yu, in *The Natural History of Infixing* (2007), specified the conditions for "true" or Homeric infixing in various languages. Homeric infixing is characteristic of Homer Simpson, not the Greek epic poet, and the stress in *Homeric* here is assigned to the first syllable, rather than the second. (Note, though, that Simpson is figuratively blind to many things and sometimes, as when infixing, a poet though he doesn't know it.) Yu includes infixing among "language play and disguises" (linguists call them *ludlings*, *lud-* from Latin *ludus* 'play' + the double diminutive -*l-ing-*, as in *underling*) common in the world's languages, and he provides examples of infixing as language play not only from English and, via Prokem, Indonesian, but also from Estonian (a Finno-Ugric language), Tigrinya (an Afro-Asiatic language), and Tagalog (an Austronesian language). Reverse or back slangs and other lexical remixes are ludlings, too.

In a classic article, "Plain Morphology and Expressive Morphology" (1987), Arnold Zwicky and Geoffrey Pullum argue that "closely allied to the artistic use of language is the playful use of language — in secret languages, riddling, punning, insult games, and the like. Just as the restrictions and deviations of poetic language are extraordinary from the point of view of the grammar of prosaic language, so are the deformations, extensions, and restrictions found in verbal play." Zwicky and Pullum include infixing in "expressive morphology," processes of word formation with strong pragmatic effects, words formed playfully and aesthetically against the conventions of "plain morphology." On the other hand (Shakespeare and our brains might be surprised at this), they don't consider functional shifts from noun to verb and so on as expressive. Slang, it seems, covers a range of linguistic practices, some of them expressive in morphological terms and some of them not, though the latter are quite possibly expressive in linguistic dimensions other than morphology.

The anthropologist Henri Chambert-Loir noted of one bit of conversation in Prokem that its intention "was not to deliver a message but rather to convey an impression," that it had "no content other than the expression of a feeling of intimacy." Slang often promotes social rather than lexical meaning, as we've discovered at different points in preceding chapters, whether focused on slang and social organization or the aesthetic uses of slang. And as play, language serves social functions, of course: just as many languages have back slang and infixing, they also include forms of verbal contest, like the Dozens in African American discourse. In the Dozens, competition is obvious, but slang is often competitive beneath the surface; for example, when the Queen Bee clips phrasal verbs, as discussed in chapter 2, or the Adams family plays its rhyming game, as discussed in chapter 3, slang speakers sally forth in their ongoing battles with everyone around them for social place and face.

The competition can be fierce or friendly, or friendly with a hint of fierce, or fierce with a friendly demeanor. "The objective of the Dozens," writes Geneva Smitherman, "is to better your opponent with more caustic, humorous 'insults.' Played for fun or viciousness — and it can be either — the Dozens is a competitive oral test of linguistic ingenuity and verbal fluency." The Dozens and all of these others are not just language play but language games, not just play with language for the sake of that play, or for the sake of controlling the language, but games that operate according to extralinguistic social rules. The motive for playing such games is rarely just fun, though someone's fun is usually involved.

When language is used to disguise, it is a type of ludling, a type of play. But ludling conversely can be a disguise, as with criminal argot. Chambert-Loir proposed that marijuana underlies Prokem: the slang and what it disguises, the illicit activity, are among "numerous indications of the restlessness of today's young people." As a result, Jakarta is gripped with Prokem madness. Chambert-Loir's article was published in English in 1984, but young people were restless in the 1950s (think James Dean in *Rebel without a Cause*), the 1960s (think Dustin Hoffman in *The Graduate*), the 1970s (think John Travolta in *Saturday Night Fever*), as well as the 1980s (think Jennifer Beals in *Flashdance*) and 1990s (think River Phoenix, period). Kids are still pretty restless, and they may be restless well into the future (think Luke Skywalker). Slang is certainly related to the interlude of Youth, in all its restlessness; slang is also a category of language play; marijuana's in there somewhere, too. Prokem, Chambert-Loir concluded, "should be studied as a language phenomenon and, more importantly, as a social symptom. A code or a jargon does not come into being as the result of games but because of the needs of a segment of society."

In fact, though, language play does arise for pleasure and because it serves linguistic purposes rather than or in addition to (though not opposed to or exclusive of) social ones. Sometimes, in other words, slang is the sort of play that actually helps us to understand how our language works. For instance, in what ways can you rearrange parts of words so that meaning is simultaneously concealed from some and apparent to others? The focus here is not on the social motivation for concealing, but on the efficacy of word structure for productive concealment. What are the limits? How far can you go before no one understands what you mean? How far must you go to ensure that those you don't want to understand can't? What are the relations among sound, metaphor, and cultural material, so that rhyming slang is a possible means of communication? Can you infix in English, and, if so, within what constraints?

In the previous chapter, I considered Mark Peters's recent work on the infix *-diddly-*, which began as a Flanderism from *The Simpsons* but is actually Homeric, in Yu's sense. The infix *-diddly-* has become quite productive in Web communication particularly, since the television show made it familiar. Many of Peters's examples are phrasal: *Hi diddly fucking ho* (what the Seven Dwarves really said before Disney got hold of them) or *Have a nice diddly fucking day* (what I'm often really saying in my head until Disney gets hold of me). In other words, they are examples of interposing rather than infixing, and there's nothing wrong with that. Viewed as an element of language play, however, -*diddly*- is more than an infix, more than a euphemism: it is the solution to a linguistic problem.

Here is the problem: Can you infix a single-syllable word with an expletive? Remember that, in English, infixes are inserted within a matrix at a juncture appropriate to syllable and stress. *Absofuckinglutely* inserts -*fucking*-, so that the infixed form preserves the alternating stress of the matrix. Yet consider the possible but unlikely forms **bifriggingig* and **whafuckingat* (both of the vowels in the second example are schwas). Wouldn't you prefer the alveolar nasal /n/ to the velar nasal we spell *ng*? So **bifrigginig* and **whafuckinat*. These are not ridiculous infixings in principle: either might suit a particular context as an emotional stress amplifier. At the zoo you might watch an elephant pee and say, "That elephant's stream is bifrigginig." Someone might say something absolutely shocking or absurd, so that you respond, "Whafuckinat?"

In fact, you don't hear these forms because they have a lot going against them: they require reduplication of the vowel at the center of the syllable, and the nasal stop is not the easiest transition from insert to the second half of the matrix — possible, but not likely. *Diddly* is the solution to the problem of the one-syllable matrix: in *bididdlyig* and *whadiddlyat*, you can stretch -*diddly*- to three syllables, which makes the stressful nature of the infixing transparent (otherwise it might go by too fast); the -*y*- is a glide, and it's much more pleasant to enter the second half of the matrix by gliding into the reduplicated vowel rather than stopping in front of it; and -*diddly*- has a pragmatic value, insofar as it lightens the expletive mood.

The problem is even more vexing if the single-syllable word you hope to infix is itself an expletive. *What?* is close, but can you credibly infix *fuck*, *shit*, or *bitch*?[4] The answer is "Of course, you can, with -*diddly*- at your infixational beck and call." Consider: Could you really say **fufuckinguck*? That is, could you say that expletive without an ironic understanding of the expletive moment? You could, of course, undergo something so horrendous that it warranted an

---

4 It's not clear whether forms like *biyotch* are infixed with an expletive, though, as with -*zn*- forms like *shiznit* and *fuznuck* there is some emotional stress amplification.

expletively infixed expletive, but, in such a case, you'd be unlikely to infix at all. In all likelihood, your response would not be a slang response. Were you in any position to produce *fufuckinguck* or *bifuckingitch*, you'd start to laugh at yourself before you finished either, your mouth slowed by the complex phonetics of the words just long enough for you to realize what you were doing. Of course, -*fucking*- is such a familiar infix that we think first of inserting it into all of the other expletives, but the alternatives are even less likely in the universe of real speech: *bibitchinitch*, *bishittinitch*, *shibitchinit*, or *shishittinit* don't exactly roll off the tongue. The infix -*diddly*- saves the day: rather than twist and slap the tongue around to produce an implausible infixing, the speaker inserts mellifluous irony into the matrix. Better than that, the speaker controls the irony, which is what every speaker desires. You can't be hip and worry about how you lost lexical control.

The implausible *fufuckinuck* presents two problems; *fudiddlyuck* solves both of them. One is an internal, structural problem about infixing in English, a problem of what the rules of word structure are. The structural problem comprises three subproblems: (1) Can you infix a one-syllable word; and, if it's possible to do so, (2) can you infix an expletive with that expletive; and, whether it's possible or not, (3) can you infix an expletive with another expletive? The other problem is external and social: What will people accept if you attempt to infix a single-syllable word? What will they accept if you attempt to infix an expletive with the same or another expletive? If it is possible to produce any such infixed forms, are some preferred to others, for social or stylistic reasons?

The social interface in which slang plays a part comes at a late stage of the total process of language acquisition; it bridges linguistic competence, the innate human ability to learn language, and communicative competence, the ability, whether innate or learned, to use language effectively in social settings, to achieve the range of communicative goals. Speakers of English may well have discovered everything necessary to English phonology and phrase structure by the age of six, but they haven't learned how to use language in socially "productive" ways, to cooperate, to trick, to manipulate and construct social realities. Slang is a means of finishing our formal or structural training in some of the more esoteric problems of language, like that of infixing a one-syllable matrix. While we're in this linguistic finishing school, the social meanings of prosodic and semantic tricks we've been practicing and refining more or less since birth become important: in the tweens, when we begin to establish our mature social identities, there is suddenly a lot more at stake in our use of language than earlier in life, and for many of us the stakes remain pretty high well into our twenties, after which most of us are just too tired to care.

One distinction between jargon and slang is that jargon is an assured innovation, one that often resembles slang but depends on the slang training we get at an earlier stage of life. We need experience in slang to create language of social utility and aesthetic value that literally WORKS, that helps us do jobs rather than to live large, as slang is wont to do. We work more in later life, and as we work slang starts to wane in our speech, and jargon waxes, with our first job serving food in a restaurant, for instance. As we get older, we invest in our hobbies (progressively less snowboarding and more philately), and the more we're into them, the greater role jargon plays in our lives as users of language. But we have to be careful not to overlook the playful aspects of adult language. As Guy Cook puts it:

> When we turn our attention to adult behaviour, we are likely to assume that play has disappeared, or at least shrunk to a minor role, overwhelmed and replaced by the more serious and necessary aspects of adult affairs. Yet is this actually the case? Are all the adult activities, and the uses of language to which we devote time and accord value, any more necessary than children's play, or is it just that we take them more seriously?

Literature is adult language play: adults play language games, some from boxes and others off the tops of their heads. And even if they don't create much of it, adults indulge in the language of the young all around them. Occasionally they even remember items of their own generation's slang.

As Cook insists, from crib play to nursery rhymes, from back slang to the Knock Knock slang flash cards, "though language play is manifested through a variety of different activities, these are expressions of a single underlying phenomenon, which is of particular relevance to mental adaptation for individuals, for societies, and for the species. Though it appears superfluous, it is not actually so." That "underlying phenomenon" is the need for language to test its formal and functional possibilities. Our brains develop throughout our lives, and the language in them does too, at different rates and to different effects at different stages. But the accumulated effect is to refine language, first in one person's experience of it, and then, through time and space, in its very nature.

What must be true of language play for it to have these salutary effects on language structure and language use? Cook has the following characteristics in mind: "Disconnection from reality, disruption and subversion of social structures, and the introduction of random elements have particular benefits for all of us, and that is perhaps why we are so fond of them, even when they are forbidden.

They are there to be exploited to our advantage in many areas of human activity, including language learning." Slang and language play so easily converge; it's difficult to accept that convergence as mere coincidence. Once we've learned all we NEED to know about language, once we've plumbed what's innate, don't we retain the impulse to test it, to see if language is up to what it claims for itself, to confirm that we've learned well what we were destined to learn? Slang is perhaps a built-in heuristic: it reassures us that we still know what "it" is, after all these years.

"MY BAD" MEANS NEVER HAVING TO SAY "I'M SORRY"

Of all the things Walt Whitman said about slang (twice quoted at length already in this book, so not quoted here), the notion that slang is indirection is perhaps the least noticed. Our own experience confirms that most slang is ephemeral though effervescent during its short life among "permanent" language. We grant that the effervescence enriches the total language at the time it's spoken and in less obvious ways influences the history of English. And we are impressed with the role of slang in poetic language; naturally, we assume that Whitman proposes the connection between slang and poetry, viewed both conceptually and practically, as the fundamental issue, he being a magnificent poet and all, having been hip to poetics in ways that most of us are not.

From an anthropological point of view, however, Whitman's really interesting observation is the one about indirection, partly because indirection is a problematic fact about language (it covers a very broad area of linguistic activity), and partly because considering the problem (probably not "solving" it, however) clarifies slang's role in language as a whole: indirection, though a particularly important feature of both slang and poetry, is nonetheless a prior condition for either, a linguistic potential exploited early in our history as a talkative species. Indirection manifested in slang and poetry extends a general property of human language and much other behavior associated with it; it's not unreasonable, in both cases, to see these extensions as refinements, various social demonstrations of indirectional skill, as misrepresentation in the service of truth, beauty, and all you need to know that can't be said as effectively, if straightforwardly.

Indirection is part of the very structure of language. For one thing, metaphor is a type of indirection, and language is chock-full of metaphor. I don't mean just the very obvious metaphors, as when a conservative politician is rabid, or a liberal politician has a bleeding heart, or either is caught with his hand in the cookie jar so that his goose is cooked. Metaphor is so thoroughly entwined with the rest of language that we don't even hear it as metaphor: your rich parents cut you off (but they don't use knives or scissors), and your finances are suddenly in the red (but there isn't an actual ledger with entries in red ink), but, fortunately for you, a generous friend bails you out (but you're not in a boat), at least until you can get back on your feet (though you were never literally knocked down).

Metaphor is often so conceptual that we can't imagine how to say anything without it. As George Lakoff and Mark Johnson explained in their landmark study, *Metaphors We Live By* (1980), "Metaphor is pervasive in everyday life, not just in language, but in thought and action.... Primarily on the basis of linguistic evidence, we have found that most of our ordinary conceptual system is metaphorical in nature." Metaphors behave systematically, are internally coherent, and interact with one another coherently—in other words, they make sense of one another, matching meaning with experience of the world around us, in effect structuring that experience coherently in all sorts of symbolic action, including language. But, paradoxically, all of this coherence is founded on indirection: we understand things not on the basis of what they are (which is probably beyond the grasp of human cognition), but on the basis of what they are like.

We find it difficult to imagine language without indirectional structure because indirection is both a fundamental and a subtle property of language. Think about prepositions, for instance: if I'm in a tizzy, am I in it like the seed is in the apple, or like plenty of other fish are in the sea? Yes. And no. It's got to be both: there has to be enough similarity for metaphor to operate, and there has to be room for distinctions to appear in the process of comparison. Words like *in*, *at* (*at the door*, *at bat*, *at attention*, *at last*), and *on* (*on the table*, *on duty*, *on drugs*, *on time*) are constantly stretched and extended to supply meaning—if not all meaning, at least a lot depends on indirection.

Such deeply embedded metaphor suggests our deeply embedded inclination toward it and toward the indirection of which it is an important example, though certainly not the only one. Sometimes, though, our metaphors are superficial, that is, on the surface of our discourse and used with at least some awareness that they are metaphors. We create "new meaning," as Lakoff and Johnson put it, in contrast to "conventional metaphor," in order to organize our social and political experience, and for aesthetic reasons, too. Of course, that last includes metaphor in poetry, "but aesthetic experience is not thus limited to the official art world. It can occur in every aspect of our everyday lives—whenever we take note of, or create for ourselves, new coherences that are not part of our conventionalized mode of perception or thought." Flamboyant metaphor, such as the restaurant server's *in the weeds*, the chat room's *four-lettery*, and the like, are the apotheosis of a linguistic habit we have no desire to break, which is a good thing, because we couldn't break it if we wanted to. As the neurobiologist Semir Zeki has argued (ultimately in agreement with William J. Frawley), "Aesthetics, like all other human activities, must obey the rules of the brain of whose activity it is a product, and it is my conviction that no theory of aesthetics is likely to be complete, let alone profound, unless it is based on an understanding of the workings of the brain."

Language skates back and forth, forward and backward, along our conceptual plane, occasionally cutting a figure eight. It expresses our metaphorical frame of mind because it is lithe and ambiguous. The philosophical linguist Harald Weinrich has laid out the following semantic principles: (1) Every lexical meaning is broad; (2) every lexical meaning is vague; (3) every lexical meaning is social; and (4) every lexical meaning is abstract. We can't verify these principles by running through the entire English lexicon here and now; however, a sample word is probably enough to illustrate their plausibility.

Take, for instance, a common word such as *cat*. It covers a lot of cats, from Persians and Siamese to calicos and Manx (who differ from the stereotyped cat because they have no tails); besides these domestic breeds, each representing a different set of cat characteristics, *cat* covers feral cats and big cats like lions and tigers, and lots of cats in between; it also covers Gumbie Cats, like Jennyanydots, and Mystery Cats, like Macavity, that is, all fictional as well as all real cats. In other words, the lexical meaning of *cat* is broad.

In order for the lexical meaning of *cat* to be broad, it must also be vague — it must be vague enough to mean not just your cat or my cat, but all cats. And we agree on what counts as a cat and when the word *cat* applies conceptually. Because *cat* is not a natural fact but a sign used by speakers to signify a class of things and concepts as long as speakers agree to use it for that purpose, the lexical meaning of *cat* is social. In order for the first three conditions to be true, the meaning has to be abstract, but obviously it has to be abstract if we use it to "refer" to the nonexistent cats of T. S. Eliot's imagination — abstract meanings, in other words, for abstract "things." As abstractly, but in a different metaphorical direction, *cat* extends metaphorically to mean 'cool guy'.

Thus ambiguity (perhaps the inevitable effect of broad, vague, social, and abstract lexical meaning) and the negotiation of ambiguity are central to language behavior. Ambiguity is what allows the characters in *Buffy the Vampire Slayer*, as described in chapter 2, to negotiate their way through similarly ambiguous social relations. *Buffy* is fiction, and the language of its text may not perfectly represent language in the real world; nevertheless, it represents the sorts of sociolinguistic negotiation that occur every day among all of us. Slang depends on Weinrich's principles for its value as currency in such negotiations, as a cursory glance over a list of slang items suggests: *awesome* 'excellent', *bad* 'excellent', *chill* 'relax', *on the down low* 'secret', *excellent* 'awesome', *far out* 'excellent', *game* 'skill', *hot* 'sexually attractive', *ill* 'excellent', *jammed* 'intoxicated', *killer* 'superlatively excellent', *lowdown* 'inside story', *mack daddy* 'bad, hot man with game', *no way!* 'absonotly', *props* 'respect', *q.t.* 'down low', *ridiculous* 'excellent', *sick* 'excellent', *tizzy* 'confused or panicked state', *up yours!* 'fuck you!', *vu ja de*, 'never seen (this) before', *way* 'absolutely yes', *x* 'Ecstasy, MDMA', *yo!* 'hey; yes', *zit* 'pimple'.

Any outright code meant to cover the underworld's underbelly obviously depends on indirection: *on the down low* (even more deeply coded as *on the d.l.*), *jammed*, *q.t.*, and *x* are supposed to be indirect enough that only those hip to the code can understand them. The best test of code in reality is that it confuses the uninitiated: "I'm down low with that, way low," someone outside of the coded subculture says. He may have known what "it" was once upon a time, but "it" eludes him now. Of course, some people actively pursue the hip aesthetic (not, in fact, a hip thing to do), so the criminal code constantly changes, its elements downgraded or upgraded, depending on one's perspective, to serve everyday social purposes instead.

This subtler social code (or set of codes) also continually changes so that we can sound *cool* 'casually rebellious'. It circulates in one group and out the other; it's the code that supplies contextually useful nuance; it hits an attitude on the head by appropriating old terms and using them in new ways, taking advantage of semantic breadth, vagueness, and abstractness. So *awesome* is brought down to merely 'excellent', its original meaning diluted by adolescent casual disregard for conceptual precision; *excellent* is used so enthusiastically as to ascend to 'awesome'; *ill*, which is the opposite of 'excellent', surely, is pushed far away from any historical sense; and *killer* is enlisted to mean 'so excellent as to be destructive', though it's obviously an unlikely choice to mean 'excellent', but that's the role of indirection in slang. Through the exaggerated tendencies of slang we're reminded of the indirection rife in all language use.

How many words do we need for 'excellent'? And how does one react to the whole collection of them? One could say, "Yay, synonymy!" Or one could note that each synonym, in its established or contextually controlled connotations, is an example of deliberately NOT saying *excellent*. The motives for that indirection are various, from social ones, such as fitting in with a group partly on the basis of lexical choices (or, as Lighter would have it, thoughtless lexical habits), to semantic ones, such as trying to get that extra shade of meaning in there. It wasn't the best concert ever; it was *like* the best concert ever. You went with someone who wasn't *cool*, but he wasn't *uncool*. And augmentation, even that which adds pragmatic but no lexical meaning, is a form of indirection because you don't get the base word directly. It wasn't *unbelievable*; it was *unfuckingbelievable*. It wasn't *the shit*; it was *the shiznit*.

The lexical items, morphological quirks, and syntax bending discussed in this chapter are all examples of indirection, though indirection of various kinds:

- *Metaphory* and all sorts of *-y* suffixed forms start from the meaning of the base (*metaphor* in this case), but indicate an oblique relationship to the base. It's not so much metaphor as kind of metaphory.

- *Co-y*, from *codependenty*: What could be more indirect than clipping the actual point right out of the word and assuming that it would still make sense to members of some social group somewhere, at some time?

- *Stay iny* is an indirect way of announcing one's intention not to *come out*, which as a clipping of *come out of the closet* is itself an evasion, whereas *come out of the closet* is a metaphorical evasion for *gay*, for God's sake.

- *WTF* is a Web euphemism for *What the fuck!* so is indirect in its very construction as a slang item, and *ROTFLMAO* is a particularly demanding euphemism, one that requires a certain hipness to know how it's a euphemism and simultaneously, indirectly, and ironically makes fun of alphabetism and other hip Web slang strategies.

- *Pathetic much?* could be asking "Are you pathetic often?" or "Are you very pathetic?" or "Are you both?" Even more, *Tuna much?* and *Curb much?* are, one must admit, very indirect ways of saying, in their respective contexts, "We don't brown-bag it in this clique" and "Do you even know how to drive?"

These last two paradoxically sound more direct than their expanded, denotative counterparts. That, of course, is their slanginess, the power of extreme metaphor and compact utterance to rebel against the norms of speech playfully and skillfully, in both cases, one from the movies and one from the real world, exhibiting the highest level of sprezzatura.

My bad is a particularly good example of slang as skillful prevarication. Every use of *My bad* is a speech act, and every speech act has within its performance a locutionary, an illocutionary, and a perlocutionary act. The locutionary act is the statement's straightforward meaning, its denotation, its literal sense. As locution, *My bad* is just another way to say *I'm sorry*: "Oh, you were ahead of me in line? My bad"; "Oh my God, I did your line? My bad"; "Oh my God, you're pregnant? My bad." In every case, in the case of every speech act, the perlocutionary act is what the person addressed understands the utterance to mean. In all of these cases, the person addressed probably expects something on the order of an actual apology, but apology isn't exactly forthcoming: the illocutionary act is not what the locutionary act seems. *My bad* substitutes a bare acknowledgment: the situation is confusing, signals get crossed, shit happens. *My bad* always suggests a little reservation — call it verbal flinch, a turning of the head away from ... whatever.

The person addressed is skeptical because the illocutionary act is the instrument of indirection, what the speaker "really means" underneath the locutionary act. Arguably, someone who says *My bad* in some context may sincerely mean *I'm sorry* in that phrase's most literal sense, but probably not. In fact, almost never, because *My bad* is a casual (often glib) acknowledgment of fault. The speaker is clearly implicated, somehow, in whatever went wrong, but is it worth an apology? Not so much. *My bad* is casual but paradoxically also formal, like acknowledgment of a foul in basketball. Rarely is the player who commits a foul sorry for committing it (it may well have been deliberate), but he or she has to raise a hand and accept responsibility, even if responsibility, in any moral sense, is not what he or she is accepting. Rarely does the other team take a raised hand, a mere acknowledgment, as an apology, nor do most on the receiving end of *My bad*. Though nobody is ever really deceived by *My bad*, it's nonetheless an attempted deception.

Language as a means of deception is perhaps rooted deep in evolutionary anthropology. Deception certainly is. As the paleoanthropologist Leslie C. Aiello explains:

> Males and females have fundamentally different and potentially conflicting reproductive strategies. . . . Whereas females are limited in the number of children they can conceive, bear and raise to maturity, males are only limited by the number of females they can inseminate. There would be a strong incentive for females to use deceptive tactics to encourage provisioning from the male (in possible return for sexual access) while at the same time there would be a strong incentive for the males to use deceptive behavior to gain sexual access to the female without engaging in the levels of provisioning that might be to her best benefit.

Prehistoric men lied to have sex and avoid work; prehistoric women lied to put men to work while they were busy rearing children. As the linguist Jean

Aitchison points out, many animals are capable of deception but humans have "a propensity for lying," and lying is not mere deception but "tactical deception."

Lying is inherently problematic: a lie is open to exposure because the truth will out, and that leads to serious social consequences. People shun liars, not always to the greatest possible degree, but to some degree. Lying carries a lot of risk. Indirection, then, is better than lying: we can deceive, mislead, insinuate, challenge, and prevaricate without being disproved, without having to accept much responsibility if challenged. Adept indirection, in all its varieties, is a leadership quality, a skill that raises one's status within a group. Queen Bees get to pronounce on slang, what's in and what's out within their domains; they also manipulate their groups by means of slang, among other means.[5] One of the most important discourses of indirection is gossip: you don't say that Katerina and Aloysius hooked up, you say that you HEARD that they hooked up. From whom did you hear it? You don't remember. Everyone's talking about it.

Robin Dunbar in *Grooming, Gossip, and the Evolution of Language* (1996) argues that there is "strong support for the suggestion that language evolved to facilitate the bonding of social groups, and that it mainly achieves that aim by permitting the exchange of socially relevant information." Indeed, "about two-thirds of conversation time is devoted to social topics. These include discussion of personal relationships, personal likes and dislikes, personal experiences, the behaviour of other people, and similar topics": gossip. "Could it be that language evolved as a kind of vocal grooming to allow us to bond larger groups than was possible using the conventional primate mechanism of physical grooming? . . . In a nutshell, I am suggesting that language evolved to allow us to gossip." Lying is not the only tactical deception available to humans: gossip fits the category, too, as does some slang, though *My bad* may not fool anyone.

Gossip is an instrument of social efficiency, which is why, arguably, it appeals to natural selection, though, as we'll discover in the next section, many prominent linguists find the appeal to natural selection implausible: it allows us to sort liars and free-riders from supportive and reliable friends, to draw the line between who's in and who's out quickly, while serving other sociable needs. If Aiello and Dunbar in combination are right, then indirection has been a feature

---

5 Or, as Jean-Louis Dessalles says, "Performance in conversation is a 'good' alliance criterion, for it demonstrates the ability of a speaker to get biologically relevant information from the environment; it is assumed that this ability is correlated with the ability to influence the coalition in the right ways."

of language from the outset, with slang and poetry (and lying, of course) as extreme and stylized exercises of an indirection natural to us as talkative primates, an indirection hardwired into us as we emerged from primate ecology.

Not everyone agrees with Dunbar's theory. For instance, Jean-Louis Dessalles in *Why We Talk: The Evolutionary Origins of Language* (2007) argues against it:

> It is unlikely that the scope offered by language to praise or disparage the actions of others had any direct influence on the evolution of language behaviour. After all, language also serves for speaking of many other types of subject matter, factual, psychological, imaginary, etc. The diversity of topics of conversation is infinite; and the emergence of language during the course of evolution cannot be accounted for by any one of these various uses on its own. . . . The role played by language in social bonding or as a way of controlling the doings of members of the group is not up to explaining language behaviour as a whole.

One readily admits that language is used for more than gossip today, yet it's not clear that language has always been used for everything Dessalles lists in competition with gossip. What were the relative claims of fact and gossip in prehistoric times? Did internalized monologue precede social communication? Slang as an aspect of gossip (which is partly fictional or indirectional) is imaginative language devoted to imaginary subjects. In any event, there's a point at which Dessalles's and Dunbar's theories converge: indirection.

For, as Dessalles correctly notes, participants in any communicative act rarely share interests absolutely, so to whatever degree they are cooperative, they are also to some degree (perhaps a very small degree) competitive: "What we must envisage . . . is the speaker who has something to gain and the hearer who holds back. In other words, the real difference between the cooperative relationship and the way language is observably used in real life is to be found where the risk lies." Of course, outright deception constitutes the greatest risk, but gossip, slang, and poetry are types of discourse that ameliorate deception and minimize risk without eliminating either.

Dessalles views language behavior, even in its social manifestations, as cognitively based: "What we are unconsciously exercising in our conversations is a part of our biological programming. Behind the immediate stimulus of exchanging relevant information, what we are doing is assessing others' ability to decide what is good for the set of people who will choose to ally with them." This is ultimately of evolutionary benefit to the many, whereas natural selection is of benefit only to the fittest:

Human beings turn into interlocutors for a fifth of their waking lives because they are in a game which, when played under nature's conditions, is essential to their survival and procreation. The aim of the game is to discover whom to choose as allies and to determine who will influence collective decisions. It is a game which differs from the other one, the game of natural selection, because the winners are not the only ones who get to propagate their difference.

Though we assess speech from a biological foundation, we do so for social and personal reasons. There's certainly nothing in Dessalles's last statement that disagrees with Dunbar, for social alliances can develop from QUALITY of gossip exchanged, not so much from its content as from the judgments and attitudes that align some participants and separate others. We make decisions about social leaders and confederates not merely on the basis of facts and information, but also on the basis of style. Slang is indirection zooted up for public discourse: the more stylish the slang, the more risky the indirection, the more powerful the speaker, who gets away with things, manipulates social reality with speech, and so is competitively attractive as the focus of social alliances.

What Aiello, Dunbar, and I see as natural and humane disappoints Dessalles: "Let us assume," he writes, "that whatever benefit speakers derive will increase with the salience of the situations they speak of. This makes for a strong temptation to exaggerate or even tell lies." Heavens! "There is an argument, advanced by John Krebs and Richard Dawkins, which says that communication, when it is of benefit to the sender of a signal, evolves into signals that are exaggerated, repetitive, and costly," so "evolution must endow hearers with an ability to resist, which would mean that language should either disappear or evolve into signaling that is exaggerated, repetitive, and costly. Yet clearly this has not happened." Of course, Dessalles is French, but, in a metaphorical sense, I wonder if we speak the same language.

Signaling is, in fact, often exaggerated, repetitive, and costly, for instance, in slang. Ultimately, Dessalles's approach to the question of language origins and the fundamental quality of language is reductive and binary — I would say inevitably so, but that should be obvious. Of course, language isn't ALWAYS exaggerated, repetitive, or costly, but why should it be? Dessalles assumes that, within the evolutionary model, if language develops it has to develop toward an end. But that assumption is not sound: successful adaptations have to promote evolutionary success, but surely the ability to skate along the line between a lie and poetry, the line we call *slang*, is of benefit to us. Why can't we all just get along?

Well, we can and we can't: we can and must because we have evolved into social beings, and social relations (as Dessalles admits) promote "everyone's" evolutionary success; we can't because we're competitive and because our successful version of social behavior (arguably that of all primates, though some think bonobos are an exception) involves competition. That's the paradox at the heart of human nature. Slang helps us get away with it.

What does it mean when someone walks into the room, looks you up and down, and says, "How's it goin', protozoan?" Why doesn't he just say "Hello!" or "I'm so glad to see you!" if that's what he means. If he chooses to conceive of you as like a one-celled animal, if he establishes his own casual cleverness in rhyme, then what does he really mean? "I want you to find these sounds sexy so that you allow me to have sexual relations with you?" Or "If you think I'm going hunting and gathering for that brat again, you are sorely mistaken, but I don't want to be unpleasant." Or "Listen to my totally awesome rhyme that you've never heard before because I just made it up — I am so the shit." Indirection enacts our social and aesthetic uncommitments. We're too cool for school or for the textbook semantics they teach there. Is that wrong for a college professor to say? Should I appear to approve of lies, and slang, and poetry? My bad.

SLANG AS LINGUISTIC SPANDREL

In his *Passions of the Soul* (1649), indeed in several works published over the course of his lifetime and after, René Descartes located the soul in the pineal gland. The pineal gland, about the size of a pea, fits snugly between the brain's two hemispheres, just behind the eyes. We're pretty sure that the pineal gland isn't the seat of the soul. In fact, it's likely that the pineal gland is largely vestigial, an organ that used to have a purpose but doesn't much serve modern human needs, like the coccyx or appendix. In the case of the pineal gland, the exception might be production of melatonin, which regulates our circadian rhythms. I don't want to make a mistake of Cartesian proportions, so I'm not suggesting that slang has a cognitive basis because it resides at some location in the brain, or even a nearly cognitive one because it emanates from the pineal gland.

In fact, language (which is "bigger" than slang, so harder to fit into the pineal gland, though, obviously, easier to fit than the soul) isn't confined to any one cortical location. We know that much language activity occurs in the brain's left hemisphere (for most people); we know that if certain centers in the brain are damaged (Broca's area or Wernicke's area, for instance) language is also impaired, and impaired in specific ways (loss of syntactic capacity in the case of Broca's area, loss of lexical capacity in the case of Wernicke's). But we also know that language stuff happens in the right hemisphere, too. And the language "organ" apparently cooperates with other complex cognitive functions, such as gesture, memory, and computation. When slang surprises it, points light up in laboratory images of the unsuspecting brain — but those points aren't slang centers. When we talk of language as a cognitive function and of slang as therefore cognitively based, we aren't saying that we know where or how slang happens. It will be a long time before we can say anything much on the subject.

We also cannot say that slang functions like syntax or other linguistic elements absolutely essential to language. Because syntax is in some sense fundamental (Chomsky would say it is the finally important sense), it must be an inextricably cognitive element. In the twenty-first century language is what it is: we can't (and shouldn't) imagine historical language without slang. Importantly, though, one CAN imagine an I-language without slang, indeed, one can even imagine an E-language (language external to the brain) without slang, whereas one cannot imagine language without syntax: it's a structural truism that, where there's no syntax, there's no language.

Consider, though: Can one imagine language without indirection, that is, without metaphor or prevarication or misrepresentation? That's a more complicated question. It's hard to imagine human society without lying, of course, but one could write science fiction about a perfectly honest society; living in it might prove unbearable. Not every social use of language is a necessary consequence of indirection, however, and lying is only one type of indirection, surely the least complicit in the very nature of language. Metaphor and the pragmatics that allow indirection, however, are fundamental to meaning, even if they aren't prior to syntax: they are fundamental to language as we know it. We can talk of syntactic structure abstracted from any meaningful context, but unmeaningful sentences are symptoms of language pathology; meaning, too, is fundamental to language, and, anyway, meaning and indirection depend in part on syntax.

Slang is a social and aesthetic reinterpretation of fundamental elements of language: word structure, sound, syntax, lexical meaning, and the characteristics of discourse, like indirection, that depend on them, sometimes in cooperation with other cognitive abilities. Slang draws from these elements and integrates them for meaningful social and aesthetic purposes, yes, but for its own sake, too, for the sake of reiterating what's possible in language. The problem with I-language is that it's just there, like a fallen tree whose falling made no sound because no one heard it. Unless language makes a sound, so to speak, unless it is manifest in practice, it's irrelevant, much as the code DNA is irrelevant until it is expressed in living organisms.

But surely the very existence of I-language can't depend on our knowing about it. Surely the whole point of identifying I-language is that we "know" it whether we know it or not! We produce language without conscious effort or any particular awareness of language phenomena. Language is innate, but linguistics is not. Yet having admitted this, one should also admit that I-language is a code in the brain, and the code's existence is not the same thing as the existence of language, no matter how necessary the code is for the production of language in everyday use. Again, to say that X is competent isn't particularly informative unless that competence is affirmed. In Chomsky's theory, I-language undergoes a series of transformations, from an inaccessible "deep structure" to the "surface structure" of everyday language, and affirmation of competence comes with acquisition. As Guy Cook has argued, and as I suggested earlier in this chapter, acquisition properly understood may be a more protracted and complex process than we have envisioned so far. Slang may have a role in extended acquisition; indeed, slang may be evidence of it.

Reiterating what's possible in language by using language (perhaps by using it in particular ways) is essential to the ontology of language, that is, to the terms on which it exists at all. At least that's what I'm inclined to believe, but I'm what philosophers call an antirealist. Realism is the broad philosophical position that affirms an old rule of logic, the Law of the Excluded Middle: statements of belief, of ethical value, and those asserting the existence of something are always only either true or false (here comes a really important part of the position, in small capital letters, just for emphasis) INDEPENDENT OF WHETHER WE KNOW IT. For the realist, verification is external to the process of knowing or understanding, whereas for the antirealist, it's all part of the process.

An antirealist rejects both the "always only either/or" formula, as well as any small-capital dogma. Just as there are many types of realists, there are many types of antirealists. For instance, if you are a mathematical realist, you believe that numbers exist independently of whether we know it, indeed, that the very concept "number" exists in some Platonic world where concepts thrive, and that mathematical truths are true whether we figure out how to prove them or not. Mathematics, on this model, is a process of discovering whatever mathematics is out there. But constructivists, the antirealist mathematicians, believe that mathematical truths are true when and because we prove them: proof constructs truth and existence. There may be some code in the brain we call I-language (I don't mean to sound glib; it's a very powerful code, and the theory that proposes it is a very powerful theory), but it exists because the language of everyday use allows us to prove that it must exist for language to occur on the terms it does.

Slang is a show or a performance; it's language on the edge of acceptability. If slang exists (and it does), then language of a certain kind, language with indirection, rhyme, a pragmatics of nonsentences (like "Broken record much" or "Curb much?") must also exist. Sometimes you're not aware of what language is until slang provides extreme evidence of its character and capacities, much as terra firma never feels so good to Wile E. Coyote until he skids to the edge of a canyon cliff. In fact, slang isn't all that edgy; it doesn't lead to any linguistic abyss. Indeed, slang is mostly predictable. For instance, English slang words form pretty reliably according to the rules that govern word formation in English generally. That's as it should be if slang is part of a language, because language is systematic. But slang pretends to be unsystematic and unpredictable: it trades on the illusion that it's edgy or unacceptable, even though, as we know, it doesn't take long for most slang items to lose their edge or for some slang items, the less ephemeral ones, to become acceptable within colloquial discourse. New slang is always popping up: there's an explanation for how the rabbit got into the hat, but we're distracted from that explanation because a rabbit is being pulled from a hat!

Surely, though, we have lots of reasons to believe that language exists, that it is what it is; slang seems to be more proof of language than we need. There's no doubt that slang makes a virtue of superfluity: it's always language we don't "need" in the narrowest sense. We don't "need" both *chill* and *chill out*, or one hundred synonyms for *excellent*, and some (not me, though) might insist that *Pathetic much?* is a poor substitute for a precise sentence. Indeed, the point of slang might be that we need occasional superfluity, that the extra and ephemeral bits of language serve purposes. Those purposes may be expressive, that is, social or aesthetic, or even political, as slang is an instrument of low-level resistance, called "sticking it to The Man." It may also, as I've suggested in this chapter, be a means of testing the limits of language. We can use language to accomplish more than one thing at one time, and a little superfluity goes a long way to serve purposes that aren't strictly matters of communication.

It's not clear that we need slang to challenge conventions and rules in order to reassure us that we know about language or to certify that language is what it is. Linguists already know that and what language is by describing and reconstructing it, from dialect to I-language. If we want to know about language, if we want confirmation that language is such and such a thing with this and that characteristic, all we need to do is ask a linguist. You know, though, there's never a linguist around when you need one. Everyday people, especially teens, who are naturally and rightly skeptical of authority, linguistic and otherwise, test the ontology of language as they use it by means of slang, among other aspects of language. Slang is part of the people's linguistics.

Most language is automatic; remember that Steven Pinker calls what prompts it "the language instinct." One difference of too many to count between I-language and slang is that I-language must be unconscious. How many linguists does it take to unscrew an I-language? So far it has taken thousands of linguists some fifty years (including weekends) to work out some of what it is, and the job's still not done. Confirming the existence of I-language and describing it properly is organized science — to the extent that linguists, psychologists, evolutionary biologists, cognitive scientists, philosophers, and the like can be organized. Much E-language, the external-to-the-brain language we use to communicate, comes so freely or automatically that it must operate below the level of consciousness, too.

Jonathan Lighter, you'll recall, argues that slang tends to "short circuit reflection and exalt snap judgments and habitual attitudes among social peers" — literally thoughtless language. But as I've suggested throughout this book, slang is not only hip but hip to itself: it's as often conscious, purposeful language as it is MERELY habitual. Slang often resists the automatic for social or aesthetic reasons; it's also often a play on language that substantiates language and its properties, not in linguistics seminars but for us in the everyday world. We're not all going into it as deeply as the linguists, but we understand a great deal about language, enough to be going on with, from daily personal experiments in the systems and limits of discourse. Slang figures in those experiments.

Identifying what slang IS isn't the same as explaining what it's FOR. Is slang meant to promote cliques or social networks? After all, homo sapiens is a social animal. Is it merely "like" poetry, or, as Whitman suggested, is it the source of poetic language? Is it "for" poetry? Do the bits and pieces serve concrete purposes, or are some aspects of language purposeless, sufficient unto themselves? These are anthropological questions, and it's difficult to know whether the slang

IT'S ALL IN YOUR HEAD ·

to which they refer is a late social development, and so an artifact of human culture, or, like language play and indirection, a product of evolutionary forces. That's not to say, by the way, that language play and indirection may themselves be the result of natural selection or evolutionary adaptation: they are second- or third-order developments within language. It's unclear whether language itself is an adaptation or an effect or consequence of cognitive features for which nature selected. If the relationship between natural selection and language is unclear, the corresponding relationship between natural selection and slang is obscure.

The evolutionary purpose of language is problematic, and for well over a century linguists have doubted that the origins of language were relevant or discoverable or worth going into. Chomsky, for instance, held out against viewing language in evolutionary terms for most of his career. In the past few years, his previously hard line has softened, but not much. Recently language origin has been the focus of lively debate. In 2005 Marc D. Hauser, Chomsky, and W. Tecumseh Fitch published an article titled "The Faculty of Language: What Is It, Who Has It, and How Did It Evolve?" in the journal *Science*. Steven Pinker and Ray Jackendoff, directly in response to this article, more aggressively proposed relations between the nature of language and evolutionary purposes in the journal *Cognition* (2005). Chomsky and his colleagues issued a rebuttal in the same journal in the same year, accompanied by a further response from Pinker and Jackendoff.[6]

Chomsky and his colleagues reject most argument about the origin of language as speculative and unimportant to describing the biological foundations of language: language is what it is biologically, even if it isn't a product of natural selection or evolutionary adaptation. They insist that, "without further specification, the statement that 'language is an adaptation' is . . . vague enough to have few empirical consequences. In our opinion, there is no question that language evolved, and is very useful to humans for a variety of reasons." Similarly, in some vague sense everything about us evolved: nostrils, I-language, pineal

---

6   The argument between these two teams, though technical, makes good reading and is like the linguistics playoffs to us spectators. Unfortunately, there's no space for a replay in these pages, and no chance of an instant one (it's not an instant subject). I pick up the thread of Hauser, Chomsky, and Fitch's argument because it's relevant to this book; I am not supporting Fitch, Hauser, and Chomsky against Pinker and Jackendoff, by any means. Though I'm waving a pennant with PJ on it from the cheap seats, I'll adopt the more conservative position for the sake of argument.

gland. Remember that the language Fitch, Hauser, and Chomsky have in mind is I-language, a set of cognitive abilities fundamental and prior to any spoken language: if we say that spoken languages like English evolve, we aren't using the term *evolve* in a biological way.

For Fitch, Hauser, and Chomsky the only identifiable linguistic adaptation is the general cognitive ability called *recursion*. Recursion is a syntactic structure; for instance, the sentence "Bob said that Amber thought that Kimmie should chill out" is really a progression of sets: (Bob said that (Amber thought that (Kimmie should chill out))). In this regard, language shares features with logic and mathematics, but recursion is also part of our spatial reasoning. Fitch, Hauser, Chomsky point this out, but I have my own example, from one of my favorite camp songs (which is partly call and response):

And on that twig
And on that twig,
There was a nest,
There was a nest,
The coziest little nest,
The coziest little nest,
That you ever did see
That you ever did see. (All together now!)
And the nest on the twig and the twig on the branch and the branch on the limb
    and the limb on the tree and the tree in the hole and the hole in the ground
    (breath),
And the green grass grew all around, all around, and the green grass grew all
    around.

As you know some things about language from using and understanding slang, you know something about your profound recursive powers when you sing this song.

The relation of other recursions to linguistic recursion suggests that recursion itself is the adaptation and that recursion's general utility extended into specific recursions. Or, as Fitch, Hauser, and Chomsky suggest, "in addition to its clear utility for cognitive functions like interpreting mathematical formulas that are not plausibly adaptations at all, recursive thought would appear to be quite useful in such functions as planning, problem solving, or social cognition that might themselves be adaptations." But if recursion counts as an adaptation, it had a specific value or purpose when it emerged to amplify human cognition;

in the event, however, it much more likely accompanied or enabled spatial recursion than the linguistic kind, since our vision and the capacity to interpret visual evidence must have evolved long before we had the evolutionary down time to develop language.

It's all right to ask what language is FOR if you'll accept answers about what language IS. "Questions about current utility," Chomsky and his colleagues write, "are (at least in principle) empirically testable." Do we use language to communicate? We sure do. Do we use it to organize our internal lives? We do that, too. Is it a medium of art? Why, yes, it is. (Of course, I'm overgeneralizing the terms of current utility.) "But questions about original function are of a different logical type." We cannot easily extract information about the original functions of language from current utility: What is the appendix for? What is the pineal gland for? What are nostril hairs for? Maybe they aren't for what they were, even if they're still for something. Clearly, in a case like the appendix, they aren't for anything at all, at least as far as we can tell. So "empirically addressing specific hypotheses concerning adaptation requires equally specific hypotheses about function. . . . 'Communication' is far too vague to constitute such a hypothesis, and none of the other candidates on offer seem much better. So why argue about them?" The same applies for gossip, even for indirection: these are the socially extended outcomes of fundamental adaptations like the capacity for recursion.

Chomsky and his colleagues compare the question "What is language for?" to another: "What is the brain for?" We know about many things the brain does, but beyond its being for what it does, there isn't much to say. It certainly isn't easy to explain what the brain was originally for, even though we might find some traces in the fossil record. It's impossible to find the fossil remains of language, so the anthropology of language origins depends on indirect evidence and conjecture. Writing is too late an invention to reveal anything about the origins of spoken language; even if we had cave paintings of ancestors using sign language, they, too, would prove uninformative about the question of language's original purpose. Fitch, Hauser, and Chomsky further note that, if the question "What is the brain for?" is nearly impossible to answer sensibly, questions like "What is the cerebellum for?" are even less important. "What is slang for?" is in a similarly subsidiary position to "What is language for?"

It's only natural to ask such speculative questions, even if we can't really answer them. Such is the nature of human curiosity, so it's a good thing that we have archempiricists like Chomsky to slap us down. Even scientists like Pinker and Jackendoff ask and attempt to answer such questions seriously.

Thomas Eisner, the Schurman professor of chemical ecology at Cornell University, in a special issue of the *Virginia Quarterly Review* titled *Why Darwin Is Still Right* (2006), explains how he began to study the scales on butterfly wings: "As a budding evolutionist, I was certain that lepidopteran scales had 'survival value.' As products of natural selection, I thought, they had to have a function. But what might that function be? . . . One hypothesis that I liked was that the scales served to trap a layer of 'dead air' next to the wing surface, thereby providing the airborne insect with added lift."

But in the end, Eisner discovered, there's a lot more about butterfly wings than meets the eye: "There was something else about lepidopteran scales that I thought needed explanation. Scales in butterflies, typically, come in a variety of colors, while those of moths, as a rule, do not. This accounts for a basic difference between butterflies and moths. Butterflies tend to be gaudy, while moths, more often than not, are drab." This leads inevitably to the question "What do butterflies gain by being gaudy?" Gaudiness is superfluous, right? Embellishment on the otherwise functional butterfly, the colors themselves need not be an adaptation motivated by natural selection. Birds aren't generally interested in butterflies; they can't catch them easily because butterflies are erratic fliers. So, Eisner concludes, "butterflies could thus be thought of as constituting a gigantic mimetic assemblage, in which gaudiness and elusiveness are the defining traits, and safety from birds is the payoff."

Slang is often offensive, but it's really defensive: the best defense is a great offense. Slang that's meant to deflect ("My bad!") or distract ("Yeah, whatever, that's cool") or disturb ("Dude, I couldn't man, she's got chrome labia") is offensive and defensive in ratios calibrated to context. If we are thinking of slang in analogy to butterfly wings, then Labov may be correct that it's merely the paint on the hood of the language car, but color isn't the paint's only purpose: it protects from rust, reflects lights, stimulates envy in those who drive less flashy cars. The value of paint on a car or slang in a language needn't be entirely a matter of function or "present utility" anyway. As scales contribute "sheer splendor" to the lepidopteran wing, so verbal color makes language a many-splendored thing: "The diversity of color and pattern, and of scale arrangements and shapes, was stunning. There was a world of hidden dimensions in these images, a treasury of abstract art, unique in execution and gripping in its impact." Few would speak with the same enthusiasm of slang, but butterfly wings have no social significance to humans and don't threaten any established order. What birds think about the subversive nature of butterfly wings remains a mystery.

Michael Ruse contributed "Flawed Intelligence, Flawed Design" to the same issue of the *Virginia Quarterly Review* that contains Eisner's article. His essay attempts to explain the opaque relation between purpose and development in the context of arguing the inadequacy of intelligent design theory (IDT), which is based on the notion that some physical mechanisms (such as flagella in some single-cell animals) attributed to natural selection and adaptation by classical evolutionary theory are irreducible, that their very existence cannot be explained in evolutionary terms.[7] Ruse points out that "Kenneth Miller, a biologist at Brown University and a great critic of IDT, draws our attention to the Krebs cycle, a highly complex process with many steps, used by the cell to provide energy. It did not appear out of nowhere. It was something molecular biologists call a 'bricolage,' built bit by bit from other pieces." He quotes Miller as follows:

> The Krebs cycle was built through the process that Jacob (1977) called "evolution by molecular tinkering," stating that evolution does not produce novelties from scratch: It works on what already exists. The most novel result of our analysis is seeing how, with minimal new material, evolution created the most important pathway of metabolism, achieving the best chemically possible design.

Wherever slang came from and to whatever purpose, certainly it is not an independent development but a type of language in which bits from various other areas of language become an identifiable bricolage.

To hang my argument on yet one more evolutionary analogy, slang is thus a linguistic spandrel, a reinterpretation of other faculties that developed from adaptations forced by natural selection, for instance (and not exclusively), gossip, indirection, and language play. In their controversial article "The Spandrels of San Marco and the Panglossian Paradigm: A Critique of the Adaptationist Programme" (1979) Stephen Jay Gould and Richard C. Lewontin proposed that some traits usually (but not convincingly) attributed to natural selection are actually side effects of adaptation that arise in the course of a species'

---

7   For her recent book, *The First Word: The Search for the Origins of Language* (2007), Christine Kenneally interviewed Chomsky, who said that he found it "hard to imagine a course of selection that could have resulted in language." This is the sort of objection that intelligent design enthusiasts raise against evolutionary conundrums. I doubt that Chomsky is into intelligent design, but I was surprised to hear the similarity. I wonder if Pinker and Jackendoff heard it, too.

development. They are "evolutionary," but in a soft sense, not in terms canonized by the post-Darwin generation of Darwinian evolutionists; in other words, they aren't products of an inexorable and biologically central emphasis on the survival of species. As Gould and Lewontin put it, natural selection is assumed to be an "optimizing agent," but optimizing may occur as a result of various, even accidental or incidental influences. (This, in other words, is where Dessalles goes wrong.)

To illustrate their position, Gould and Lewontin turn to analogy, comparing the biological phenomenon to architectural spandrels. As they explain, spandrels are "the tapering triangular spaces formed by the intersection of two rounded arches at right angles" that are "necessary architectural byproducts of mounting a dome on rounded arches." It's a bit risky to draw an analogy from an analogy, I realize, but we can conceive of slang as a space constructed at the limits of more fundamental linguistic traits for no other reason than to be the space between them, like the architectural spandrel. The spandrel is not the focus of architectural design or function, but a by-product of them; the biological spandrel is not the purpose of adaptation or natural selection, but a by-product of it; and slang is a linguistic spandrel, a by-product of other elements of linguistic structure.

Once the arches are in place, you can't remove the spandrel; it's not an optional but a necessary by-product of architectural geometry. Similarly, now that language has constructed slang, there's nothing to be done about it: it's a feature of language's "design" and it can't just be pulled out from between the arches, say, of indirection and language play, without the dome collapsing into the rest of the linguistic edifice. We should admire the result of language's design, the slang spandrel, no less because it happens to be accidental. After all, slang's lexical, social, and aesthetic consequences are profound, as is the way it helps you to visualize and rationalize the arches that created it in the first place, the way in which, like trompe l'oeil, it clarifies priorities in the design first by leading the eye away from them. There's every reason to believe that slang is a late development of language, no reason to believe that it is a larger category, an arch or the dome, like indirection or syntax. But it has been part of language for a long time, not optionally, but necessarily, given the way that human language developed.

Unlike the elegant spandrels of the Cathedral of St. Mark in Venice, slang is gaudy. Take all of the dictionary descriptors of slang: arbitrary, casual, ephemeral, extravagant, facetious, forced, humorous, informal, irreverent, playful, racy, and vivid. Slang items or practices that combine two or three of these are colorful enough; the more characteristics a word or practice admits into its pattern, the gaudier it is, and the more exotic, given the linguistic norm. If by now you are looking for a fresh metaphor, you can think of the characteristics as compounds dissolved into the neutral spirits of words and linguistic practices: the more of them present in the cocktail, the more potent the slang is pragmatically. Inject a dose of slang into your conversation before breakfast and, in one sense of the term, you experience the morning glory of the day's language use.

TOWARD A POETICS OF SLANG

It should be clear by now that I'm more inclined to complicate matters than to get to the bottom of things. One could say, given the rest of this book, that slang is a register of vocabulary and various linguistic practices that are . . . (insert all of the dictionary descriptors, such as "arbitrary," "forced," "playful," etc.) . . . and are usually (but not always) synonyms for standard terms or expressions, usually (but not always) ephemeral, and that participate significantly in the construction of our social identities, in social interchange and group politics, and in our aesthetic behavior, and that also perhaps allow us to test the structural systems and limits of discourse. But a definition even this extended doesn't consider the role that slang as a linguistic spandrel plays in the shape and structure, the form and function, the ultimately whole nature of human linguistic behavior.

Slang is not, in other words, a category of language with meaning in isolation from other linguistic features. Imagine an arch, let's say the Arch of Indirection, made possible in the first place by a geometry of speech acts and metaphor and other linguistic points and lines and planes. Along one side of that arch you can imagine a "space," a nonarch space, but it's a space without geometric definition. It's not a spandrel because a spandrel is a triangular space formed by two arches reaching to support a dome. In other words, you cannot see a spandrel unless it's bounded by and participates in the geometry of arches and the other structural features that support a dome. If slang were related only to indirection, we wouldn't see it as anything distinct; if it were related only to language play, we still wouldn't see it as anything distinct. Some lines of language's architecture lead us to the slang spandrel repeatedly; being led by those lines to the same space over and over again, as a necessary consequence of structure, actually creates the space, so that we feel the need to decorate it, to fill it with color and design that depends on the surrounding structure, color, and design but contrasts with it, too.

Chomsky and those like-minded are interested in what's universal to language, what constitutes our language competence. Describing competence allows us to determine what's not universal as well, relegating it to linguistic performance. Some of what we have come to count as performance, however, might actually be universal and just as innate as the next feature of language. So Guy Cook muses:

> The issue which then arises — as with play in general — is whether this use and response to verse may be some kind of universal human behaviour, independent of the child's linguistic and cultural environment, naturally selected perhaps during the process of evolution. If so, there follows a further question: why should such a liking for verse have developed in our species? We tend to think of the socially significant genres of language use as being determined more by culture than biology, However there is no reason in principle why — despite their diversity — part of our knowledge of at least some of them (song, verse, narrative, gossip, jokes, for example) should not be innate.

Cook is not alone among linguists in thinking that innate language faculties extend much further than the grammar of I-language. For instance, the very ambitious narratologist David Herman has recently proposed "a broadly 'socionarratological' approach that synthesizes narratology, discourse analysis, interactional sociolinguistics, and cognitive science," such that the roots of story and our recognition of story structure are as much a part of our universal and innate linguistic makeup as the structure of conversation, from gossip to debate, as well as those features of language that interest the Chomskyans. Slang is not a feature of narrative per se, but, as discussed earlier, it is part of gossip, as well as a type of language play or joking, and also closely related to verse. The more of language we accept as innate, the more we value the slang spandrel as part of linguistic architecture.

The idea that linguistic structures such as narrative, poetics, grammar, meaning, and the sound structure of language are all parts of the same universal cathedral of language, a cathedral in which slang is a spandrel, is far from new. In fact, it's older than Chomsky's theory, a feature of the structuralism that originated with the Swiss linguist Ferdinand de Saussure but was then extrapolated in un-Saussurian ways by the succeeding generation of European linguists. Manifestos of the Prague school of linguistics in the 1920s and 1930s, as John E. Joseph puts it, "evince the distinctive characteristics of Prague structuralism, namely breadth." Roman Jakobson, the member of the Prague school who most influenced American linguistics, thought of linguistics as an encyclopedic science, ranging across all human expression, from everyday speech to mythic poetry: "I am a linguist," Jakobson said, "and hold nothing that has to do with language to be alien to me." As Whitman suggested, slang is part of the structure that allows passage from one linguistic manifestation to another.

Jakobson wrote a great deal more than one can read, let alone quote to support a point. He didn't write directly about slang, but his view of language is relevant to explaining the slang phenomenon. Consider the following passage from *The Sound Shape of Language* (1979), written with Linda R. Waugh:

> Since both aspects of language, the ordinary and the poetic, are two copresent and coacting universals familiar to the human being from his first linguistic steps, one could with equal right and equal one-sidedness speak about poetry and its "ungrammaticality" or on the contrary assail ordinary language for its casual, crude, and retrograde grammatical organization and character. Poetry, whether written or oral, whether the production of experienced professionals or children, and whether oriented toward or against ordinary language, displays its own peculiar sound shape and grammatical structuration.

Ordinary speech and poetry run along the same linguistic continuum: they share a sound system and grammar, but dispose them into distinctive shapes and structures. It makes sense, we think, to focus on the language most evident in acquisition as the "basic" language, the one that reveals the most about I-language or the language instinct. But for Jakobson, "the universal existence of poetry and demand for poetry find a powerful corroboration in studies of children's language."[8] Just as Cook suggests, what's evident is a matter of perspective, and poetics may be much more prominent in competence and acquisition than we have assumed. Again, if Whitman, Cook, and I are right, slang figures in the poetics of human language.

8   When Jakobson speaks of the "demand for poetry" here, he is not concerned with how many people read poetry in magazines or books, or how many copies of those magazines and books sell, but rather with the human need, apparently universal, to speak poetically. If you want to jump rope with your friends, you demand poetry; if you want to tell a sad traditional story in the right mood, you sing a ballad; if you need a clever, prevaricating farewell, you say, "See you later, alligator." The demand for poetry in our everyday lives is much greater than we notice, and slang satisfies part of that demand.

Phonology, the sound system of language, is basic to language and figures in our linguistic competence as Chomsky and other Universal Grammarians understand it. But Jakobson (quoting the linguist Edward Sapir on the poet Gerard Manley Hopkins) points to the " 'spell of the sheer sound of words' which bursts out into the expressive, sorcerous, and mythopoeic tasks of language, and to the utmost extent in poetry . . . endowing the distinctive features themselves with the power of *immediate* signification." It's not easy to understand Jakobson at his clearest, so perhaps this restatement by the Danish linguist Christian Kock will help: "What gives poetry a function in our lives is not its meanings, however ambiguous or otherwise interesting. The function of poetry is crucially dependent on how it makes us foreground sign functions as such. The very experience of unresolvable ambiguity or capriciousness in signification is at the heart of what poetry can do for us." "My bad" is the perfect example of unresolvable ambiguity, and what could signify more capriciously than *edumacation, fuznuck, yee diddly fuckin' haw,* or *How's it goin', protozoan?* All of these are examples of slang casting language's spell. Though not poetry, slang is on the way to poetry and is an important, often overlooked, element of poetics, or the overarching design of language. For more examples, starting with *mongo,* feel free to reread the entire book before continuing to the end.

Joel Sherzer has been thinking along the same lines, implicitly about slang's *razzle-dazzle* or *razzmatazz,* the *hickety pickety* of nursery rhymes, the *Turkey Lurkey* and *Foxy Loxy* of folk tales:

> Since reduplication is a type of patterned repetition, it is, potentially or actually, intimately related to the poetic function of language, which Jakobson and others have defined in terms of patterns or systems of repetition. And the ways in which reduplication moves across the boundaries of the grammatical/referential function of language, and the playful/aesthetic function of language fit quite nicely with Jakobson's very apt conceptualization of the relationship between linguistic structures and the aesthetics of language — "the poetry of grammar and the grammar of poetry."

In other words, when you stop to examine some of the playful elements of language, including slang, you realize that they not only reflect an I-language that must underlie poetry (as it underlies all language), but that poetry (and thus slang) is an element of the grammar embedded in cognition.

Of course, Jakobson, Cook, Sherzer, Whitman, and I could be wrong. For instance, Chomsky might think so. John E. Joseph sketches the relations between Jakobson and Chomsky as follows:

> The mainstream of linguistics in the last four decades of the 20th century has been shaped by the work of Chomsky, who had ties to [Leonard] Bloomfield [the leading American structuralist] through his teacher Zellig Harris, and to Jakobson through personal acquaintance and through his close association with Jakobson's student Morris Halle (b. 1923). It is widely believed that in its concern with "universal" aspects of language, Chomsky's programme is a continuation of Jakobson's; in any case, it had no precedent in neo-Bloomfieldian structuralism.

In spite of this very true history, which brings the two great minds of twentieth-century linguistics into contact, the Chomskyan revolution in linguistics depended very little on Jakobson, as James D. McCawley recognized some thirty years ago. Jakobson initiated his ambitious linguistic program well aware of language pathology, about which he wrote extensively, and he knew that language was cognitively based. Nevertheless, he wrote most of his theory long before we could observe the effects of *Coriolanus* on the brain. For fifty years Chomsky has been drilling further and further into cognition in order to get to the bottom of language; Jakobson spent fifty years and more erecting a vast, articulated, decorated cathedral of language. Chomsky has pared away an already elegant theory into a minimalist program, whereas Jakobson conceived a maximalist one.

It's quite possible to accommodate something like Chomsky's Universal Grammar into language according to Jakobson's design, if you don't worry too much about details that could be worked out later. With regard to slang, here's the fundamental difference between the two models: slang has to find a place in Universal Grammar, and it isn't clear where that would be or, more telling, what would motivate the Universal Grammarian to look for it. Slang as superfluity has a slim chance in a minimalist program, but a good chance if its space is accidentally constructed as language develops its vast cognitive, social, and aesthetic architecture. Universal Grammar feels no need to explain slang, in spite of the fact that it strives for explanatory adequacy, because slang is like paint on the hood of a car and doesn't require explanation: it isn't a significant issue in the language phenomenon, and the Chomskyan method is to sort out what counts and what doesn't and then to arrange a hierarchy of what counts.

As John E. Joseph observes, "Chomsky's avowed aim was to bring linguistics to the level of rigor of physics, at once the most mathematical and most exact of physical sciences." No wonder Chomsky is critical of evolutionary biology's imprecision, or at least applications of evolutionary thinking that wouldn't satisfy a physicist. Interestingly, in its architectural variety and expansive interrelation, something like Jakobsonian structuralism better accommodates slang, while slang contributes to a justification for the maximalist program. One might think of Chomsky as one who saw the blueprint for a cathedral of language and tried to reduce it to as few structural elements as possible, without regard for design or decoration. Jakobson saw the same blueprint and tried to build and decorate the cathedral.

Although slang may be at the third remove from linguistic competence, it is nonetheless implicated, if not in the blueprint, at least in the design. It cannot be understood without considering its relation to every relevant aspect of language, the slight but irreducible area of a spandrel amid the lines and arcs and space of the grand design of language, which is just what I have attempted in this book.

REFERENCES

The experiment with Shakespeare's *Coriolanus* was widely reported on the Web, for instance at www.physorg.com/printnes.php?Newsid=85664210. I quote from Eric Linklater's *A Man over Forty* (London: Macmillan, 1963), 15. "When Nouns Surface as Verbs," Eve V. Clark and Herbert H. Clark's classic article on functional shifting, appeared in *Language* 55.4 (1979): 767–811. Unless otherwise noted, examples of *-age* and *-y* suffixation, as well as many *much* forms, come from the alphabetically organized glossary in my *Slayer Slang: A "Buffy the Vampire Slayer" Lexicon* (New York: Oxford University Press, 2003). The example from *Six Feet Under* is from the episode "The Liar and the Whore" (May 12, 2002), written by Rick Cleveland and directed by Miguel Arteta; Ruth was played by Frances Conroy, Robbie by Joel Brooks. On the OED's concern over out-in-left-fieldy *-y* forms, see Lynda Mugglestone's *Lost for Words: The Hidden History of the Oxford English Dictionary* (New Haven, CT: Yale University Press, 2005), 77–78. Kevin Sullivan reported the earliest known use of ADJECTIVE + *much* in the June 8, 2008, entry of Language and Humor Blog, at http://languageandhumor.com/blog/. The *much* example from *Grey's Anatomy* occurs in the episode "Drowning on Dry Land" (February 15, 2007), written by Shonda Rhimes and directed by Rob Corn; Alex is played by Justin Chambers. *Juno* (2007) was written by Diablo Cody and directed by Jason Reitman; the relevant lines were spoken by Jason

Bateman and Ellen Page. Elle Bishop, played by Kristen Bell, asks her *much* in the episode of *Heroes* titled "Cautionary Tales" (November 19, 2007), written by Joe Pokaski and directed by Greg Yaitanes. *Missbehave*'s Web site is just as cool as the magazine, well worth visiting at www.missbehavemag.com. It's easy to find The Superficial, at www.superficial.com. "Broken record much" comes from the *Buffy the Vampire Slayer* episode "No Place Like Home" (October 24, 2000), written by Doug Petrie and directed by David Solomon; Buffy is played by Sarah Michelle Gellar, Dawn by Michelle Trachtenberg. I refer to William J. Frawley's address "Core Issues in Linguistic Theory: 'Cognitive' and Other Problematic Concepts," presented in the Division on Language Theory's session "Language Theory and the Cognitive Sciences" at the Modern Language Association convention in Washington, DC, December 29, 2005. Steven Pinker's *The Language Instinct: How the Mind Creates Language* (New York: Morrow, 1994) is by now a contemporary classic; I quote it from 25. For the deeply interested, I also recommend Stephen R. Anderson and David W. Lightfoot, *The Language Organ: Linguistics as Cognitive Physiology* (Cambridge, UK: Cambridge University Press, 2002). Of the many critiques of Chomsky registered in *Chomsky and His Critics*, edited by Louise M. Antony and Norbert Hornstein (Malden, MA: Blackwell, 2003), I recommend especially Ruth Garrett Millikan's "In Defense of Public Language," 215–237, and Alison Gopnik's "The Theory Theory as an Alternative to the Innateness Hypothesis," 238–254. Guy Cook's *Language Play, Language Learning* (Oxford: Oxford University Press, 2000), which won the Kenneth J. Mildenberger Prize from the Modern Language Association, is an engaging and insightful book, though, at this point in the chapter, I appear to have quoted it repeatedly only from 12. I quote Joel Sherzer's *Speech Play and Verbal Art* (Austin: University of Texas Press, 2002), 25. I borrow my account of *al vesre* from Jennifer, my wife, who learned about it while flirting with Argentine students in Madrid some years ago; she took careful notes. Then I quote Sherzer again, 27. My account of Prokem is derived largely from an article by Henri Chambert-Loir, "Those Who Speak Prokem," translated by James T. Collins and published in *Indonesia* 37 (1984): 105–117. Alan C. Yu also discusses Prokem some in his recent book, *The Natural History of Infixing* (Oxford: Oxford University Press, 2007); his discussion of Homeric infixing can be found on 174–190, his discussion of infixing as ludling on 190–206, and his appendix of infixing languages on 231–233. The quotation from Arnold M. Zwicky and Geoffrey K. Pullum's "Plain Morphology and Expressive Morphology," in *Berkeley Linguistics Society Proceedings of the Thirteenth Annual Meeting, February 4–16, 1987: General Session and Parasession on*

Grammar and Cognition, edited by Jon Aske, Natasha Beery, Laura Michaelis, and Hana Filip (Berkeley: Berkeley Linguistics Society, 1987), is on 332. After Zwicky and Pullum I quote Chambertin-Loir from 106 of the article cited above. Commentary about the Dozens is quoted from Geneva Smitherman's *Talkin and Testifyin: The Language of Black America* (Detroit: Wayne State University Press, 1977), 131. Back to Chambertin-Loir, in the first instance fusing material on 115 of the previously cited article with a quotation from 117, followed by another quotation from 117. I refer to Mark Peters's stimulating paper "In-diddly-fixing Innovations: The Ned Flanders Effect," presented at the annual meeting of the American Dialect Society, January 5–8, 2006, in Albuquerque, New Mexico. Finally, some more quotation from Guy Cook's excellent book, from 3–4, 5, and 5 again, in series. If I'm not going to quote Whitman on slang again at this point in the book, I'm not going to cite him, either; you'll just have to look for the relevant quotation in previous chapters. I quote George Lakoff and Mark Johnson's classic and very accessible *Metaphors We Live By* (Chicago: University of Chicago Press, 1980), 3–4, refer briefly to their extended discussion of metaphor and coherence on 77–114, and then quote them again, from 236. I quote from Semir Zeki's "Art and the Brain," in *The Brain*, an issue of *Dædalus: Journal of the American Academy of Arts and Sciences* 127.2 (Spring 1998): 99. Harald Weinrich's *The Linguistics of Lying and Other Essays* (Seattle: University of Washington Press, 2005) kicks off with the title essay on 3–80; the four semantic principles are introduced on 15–17. Leslie C. Aiello is quoted from "Foundations of Human Language," in *The Origin and Diversification of Language*, edited by Nina G. Jablonski and Leslie C. Aiello, Memoirs of the California Academy of Sciences 24 (San Francisco: California Academy of Sciences, 1998), 29. I conflate two observations from Jean Aitchison's *The Seeds of Speech* (Cambridge: Cambridge University Press, 1996), 20 and 68. Robin Dunbar's *Grooming, Gossip and the Evolution of Language* (Cambridge, MA: Harvard University Press, 1996) is quoted from 123 (twice) and 78–79. Jean-Louis Dessalles's *Why We Talk: The Evolutionary Origins of Language*, translated by James Grieve (Oxford: Oxford University Press, 2007) is quoted from 351 (in the footnote), 317, 327, 355 twice, 330, 328, and 329, in series. René Descartes' first published work to discuss the virtues of the pineal gland was *Dioptrics* (1637), though the discussion in *Treatise on Man*, published posthumously in 1662, was probably written first. The relevant passages in *Passions of the Soul* are easily located, for instance in *The Essential Descartes*, edited by Margaret D. Wilson (New York: Mentor/New American Library, 1969), 362ff. There are plenty of accessible accounts of language pathology, notably in various works by Oliver Sacks; Pinker discusses those mentioned here in *The Language Instinct*, 307-314, as do Anne Curzan and Michael Adams in *How English Works: A Linguistic Introduction*, 2nd edition (New York: Pearson Longman, 2009), 347-348. My treatment of realism and antirealism is necessarily cursory and oversimplified, but the division between the two orientations to knowledge and truth are significant in the history of ideas. Anyone interested in the topic should start with a classic article by Michael Dummett, "Realism," in his *Truth and Other Enigmas* (Cambridge, MA: Harvard University Press, 1978), 145-165. The intrepid (a degree in philosophy helps) may want to continue with the articles in *Realism and Anti-Realism*, a.k.a. *Midwest Studies in Philosophy XII*, edited by Peter A. French, Theodore E. Uehling, and Howard K. Wettstein (Minneapolis: University of Minnesota Press, 1988). Lighter is quoted from "Slang" in *The Cambridge History of the English Language. Volume 6: English in North America*, edited by John Algeo (Cambridge, UK: Cambridge University Press, 2001), 226. The series of articles on language and evolution mentioned include the following: Marc D. Hauser, Noam Chomsky, and W. Tecumseh Fitch, "The Language Faculty: What Is It, Who Has It, and How Did It Evolve?" *Science* 298 (2002): 1569-1579; Steven Pinker and Ray Jackendoff, "The Faculty of Language: What's Special about It?" *Cognition* 95 (2005): 201-236; W. Tecumseh Fitch, Marc D. Hauser, and Noam Chomsky, "The Evolution of the Language Faculty: Clarifications and Implications," *Cognition* 97 (2005): 179-210; and Ray Jackendoff and Steven Pinker, "The Nature of the Language Faculty and Its Implications for Evolution of Language (Reply of Fitch, Hauser, and Chomsky)," *Cognition* 97 (2005): 211-225. The quotations from Fitch, Hauser, and Chomsky (2005) are from 184, 186, 185, 185, and 185, in series. I led assorted Boy Scouts in the song that briefly interrupts those quotations, week after week, year after year, at Camp Rota-Kiwan, in Kalamazoo, Michigan (1979-1985). I quote Thomas Eisner from "Scales: On the Wings of Butterflies and Moths," *Virginia Quarterly Review* 82.2 (Spring 2006): 79, 80, 81, 84, and 85, in series. I quote Michael Ruse from "Flawed Intelligence, Flawed Design," in the same issue of *VQR*, 71. Christine Kenneally quotes Chomsky in *The First Word: The Search for the Origins of Language* (New York: Viking, 2007), 39. I wholeheartedly recommend Stephen Jay Gould and Richard C. Lewontin, "The Spandrels of San Marco and the Panglossian Paradigm: A Critique of the Adaptationist Programme," in *Proceedings of the Royal Society of London*, Series B 205 (1979): 581-598, to readers interested in — anything. In the chapter's final section we return briefly to Guy Cook's *Language Play, Language Learning* (2000), 17. David Herman is quoted from his introduction to *Narratologies: New Perspectives on Narrative Analysis*, edited by him (Columbus: Ohio State University Press, 1999), 21. John E. Joseph characterizes the Prague school in *From Whitney to Chomsky: Essays in the History of American Linguistics* (Amsterdam: John Benjamins, 2002), 57. Jakobson paraphrased a famous line from Terence, the Roman comic poet who flourished in the first century BCE: in *Heuton Timorumenos* (The Self-Tormentor) Terence wrote, "Homo sum; humani nil a me alienum puto" (1.1.25), for which see series volume 22 in the Loeb Classical Library, edited and translated by John Barnby (Cambridge, MA: Harvard University Press, 2002); Jakobson altered this to "Linguista sum, linguistici nihil a me alienum puto," translating it as I quote in the chapter, for which see "Closing Statement: Linguistics and Poetics," in *Style in Language*, edited by Thomas A. Sebeok (Cambridge, MA: MIT Press, 1960), 377. I illustrate Jakobson's views from a book he wrote with Linda R. Waugh, *The Sound Shape of Language* (1979), in *Roman Jakobson Selected Writings VIII: Completion Volume One: Major Works, 1976–1980*, edited by Stephen Rudy (Berlin: Mouton de Gruyter, 1988), 225, 230, and 234, in series; I hope to clarify them some by quoting Christian Kock, "The Function of Poetry in Our Lives: Roman Jakobson's Legacy and Challenge to Poetics," in *Acta Linguistica Hafniensia* 29 (1997): 316, proceedings of the Roman Jakobson Centennial Symposium, Copenhagen, October 10–12, 1996, edited by Per Aage Brandt and Frans Gregersen, in collaboration with Frederik Stjernfelt and Martin Skov. Joel Sherzer is quoted from *Speech Play and Verbal Art* (2002), 24–25. John E. Joseph's *From Whitney to Chomsky* (2002) is quoted from 61–62. Finally, James D. McCawley noted Jakobson's limited influence on Chomskyan linguistics in "Jakobsonian Ideas in Generative Grammar," in *Roman Jakobson: Echoes of His Scholarship*, edited by Daniel Armstrong and C. H. van Schoonveld (Lisse, the Netherlands: Peter de Ridder Press, 1977), 269–284.

INDEX

Page numbers in italics indicate references within the end-of-chapter "References" sections. Even when it seems awkward, initial articles are omitted from titles, so *Office*, rather than *The Office*, and so on. All meanings of a word (and words with the same spelling) are included under a single entry here, without distinction.

-a-, 123–124
A, 64
Abate, Frank, 50
absatively posilutely, 138
absobloodylutely, 130
absobloominglutely, 128
absofrickinlutely, 131
absofuckinglutely, xii, 68, 120–121, 127, 130, 180
absofuckinglutely not, 138
absogoddamlutely, 130
absolutely, 121, 130, 138
absoly, 138
absonotly, 138, 160, 166
absoschmuckinglutely, 130–133, 136–137, 142, 144, 160
abstraction, 185
Acapulco gold, 39
accipurpodentally, xii, 143–144
ace boon coon, 68, 70, 105
acid, 43

Ackroyd, Dan, 133, 160
acquisition, 89, 175–176, 181–182, 194, 205
Acta Linguistica Hafniensa (journal), 212
Adam, 38, 40, 43
Adam and Eve, 38, 43, 46
Adams, Jennifer Westerhaus, xv, 114–115, 209
adaptation, xiii, 197–202
addressees, 26
adolescence, 85–87, 89–91, 175–176
adolescent peak, 89
adorabable, 126
adorabubble, 126
aesthetic, 111–112, 158
aesthetics, xii, 111–112, 136, 143–145, 151, 153, 155
African American language, xi, 55–78, 151–154
afuckin'way, 131
-age, 79, 108, 166, 208
agreeage, 166

Aiello, Leslie C., 188, 191, 210
air, 22
airwavey, 168
Aitchison, Jean, 188, 210
"Alcohawk" (Allin), 109
Alcott, Louisa May, 69, 78, 80, 108, 159
Algeo, John, 52, 158, 211
-alingus, 148
all, 111
Allen, Keith, 130, 159
Allin, Olivia, 109
alliteration, 46, 118–119, 122, 149
all that, 71
"Alone Again, Natura-diddly" (*Simpsons*), 160
al revés, 176
alternative-fuel vehicle, 3
al vesre, 176–177, 209
amateur diner, 17–18
ambiguity, 185–186
America in So Many Words (Barnhart and Metcalf), 50
American Dialect Society, 142, 161, 210
American Heritage College Dictionary (Pickett and others), 8–9, 13, 50, 111
American Heritage Dictionary of the English Language (Pickett and others), 158
American Idol (television show), 70, 107
American Language (Mencken), 45, 48, 52, 158
"American Lexicology, 1942–1973" (McMillan), 52
American Libraries (journal), 140
American Notes (Dickens), 48
American Pimp (Hughes and Hughes), 87
American Primer (Whitman), 46
Amphitheatre, 28
amuse, 35
amuse-bouche, 2
Analytic Dictionary of English Etymology (Liberman), 7, 50, 123, 159
Andersen, Gisle, 85–86, 108
Anderson, Stephen R., 174, 209
and everything, 86
Angel (*Buffy the Vampire Slayer*), 97–98, 110, 135, 141
Angel (television show), 141, 161
annihilated, xi, 14–15
A. No 1, 80
"Another Effing Euphemism" (Adams), 161
anti-realism, 194
Antony, Louise M., 174, 209

app, 18
appetizer, 18
Apple, Inc., 142–143, 173
"Approaches to Lexicography and Semantics" (Read), 107
Archer, Wesley, 109
Archie (comic), 152
argot, viii, 8, 16
argot, 8, 43
"Argot of the Racetrack" (Maurer), 51
Armstrong, Daniel, 212
Armstrong, Scot, 162
"Army We Have" (Mockenhaupt), 107
"Art and the Brain" (Zeki), 210
Arteta, Miguel, 208
Artful Dodger (*Oliver Twist*), 35–36
Aske, Jon, 160, 210
AskPhil, 20, 51
assure, 56
-as usual-, 141
at, 184
Atlantic Monthly, 107
Attias, David, 160
auctiony, 168
awesome, 186
Ayto, John, 4, 34, 47, 52

ba-a-a-a-d mothafucker, 94
babe, 82, 89
baboon, 117
baby slits, 38
back, 68, 71, 76
back of the house, 19
Backs, 19, 24
backside tweak, 166
backside tweak air, 23
back slang, 37–38, 150, 176–177
bad, 59, 62, 71, 105, 157, 186, 200
Bader, Diedrich, 160
Badigi, Reza, 110
Bad Language (Battistella), 77, 108
bad motherfucker, 94
badmouth, 68
bagpipe, 149
bagpiping, xii, 147–149
bail, 82–84, 95–97
Bailey, Richard W., xiv
bail out, 95–97
bait and switch much, 171
baked, xii, 15, 113

ball, 62
Ballad of Peckham Rye (Spark), 116, 158
ballistics, 69
ballsackian, 147, 149
Balzac, 149
"Band Candy" (*Buffy the Vampire Slayer*), 98, 109
bang, 10
bangin', 59, 83
bapak (Prokem), 177
barf, 15
Barnby, John, 212
Barnhart, Clarence, L., 50
Barnhart, David K., 2–3, 50
Barnhart Dictionary Companion (BDC), 2–3, 50
Barrett, Grant, 4–6, 50
bartendery, 168
Bart Simpson, 38, 41
bash, 120
bash the bishop, 118–119
bat, 120
Batali, Dean, 108, 110
Bateman, Jason, 208
Bates, Karen Grigsby, 51
Battistella, Edwin L., 77, 108
Baugh, John, 75–76, 108
BE, 75
beak, 35
Beals, Jennifer, 179
bean, 38–39
beat the beaver, 118
be bout, 154
Becker, Walt, 162
"Becoming, Part 2" (*Buffy the Vampire Slayer*), 110, 135, 160
bedhead, 3–4, 153
B. E. Gent., 34, 36
Beery, Natasha, 210
bee's, 154
bee's knees, 154
bees, 154
begitu (Prokem), 177
begokit (Prokem), 177
beliefy, 168
Bell, Kristen, 209
Belushi, John, 133
Benjamin, 39
Bennett, Jeff, 51
bennie, 39

Benson, Larry D., 107
bent, xi, 14–15
Benzedrine, 39
Beowulf (poem), 148
bepi (Argentinian *al vesre*), 176
Bermudez, Nancy, 106
Beyond Ebonics (Baugh), 108
bheer, 127
bibitchinitch, 181
biddy, 69
bididdlyig, 180
bifriggingig, 180
bifrigginig, 180
bifuckingitch, 181
binding, 21
Birnbach, Lisa, 55, 106
biscuit, 38–39, 41, 43
bishittinitch, 181
bitch, 126, 180
Bitch (magazine), 142, 161
bitter much, 170
biyatch, 126, 180
biyotch, 126, 180
biz, 154
bizatch, xii, 126
biznatch, 126
biznitch, 126
bizounce, 126
bizzomb, 126
"Black English Semi-Auxiliary *come*" (Spears), 108
Black on Black (Himes), 115
Black Talk (Smitherman), 72, 74, 107, 154
blah, 82–83
blasted, xi, 14–15
blender tender, 16, 41
blending, 136, 164
bling, 56, 64, 94
-*bloody*-, 126, 134–136, 143
Bloomfield, Leonard, 207
bloomin' emag, 37
-*blooming*-, 126, 128
Blount, Roy, Jr., 131, 160
Bloustien, Geraldine, 90
blow, 44
Blowfish, 136, 160
blue balls, 149
Blues Brothers (Landis and Ackroyd), 133, 160
blustery, 166

board, 21, 25
boarder, 21–22
bob, 35
Bob ("Slang Gang"), 57
boho, 83
bokap (Prokem), 177
Bolivian, 39
bolonki (Argentinian al vesre), 176
Bolton, W. F., 52, 159
bomb, 126
bombed, 14–15, 68
bone, 23, 69, 71
bone out, 23
bongo, 1–2
boobs, 83
boog, 69
Book of the Courtier (Castiglione), 156–157
boomin', 154
boon coon, 68
boonmost, 68
booty, 62
booty call, 82
booty juice, 38
booze, xii, 86, 154
Boreanaz, David, 110
Borg (Star Trek), 60–61
born bloody survivor, 134
boss, 120
bossy, 120
Botha, Ted, 5, 50
boujie/bougie, 68
bounce back, 97
bout it, 154
Bowers, Angus, xiv
box, 149
box out dealin', 147
"Boys Want Sex in the Morning" (Uncle Bonsai), 158
bracelet, xi, 31
Bradley, Henry, 45, 52, 115, 158
Brady, 135
Brady, Marcia (Brady Bunch), 136
Brain (special issue of Daedalus), 210
Brandon ("Slay the Critics"), 140–141, 161
Brandt, Per Aage, 212
Brave New Words (Prucher), 127, 159
Brendon, Nicholas, 110
Brest, Martin, 160
brim, 62
bring down, 62

bro, 70
Broca's area, 192–193
broken record much, 169, 171, 195, 209
Bronze (posting board), 140
Bronze: Beta (posting board), 140
Brooks, Joel, 208
brotha, 69
brother, 70, 72, 105
brotisserie, 147–148
Brown, James, 133
Brown, Lyn Mikel, 90, 109
Brown, Tina, 142
brumsky, 147–148
BTW, 172
bubble, 27
bubble and squeak, 37
bubble economy, 2
Bucholtz, Mary, 88, 106, 109
buddy, 69
buenos ding dong diddly dias, 125
buff, 83
Buffdom, 167
Buffkin, 167
Buffy, 140
Buffy-comic, 140
Buffy-comicverse, 140–142, 161
Buffyness, 167
Buffy-pencil, 140
Buffy the Vampire Slayer, vii, xii, 79–80, 95–103, 108–110, 128, 135, 140–142, 159, 166–167, 169, 171, 185–186, 209
Buffy the Vampire Slayer #43 (comic), 161
Buffyverse, 140–141, 161
bug, 63, 69
bumped, 30
Burridge, Kate, 130, 159
busser, 19
busting out, 68
butt, 83
Butters, Ronald R., xiv, 11, 50
buzz, 154
by-pass smalls, 26

Cabellerial, 24
Caballero, Steve, 24
caj, 10
Calendar, Jenny (Buffy the Vampire Slayer), 97–98, 110
Californian, 38–39
-cama-, 122

Cameron Crazie, xi, 30
campaigny, 168
camper, 18
Camping Crazie, 31
Camp Rota-Kiwan, 115, 211
Camp Snoopy, 131
"Camp Snoopy" (Peppermint Pat Eye), 160
candy flip, 38
cannot, 103
cant, viii, 8
Canterbury Tales (Chaucer), 71
Cantonese slang, 85
Carell, Steve, 58, 106
Carpenter, Charisma, 110
Carpenter, Jeannine, xiv
carpetmuncher, 111
Carter, Philip, xiv
carving, 21
"Casino Night" (*Office*), 58, 106
Cassell's Dictionary of Slang (Green), ix, 3,
    10–11, 47, 84, 114, 149–150, 158
Castellaneta, Dan, 109
Castiglione, Baldassare, 156–157
casual, 10
cat, 70, 72, 185
catching air, 21
cathedral, 28
"Cautionary Tales" (*Heroes*), 209
cazh, 10, 19, 24
Cecil, 39
celeb, 83
center slang, 37–38
CFO, 26
Chabert, Lacey, 109, 160
Chadwick, Alex, 51
Chalke, Sarah, 107
Chambers, Justin, 208
Chambert-Loir, Henri, 178–179, 209–210
changes, 62
chap, 86
Chapman, Robert L., 47, 63–64, 106
Chappelle, Dave, 94
characteristics of slang, 9–13, 32–34
Charlie, 39
Charnes, Linda, xiv
Chase, Cordelia (*Buffy the Vampire Slayer*),
    96, 99–102, 110
chat room, 2
Chaucer, Geoffrey, 8, 71, 107
chefy, 168–169

cherryoke, 147–148, 164
chiche, 66
chick, 89
chicken salad, 23–24
chill, 10, 25, 89, 97, 101, 157, 186, 195
chillax, 10
chillin'/chilling, 10, 44, 154
chill out, 10, 97, 195
China white, 38, 42
chinch, 65–67
chinche (Spanish), 66
chinchy, 65–67, 105
chintz, 66
chintzy, 66
chocolate chip cookies, 38
chocolate chips, 38
Chomsky, Noam, 174–175, 193–194, 197–199,
    201, 204, 206–208, 209, 211
Chomsky and His Critics (Antony and
    Hornstein), 174, 209
chrome labia, 147, 149, 164, 200
clarity, 38, 41, 43
Clark, Eve V., 164, 208
Clark, Herbert H., 164, 208
Clement, Nic, 115
Cleveland, Rick, 208
-clickin'-, 143
climby-thing, 168
Clinton, Hillary, 142
clipped phrasal verbs, 95–103
clitorically speaking, 147
"Closing Statement" (Jakobson), 212
cloud nine, 38
Coach K., 30
cocaine, 39, 170
cocaine much, 170
cock, 157
cock-a-doodle-do, 127
"Cock a doodle doo!" 124
cock holster, 147–148, 157
Cockney, 36
co-dependent, 167
co-dependenty, 167, 187
code-shifting, 55–60, 75–77
Cody, Diablo, 208
cognition, xii–xiii, 163–165, 174–175, 190,
    198–199
Cognition (journal), 197, 211
Cogshall, Libby, xiv
coin-slot, 84

coke biscuit, 38
coke burger, 38
Colbert Report, 143, 161
Colbert, Stephen, 143, 161
cold, 56, 71, 76, 105
Coleman, Julie, ix, xiv, 8, 50, 52
Collected Poems of Wallace Stevens, 161
Collectors Club of Chicago, 20
Collins, James T., 209
come, 76, 107
Come and leap, leopard, 116
Come and wriggle, snake, 116
Comedy Central, 161
come out, 167, 187
come out of the closet, 187
-comic-, 140
comicverse, 140
commit, 120
commoner, xi, 28
communities of practice, 105
compensate, 120
Complete Poems and Plays 1909–1950 (Eliot),
    49, 158
Complete Snowboarder (Bennett and
    Downey), 51
Congo, 1–2
Connection (National Public Radio), 5, 50
Conroy, Frances, 208
consider, 120
Continental Airlines, 142
Contner, James A., 110, 161
control freak much, 171
Cook, Guy, 175, 182–183, 194, 204–205, 207,
    209–211
cool, 58–59, 157, 186–187, 200
cop, 91
coping, 23
copulate, 10
Cordettes (*Buffy the Vampire Slayer*),
    99–100
"Core Issues in Linguistic Theory"
    (Frawley), 209
Coriolanus (Shakespeare), 163–164,
    207, 208
Coriolanus, Caius Marcius, 163
Corn, Rob, 208
Corpus of London Teenage Language
    (COLT), 85–88
Costley, Eleanor, 93
Cotton, John Hamden, 36, 52

Couric, Katie, 142
cove, 35
cover, 18
covey, 35
co-y, 167, 187
Coyote, Wile E., 195
crack, 80
Cranch, W. T., 151
crayon-breaky, 167
Crazie Talk, 31
creep, 97
creep out, 97
crib, 154
Crowe, Cameron, 107
crow's feet, 38, 42
Cruel Intentions (Kumble), 134–136, 160
cruisin' for a bruisin', 114
crunk, 56
Crystal, David, 52, 159
Cukor, George, 160
cummings, e. e., 129, 139, 142
cunt, 86
cunt cuddling, 118
curb much, 171, 187, 195
Current Trends in Linguistics (Sebeok), 107
Curzan, Anne, xiv, 50, 211
custard, 44
custard cream, 44

da bomb, 56
Daedalus (journal), 210
dago, 79
Dalzell, Tom, ix, xiv, 10, 32, 34, 47, 49, 51–53,
    114, 158–159
Dana, Richard Henry, 48, 53
dance nazi, 104
dandelion, 123
D'Andrea, Kristy, xiv
Danesi, Marcel, 89, 109
Daniele, Chris, 25, 51
D'Arcy, Alexandra, 13, 51
Dark Horse Comics, 140
David and Lisa (Perry, F.), 118, 159
Davis, Philip, 163
dawg, 70
Dawkins, Jack (*Oliver Twist*), 35–36, 52
Dawkins, Richard, 191
Day to Day (National Public Radio), 11, 51
D. Bone ("Slang Gang"), 57
-de-, 123, 159

de (French), 123
deal, 82–83, 102–103
Dean, James, 179
decadence, 38
deception, 188
"Deconstructing the Tindy" (Daniele), 51
dediddlyighted, 125
definitions of slang, vii-viii, xiii, 7–8, 203
degerredation, 122
déjà vu much, 171
delle (German), 104
Delpit, Lisa, 108
democra(caveat emptor)cy, 129, 139
De Niro, Robert, 134
Dennis the Menace, x, 38, 41–42
dent de lion, 123
Dent, Susie, 84, 108, 145, 150, 161
Descartes, René, 192, 210
Des Hotel, Rob, 108, 110
Dessalles, Jean-Louis, 189–192, 210
deuce, 18
Dexedrine, 38, 42
diacope, 130, 132, 139, 142, 148
dialect, 29
Dialects and American English (Wolfram), 108
diamond, 38, 148
diamond turd cutter, 147–148, 156
dick, 131
Dickens, Charles, 35, 48
dictionaries of slang, ix, 47
Dictionary of Afro-American Slang (Major), 106
Dictionary of American Slang (Chapman), 47
Dictionary of American Slang (Wentworth and Flexner), 47
Dictionary of Australian Underworld Slang (Simes), 47
Dictionary of Slang and Unconventional English (Partridge), 47
Dictionary of the Underworld (Partridge), 47
"Diddlety, diddlety, dumpty," 124
-diddly-, 125, 179–181
dididdlyemma, 125
dig it? 93
dilemma, 125
Dinin, Aaron, 52
dinkin flicka, 58
Dioptrics (Descartes)
disafuckin'pear, 130
disco biscuit, 38
Disney, 180

dispar, 28
disparity, 28
disper, xi, 28
dispertio (Latin), 28
dissed, 56
div, 28
division, 28
Division on Language Theory (Modern Language Association), 209
Dixie Chicks, 128
"Dixie Chicks" (Lynskey), 159
doctor, 38
doing laundry, 147
do it, 10
-dom, 167
domex, 38
donkey dick, 10
Don't be silly, tiger lily, 118
Don't make me laugh, you big giraffe, 116–117
Don't rock the boat, you billy goat, 116
Doolittle, Eliza (*My Fair Lady*), 130, 160
"Doomed" (*Buffy the Vampire Slayer*), 141, 161
dope, 56
dork, 131
double cherry drop, 38
double eye blinky, 147–148
double stacks, 38
double stack white Mitsubishi, 38, 42
dove, 38, 42
down, 157
Downey, Scott, 51
down low, 25, 186
down with, 154
D'Oyly, 37
D'Oyly Carte, 37
Dozens, 178–179, 210
dramatic much, 170
driver, 38
"Drowning on Dry Land" (*Grey's Anatomy*), 208
drunk, 13
drunky, 92
DSL, 2
Duchess of Fife, 37
duck, 113
dude, 70, 72–73, 89, 91, 105, 200
"Dude" (Kiesling), 107
Dude, Where's My Car? (Leiner and Stark), 107
Duke University, xiv, 30

Duke University jargon (or slang), 30–31
Dumas, Bethany K., ix, 47–48, 52
Dummett, Michael, 211
dump, 83
Dunbar, Robin, 189–191, 210
dysphemism, 130–132

e-, 41
E, 38, 41
e-anticiparcellation, 143
e-appreparcelhensive, 143
East and West, 38
e-ball, 38
Eble, Connie C., ix, xiv, 4, 11, 16, 46, 50–52,
    63, 106, 112, 114, 158, 161
e-bomb, 38
Ebonics controversy, 76–77
echo, 38–39
eck, 39
ecker, 38
Eckert, Penelope, 73, 105, 107, 110
ecky, 38–39
ecstasy, 38–40, 43
ecstasy slang, 38–44
-ed, 120
edge awareness, 23
Edlund, Ben, 161
education, 121
edumacation, 120–121, 166, 206
Edward, 38–39
Edwards, Lisa, 106
effective edge, 22
-effing-, 131
egghead, 47
Egyptian, 38
eh, 87
eighty-sixed, 37–38
Eisner, Thomas, 200, 211
Elaine, 38–39
E-language, 193, 196
El Cid, 43
Eliot, T. S., 1, 31, 36, 49, 118, 158, 185
Ellington, Duke, 152
embalming fluid, 42
Embleton, Sheila, 52
Emerson, Ralph Waldo, 45, 52, 151
Emmons, Ron, 77
Encarta World English Dictionary
    (Soukhanov, Rooney, and others), 7,
    9, 13, 50

English in North America (Algeo), 46, 52,
    158, 211
English Journal, 52, 158
English Language (Bolton and Crystal), 52, 159
Entertainment Weekly, 140
ephemerality, x, 14–16, 40, 64, 158
-er, 120
erecstasy, 38–39
Eric B., 146–150
escarole, 113
Espenson, Jane, 109, 161
essence, 38
Essential Descartes (Wilson), 210
Essential Uncle Bonsai (Uncle Bonsai), 158
-est, 120
Estonian, 178
-et-, 124–125
et Botoxed cetera, 142
euphemism, 118–119, 128–132, 134–135,
    137–138, 140
Euphemism and Dysphemism (Allen and
    Burridge), 160
euphemistic dysphemism, 130, 132
euphoria, 38
eva, 38
Eve (*Paradise Lost*), 43
Eve, 38, 43
evolution, xiii, 188–192, 195–201, 208
"Evolution of the Language Faculty" (Fitch,
    Hauser, and Chomsky), 211
ex, 41
excellent, 186, 195
exiticity, 38
expediter, 19, 26
expletives, 128–143, 180–181
expressive morphology, 178–181
extreme, 82

fabflippintastic, 129
fabulous, 129
faced, 14, 39
"Faculty of Language" (Hauser, Chomsky,
    and Fitch), 197–199
fag, 86
fair warning, 20
Faith (*Buffy the Vampire Slayer*), 102, 110
"Faith, Hope, and Trick" (*Buffy the Vampire
    Slayer*), 110
faithy, 168
fake tan much, 170

fakie, 23, 166
fanbloodytastic, 128
Fanboys and Overdogs (Dent), 84, 108, 145, 161
fanfuckingtastic, 120, 130
fantasia, 38
fantastic, 129
FAQ, 172
Farmer, John Stephen, 47
"Farmer went trotting," 124
far out, 186
fart, 148
fashionista, 2
fast in, 38
Fast Times at Ridgemont High (Heckerling and Crowe), 73, 107
Feeling frail, nightingale? 116
fella, 82
Female Chauvinist Pigs (Levy), 146, 162
femur, 117
fetch, 95, 138
Fey, Tina, 109, 160
fido dido, 38, 42
figmajig, 123, 159
fig my jig, 123
Filip, Hana, 210
fine example of maturity to the pupils of Sunnydale High much, 171
Fine-Very Fine, 20, 24
finger fun, 118
fingery, 168
First Word (Kenneally), 201, 211
fishies, 38
Fitch, W. Tecumseh, 197–199, 211
fix, 120
fixin to, 68
Flaherty, Erin, 82, 108
Flanders, Ned (*Simpsons*), 125, 138, 160
Flashdance, 179
"Flawed Intelligence, Flawed Design" (Ruse), 201, 211
fleece it out, 58
Flexner, Stuart Berg, 47
-flippin-, 129
flipping, 129
flipping out, 129
flirt buddy, 81–82, 84
"Flirt Buddy vs. a Friend with Benefits" (Flaherty), 108
flit your clit, 119
floor, 24

flower flipping, 38
fly, 55
Flying Squad, 118
folk etymology, 11, 13, 67, 132
food, 166
foodage, 79, 166
-for-, 143
-forall, 143
Forever Young (Danesi), 89, 109
fork out, 35
Forrester, Brent, 109
"Foundations of Human Language" (Aiello), 210
four-lettery, 169, 185
Fourteenth LACUS Forum 1987 (Embleton), 52
four-top, 18–19
Foxy-Loxy, 206
Franken-, 3–4
Frankenfood, 3
Frankenfruit, 3–4
Frankenstein, 3
Frawley, William J., 173, 185, 209
freak, 95, 97
-freaking-, 126, 131
freak out, 79, 95, 97–98, 101
-free-, 143
free for all, 143
freestyle, 23
freestyler, 21
freestyling, 24
fresh, 68
freshfish, 24
-frickin'-, 129
fried, 113
friend, 69
Friends (television show), 103
friend with benefits, 81
-frigging-, 131
frisk, 47
From Whitney to Chomsky (Joseph), 212
front, 17, 19
frontside, 23
frontside edge, 25
fry, 42
fubar, xi, 14–15, 89
fuck, 111, 126, 129–130, 180
fuck buddy, 82–83
fucked up, 14–15
fuckin'-A, 134, 136, 143

-*fucking*-, 121, 126, 128, 130–132, 135, 137, 142, 180–181
fucking, 129–131, 135–136
fuddy, 137
fudiddlyuck, 181
fufuckinguck, 180–181
fufuckinuck, 181
-*fugging*-, 131
Fulk, Rob, xiv
"Function of Poetry in Our Lives" (Kock), 212
functional shifts, 150, 163–164, 173
fundage, 79, 166
funds, 166
Fung, Victor, 106
fungi, 137
funky, 62, 137
funny, 137
Fury, David, 160–161
fussy, 137
Futrell, Allan W., 51
fuznuck, 126, 180, 206
fuzzy, 137
F-Word (Sheidlower), 130, 134, 160

G & T, 39
Gable, Ashley, 109–110
gacked, 15
gaggler, 38
gag me with a spoon, 105
Gallo, George, 160
gallop the antelope, 119
game, 186
Gaston, Thomas E., 46, 52
Gay, 187
Geez, 154
Gellar, Sarah Michelle, 110, 160, 209
gender, xi, 78–88, 149
"Gendered Aspects of Lexicographic Labeling" (Martin), 108
Generative Grammar, 174
gent, 82–83
Gergersen, Frans, 212
Gershman, Michael E., 109
get down, 62, 82
get it on, 10
get over, 64
Ghod, 127
ghood, 127
Gilbert, W. S., 37

Giles, Rupert (*Buffy the Vampire Slayer*), 96–98, 110, 141–142, 161
ginger, 37
ginger pop, 36–7
girl, 71
Girl Making (Bloustien), 109
Girls Gone Wild, 145, 149
Gizzoogle.com, 126
Glorificus (*Buffy the Vampire Slayer*), 128, 160
glum, 79
go, 38, 43, 86
Go! (Liman), 43
gobbledegook, 123
going bananas, 147
Goldberg, Brent, 162
gone, 14
gone Borneo, 14–15
Goodfellas (Scorsese), 40
Good Housekeeping (magazine), 142
goofy, 23
goofy-foot, 23
Google user groups, 169
Gopnik, Alison, 209
Gordon, Dick, 5
gossip, 189–191, 201, 204
Got a pain, panda? 116
Gould, Stephen Jay, 201–202, 211
grab, 25
grabbing, 21
Graduate, 179
Graham, Heather, 107
Grant, Elizabeth, 80–81, 85, 108
green, 35
Green, Bruce Seth, 109–110
"Green Grass Grew All Around," 198
Green, Jonathon, xiv, 10, 47, 84, 145, 150, 158, 161
Greenwalt, David, 109–110
Gretchen (*Mean Girls*), 95, 109, 138, 153, 160
Grey's Anatomy (television show), 170, 208
Grieve, James, 210
Grieve, Michael, 161
Grimes, Drew, xiv
grip the gorilla, 118
groin grabbingly good, 147, 149
Grooming, Gossip, and the Evolution of Language (Dunbar), 189, 210
grope the grotto, 118

group identity, xi, 41, 55–61, 67–68, 70–71,
    73–75, 83–85, 89–91, 95, 99–100,
    104–106, 111
grow up, 97
grub, 86
grubbage, 79
guaranclickin'teed, xii, 142, 166
guaranfuckingtee, 120, 128, 130
gum, 38–39, 41
Gutman, Bill, 51
guy, 72
gymcrockery, 167

-*h*-, 127, 159
H., 132
hack it, 25
hairy clam, 10
half-cab, 24
half-pipe, 21–23
half-yapping-hour, 142
Halle, Morris, 207
ham-hock, 150
ham hocked, 147
hammered, 14–15
hammered down, x, 20
Handlist of Rhetorical Terms (Lanham),
    139, 161
hang, 10, 17, 95, 97, 100, 102–103
hanging, 44, 154
hang out, 10, 82–84, 95, 97, 100–101, 103
Hannigan, Alyson, 110
happy, 79
happy drug, 38
happy pill, 38
Hardison, O. B., 161
Harold, 133
Harris, Xander, 81, 96–97, 99, 101, 110, 141
Harris, Zelig, 207
Harry Hill, 38, 40, 44
Hasund, Ingrid Kristine, 85–86, 108
Hauser, Marc D., 197–199, 211
have a nice diddly fucking day, 180
have sex, 10
Hayakawa, S. I., 45, 52
HBO, 167
H bomb, 38
Head, Anthony Stewart, 110, 161
"Hearing Lips and Seeing Voices" (McGurk
    and McDonald), 109
Heathers (Lehmann and Waters), 133, 160, 169

heaven sent, 38
Heckerling, Amy, 107
heist, 47
hella, xii, 56, 106
"Hella Nor Cal or Totally So Cal" (Bucholtz
    and others), 106
Hello! 114
helm of the bobsled, 147
Henley, William Ernest, 47
Henry, 133
Henry Hill, 44
Henry, Scott, 70, 107
hep, ix, 152–153
Hepburn, Audrey, 160
hepi (Wolof), ix, 151
hep, hep, hep, ix
Herman, David, 204, 211
"Her Story" (*Scrubs*), 73, 107
herbal bliss, 38
Heroes (television show), 170, 209
Heuton Timorumenos (Terence), 212
hickety pickety, 124, 206
"Hickety, pickety, my black hen," 124
hicky, 124
hi diddly fucking ho, 125, 180
highbacks, 21, 26
Hilliard, Sarah, xiv
Himes, Chester, 115
Hip, ix, xii, 146, 148, 150–156
hip, ix, xii, 58, 146, 151–153
Hip: The History (Leland), 150–153, 162
Historical Dictionary of American Slang
    (*HDAS*) (Lighter), ix, 3–5, 12, 40, 47,
    49, 63, 71–72, 106, 114–115, 130–131,
    134, 158
History of Cant and Slang Dictionaries
    (Coleman), ix, 8, 50–52
History of Two Orphans (Toldervy), 48
hit, 38
hizo, 126
hizouse, 126–127
hnøggr (Old Norse), 67
ho, 126
Hob, 123
Hobbard, 123
Hobbard de Hoy, 123
hobbledehoy, 123, 159
ho diddly fucking hum, 125
Hoffman, Dustin, 179
"H. of *Jesus* H. *Christ*" (Smith), 132, 160

Ho Ho, 73
hoho plant backside, 23–24
holster, 157
homeboys, 75
Homeric, 177
Homeric infixing, 177, 179, 209
"Homerpalooza" (*Simpsons*), 109
Hominum (Latin), 132
hook up, 25, 82, 84, 89
Hopkins, Gerard Manly, 129, 142, 206
horizontalize, 10
Hornstein, Norbert, 174, 209
hot, 59, 82–83, 186
hotted, 28
House, 28
Howard, David, 67, 107
How are you? 114
How English Works (Curzan and Adams), 50, 210
How's it goin', protozoan? xii, 115, 117, 119, 155, 176, 192, 206
hug drug, 38
Hughes, Albert, 87
Hughes, Allen, 87
Hughes, Griffith, 66
hung, 111
hung like a cashew, 10
hurl, 15
Hurston, Zora Neale, 71, 107
"Hush-a-bye, baby," 123
Hutchison, Earl Ofari, 77
hydro, 38

iboga, 38
ice, 38
identity politics, 2
Iesus Hominum Salvator, 132
ietqui, 38
IHC, 132
IHS, 132
IHS (Greek), 132
I-language, 175, 193–196, 198, 204–206
ill, 186
illocutionary acts, 187–188
IMHO, 172
impletives, 141–143
imported pros, 25
I'm sorry, 188
in, 184

In a while, crocodile, 114
"In Defense of Public Language" (Millikin), 209
Indiana University, xiv
"In-diddly-fixing Innovations" (Peters), 159, 210
indirection, xiii, 183–193, 195, 201–203
Indonesia (journal), 209
Indonesian, 178
Indonesian slang, 177–179
indy, 23
indy grab, 25
inebriated, 13
infixing and interposing, xii, 120–144, 164, 166, 172–173, 177–178, 179–181
"Infixing and Interposing in English" (McMillan), 159
"Infixing and Interposing in English: A New Direction" (Adams), 161
-ing, 120, 178
initialism, 172–173
innit, 86–87
Intelligent Design Theory (IDT), 201
intelphakenlectual, 143
intensifiers, 126, 128–131, 133–137, 139, 141
interexplijective, 143
interracial conversation, 58
in the moon, 80
in the weeds, 18, 41, 185
intoxicated, 13
inversion, 138
invert, 23
Inwood, John, 107
"I'on Know Why They Be Trippin'" (Perry), 108
ironworky, 167
irony, 155
irremededially, 122–123, 166
"I Robot, You Jane" (*Buffy the Vampire Slayer*), 109
is, 75
"Is It Wrong to Date the Guy You Used to Babysit" (Marrian), 108
"Is *Slang* a Term for Linguists?" (Dumas and Lighter), ix, 52
it ain no thang, 154
itch the ditch, 119
iTunes, 142
I wanna bite that chick's ass, 147
-iz-, 82, 126, 159

-izn-, 82, 126, 180
-izzle, 126, 153, *159*
-izzy, 82

Jablonski, Nina G., *210*
jack diddly fucking shit, 125
Jackendoff, Ray, 197, 199, 201, *211*
Jackson, Randy, 70, *107*
Jakobson, Roman, 204–208, *212*
"Jakobsonian Ideas in Generative
    Grammar" (McCawley), *212*
jammed, 14–15, 186
Jane (magazine), 81, 83–86, 88–89, 91–92,
    98, *108*
jargon, viii, 8–9, 182
jargon, vii, x, 4–6, 8, 16–31
Jawbreaker (Stein), 136–137, *160*, 169
Jeepney, 92
"Jeepney Clothing" (Moeller), *109*
Jennyanydots (*Old Possum's Book of
    Practical Cats*), 31, 185
jerk the gherkin, 119
jerk your jewels, 118
Jesus, 132
Jesus Christ, 132–133
Jesus Harold Christ, 132
Jesus H. Christ, 132–134
Jesus Hebe Christ, 133
Jesus Hebrew Christ, 132
Jesus Henry Christ, 132
Jesus Holy Christ, 133
Jesus H. Particular Christ, 132
Jesus H. tap-dancing Christ, 133, 141
Jesusy, 168–169
Jewell, Elizabeth J., *50*
Joe Blow, 63
jog-trotty, 167
John Kembled, 80
Johnson, Mark, 184, *210*
joint, 82, 84
Jonah's Gourd Vine (Hurston), 71, *107*
Jones, Orlando, 57
Joseph, John E., 204, 207, *212*
Journal of English Linguistics, vii
Journals (Emerson), 45
journaly, 168
Juba to Jive (Major), 47, 64, 68, 72–73,
    106, 151
Judge, Mike, *160*
Juilliard School, 77

Juno (Reitman and Cody), 170, *208*
"Just Rewards" (*Angel*), 141, *161*

kasj, 10
Katz, Elihu, 99, *110*
K capsule, 38
Keats, George, 155
Keats, John, 155, *162*
Keats, Tom, 155
Kendall, Tyler, xiv
Kenneally, Christine, 201, *211*
Kennedy, Randall, 67, *107*
ken miller, 35
kennings, 148, 157
kew, 37
keys, 154
Keyser Soze, 81
kick, 22
Kiesling, Scott F., 73, *107*
killer, 186
killing, 79
kilombo (Spanish), 176
-kin, 167
"Kind of Poetry I Want" (McDiarmid), 145, *161*
King, Ty, *109*
Kiwanis, 115
Kleenex, 38–39, 41, 43
KM, 19
knees, 154
Knock Knock flash cards, 55–57, 59–61,
    115, *182*
know what I'm sayin', 87
Kock, Christian, 206, *212*
Kramer, Clare, *160*
Krebs, John, 191
Krzyzewski, Mike, 30
Krzyzewskiville, 30
Krzyzewskiville Tales (Dinin), *51*
Kuhn, Sherman M., *106*
Kumble, Roger, *160*
Kurath, Hans, *106*
Kutcher, Ashton, *107*
Kwapis, Ken, *106*

-l-, 120, 178
Labov, Teresa, 67, *107*
Labov, William, 6, *50*, 77, 89, 99, 104–105,
    107, *109*–110, 173, 200
Lakoff, George, 184, *210*
"L'Allegro" (Milton), 82

Lamarr, Phil, 57
lame, 25
LaMorte, Robia, 110
Landis, James, 133, 160
Lange, Michael, 109
language, 174–176
Language and Lore of Schoolchildren (Opie), 158
Language and Social Networks (Milroy), 110
"Language and Youth Culture" (Bucholtz), 109
"Language Faculty" (Hauser, Chomsky, and Fitch), 211
"Language Faculty" (Pinker and Jackendoff), 211
Language in Action (Hayakawa), 45
Language Instinct (Pinker), 174–175, 210
language instinct, 174
Language of the Underworld (Maurer), ix, 51
language organ, 174, 193
Language Organ (Anderson and Lightfoot), 174, 209
language play, xii–xiii, 111, 114–116, 125–127, 136, 138, 143–144, 174–183, 201–204
Language Play and Language Learning (Cook), 175, 182, 204, 209–211
Lanham, Richard, A., 139, 161
Larsen, Melissa, 25, 51
latch on to, 63
Law of the Excluded Middle, 194
Lazarsfeld, Paul, 99, 110
le (French), 123
Lee, Spike, 64
legless, 14–15
Lehmann, Michael, 160
Leicester bloody Square, 135, 164
Leicester Square, 135
Leist, Mia, 149
Leland, John, 150–152, 156, 162
lemon and lime, 44
lemon and limes, 38, 44
lemur, 117
l'envers (French), 177
Lerner, Alan Jay, 130, 160
Letters of John Keats, 162
lettuce, 113
Levine, Ellen, 142
Levy, Ariel, 146, 149, 162
Lewis, Robert E., 106
Lewontin, Richard C., 201–202, 211

Lexicon of Trade English, 4
lexifabricography, xii, 144, 155
"Liar and the Whore" (*Six Feet Under*), 208
Liberman, Anatoly, 7, 50, 123, 159
"Lie to Me" (*Buffy the Vampire Slayer*), 109
Lighter, Jonathan (J. E.), ix, 3, 34, 46–49, 52–53, 63, 71–72, 106, 112, 117, 130, 145, 149, 152–153, 155, 158, 162, 196, 211
Lightfoot, David W., 174, 209
like, 13, 105, 111, 187
"*Like* and Language Ideology" (D'Arcy), 51
Liman, Doug, 43
linguistic competence, 174–176, 181, 204–205, 208
Linguistic Variation as Social Practice (Eckert), 107, 110
Linguistics of Lying (Weinrich), 210
Linklater, Eric, 122, 159, 163, 208
lit, 14
little fella, 38
Little Mary Sunshine, 136
Little Women (Alcott), 69, 78–80, 108, 122, 159
lit up, 14
Livingston, Ron, 160
L. L. Bean, 55
loaded, xi, 14–15
Loaded (magazine), 159
loads of, 86
lob, 150
lobbin', 147–148, 150, 154
lochrity, 104
LOL, 172
lo-lo, 73
London Labour and the London Poor (Mayhew), 36, 52
London slang, 34–38, 85–87
Longo, 1–2
loony, 89
Lost for Words (Mugglestone), 208
love doctor, 38
love drug, 38
Love Potion #9, 38
lover's speed, 38
"Love Song of J. Alfred Prufrock" (Eliot), 118, 158
love trip, 38
lowdown, 186
Lowe, Frederick, 130, 160
LSD, 43
Lucky Charmz, x, 38

lud-, 178
ludlings, 178–179, 209
ludlings, 178
ludus (Latin), 178
Lunkers, 55
-lute-, 138
lying, xiii, 188–193
Lynskey, Dorian, 159

M & M, 38–39, 43
M25, 38
-ma-, 121–123
macamadamia, 122–123
macaroni, 62
Macavity, the Mystery Cat (*Old Possum's Book of Practical Cats*), 36, 50, 185
Mach 5, 58
mack, xii, 64
mack daddy, 62–63
mackerel, 62
mack on, 89
mad, 56
mad bastard, 38
madman, 38
Mad TV (television show), 57, 106
madwoman, 38
magaziney, 168
mage, 82
mage double whammy, 82
Magnus Merriman (Linklater), 122, 159
magpie, 35
"Mags Shift from Laddies to Ladies" (Sass), 91, 109
Mailer, Norman, 152
Maines, Natalie, 159
maj, 82
major, 82
Major, Clarence, 47, 64–65, 68, 72–73, 106
make out, 89
Making of McPaper (Prichard), 160
main squeeze, 89
Malcolm X, 38
malfunctiony, 168
Mallinson, Christine, xiv
Mambuca, Dr. ("Slang Gang"), 57, 65, 71, 153
man, 70–71, 200
man alive! 72
Manchester Guardian Weekly, 4
mandruff, 147–148
mango, 1

man, oh man! 72
Man over Forty (Linklater), 163, 208
maple bar, xii, 147–148
maquerel (French), 62
March, Amy (*Little Women*), 69, 78–79, 107, 122, 159
March, Jo (*Little Women*), 78–79
March, Meg (*Little Women*), 79, 97, 122
Marcia, 135
Marcia fucking Brady, 135–136, 137, 163
markety, 168
Marrian, Anna, 83–84, 108
Marsters, James, 160–161
Martin, Katherine Connor, xiv, 78, 108, 119
Mary Jane, 39
Masters, Alexander, 142, 161
Master Standard Data (MSD), 26, 28
masturbation, 119
"Matrix of Motives in Slayer Style" (Adams) 110
Maurer, David W., ix, 12, 51
Maxtone-Graham, Ian, 160
Mayhew, Henry, 36, 52
McAdams, Rachel, 109, 160
McArthur, Tom, 51
McCawley, James D., 207, 212
McDiarmid, Hugh, 145, 161
McDonald, John, 87, 109
McGowan, Rose, 137, 160, 170
McGurk Effect, 87
McGurk, Harry, 87, 109
McKean, Erin, xiv, 50, 158
McMillan, James B., 47–48, 52, 127–129, 131, 134–135, 138, 143, 159
McMillan's Rule, 128–129, 134, 137, 142
MDMA, 39, 43–44
Mean Girls (Waters and Fey), 95, 109, 138, 160
"Meaningful Infixing: A Nonexpletive Form" (Adams), 161
"Meaningful Interposing: A Countervalent Form" (Adams), 161
"Meaningful Interposing: An Accidental Form" (Adams), 161
Meaning of Life (Monty Python), 42
Media Daily News, 109
megadump, 3–4
Meiklejohn (*Magnus Merriman*), 122
melancholy, 23–24
Memoirs of a Highland Lady (Grant), 80, 108

Mencken, H. L., 45, 48, 52, 116, 158
-ment, 120
Merriam-Webster Collegiate Dictionary
    (Mish and others), 8, 13, 48, 50, 117, 136
messed up, 14–15, 38
metabolism, 122
metabomalism, 122, 127
metafreephorall, 143, 161
metaphor, 43–44, 46, 112, 119, 125, 148, 157,
    183–186, 193
metaphor, 187
Metaphors We Live By (Lakoff and Johnson),
    184, 210
metaphory, 169, 187
Metcalf, Allan, 2–3, 50
Michaelis, Laura, 210
Microsoft, Inc., 143
Microsoft Word, 173
Middle English Dictionary, 106
Midnight Run (Brest and Gallo), 134, 160
Mike, 58
Miller, Kathleen E., 159
Miller, Kenneth, 201
Millikin, Ruth Garrett, 209
Milroy, Lesley, 105, 110
Milton, John, 43, 82
Minimalism, 174
Miramonte High School Parents Club
    Newsletter, 43
Mish, Frederick, C., 50
Missbehave (magazine), 91–92, 98, 109,
    149, 170, 209
mitsi, 38
mitsubishi, 38
mixed signally, 169
mizzi, 39
mizzy, 64
mo' better, 64
Mo' Better Blues (Lee), 64
Mockenhaupt, Brian, 107
Modern Language Association, 173, 209
Moeller, Samantha, 91–93, 109
mongo, 1, 4–6, 9, 50, 206
Mongo: Adventures in Trash (Botha), 4, 50
Montgomery, Michael, xiv
moony, 80
Morning Edition (National Public Radio), 4
morning glory, 12, 32, 84, 113–114, 117–118
Morrice, 35
mosey, 68

much, 169–173, 208
Mugglestone, Lynda, 167, 208
mungo, 1, 4–5
Mungojerrie (Old Possum's Book of Practical
    Cats), 1, 4–5
"Mungojerrie and Rumpelteazer" (Old
    Possum's Book of Practical Cats), 50
Munro, Pamela, 4, 27, 50, 106
murder, 125
murdiddlyurder, 125
Muriel Spark Trio (Spark), 158
my, 123
my bad, 187–188
My Best Friend's Wedding/Friends much, 169
My Fair Lady (Lerner and Lowe), 130, 160
my heart is fixed, O God, my heart is fixed, 139
my main man, 70
my man, 71

Nagle, Traci, xiv
nanobe, 3
Narratologies (Herman), 212
National Lampoon's Van Wilder (Becker,
    Goldberg, and Wagner), 146, 162
Natural History of Barbados (Hughes), 66
Natural History of Infixation (Yu), 122, 159,
    177, 209
Nature (Emerson), 151
Nature (journal), 109
"Nature of the Language Faculty"
    (Jackendoff and Pinker), 211
negative capability, 155–158
Negroes, 58
-ness, 120, 167
"Never Kill a Boy on the First Date"
    (Buffy the Vampire Slayer), 110
never never come back land, 141
Neville, 104
Neville Nobody, 104
Newark, New Jersey, 142
New Canting Dictionary, 35, 52
New Dictionary of American Slang
    (Chapman), 63, 106
New Dictionary of the Terms Ancient and
    Modern of the Canting Crew (B. E. Gent.),
    34–36, 52
New England Journal of Medicine, 4
New Oxford American Dictionary (NOAD)
    (Jewell, Abate, McKean and others),
    8–9, 13, 21–22, 50, 111, 158

New Partridge Dictionary of Slang and Unconventional English (Dalzell and Victor), ix, 3, 32, 38, 40, 44, 47, 49, 92, 114, 149–150, 158
New Yorker, 39
New Yorker (magazine), 5–6, 50, 55, 77
New York Observer, 92, 109
New York Times, 76, 133
New York Times Magazine, 159
NIBM, 147–148
nice diddly fucking day, 125
niggard, 67
niggardly, 67
Nigger: The Strange History of a Troublesome Word (Kennedy), 67, 107
"Nightmares" (*Buffy the Vampire Slayer*), 110
nineteen, 39
nip slip, 84
Nissel, Angela, 107
nitty-gritty, 63
Nixon, Marnie, 160
No freakin' way! 128
No fucking way! xii, 128, 131
nollie, 23–24
nonpletives, 141–143
noon, 115
"Noooooooaaaarrgh" (Storr), 159
"No Place Like Home" (*Buffy the Vampire Slayer*), 209
North Carolina Language and Life Project, xiv
North Carolina State University, xiv
nose, 22
no shit, 82–84, 134
nosper, 37–38
-not-, 138
Notion, 27–28
Not too soon, you big baboon, 114, 117
No way! 128, 186
Noxon, Marti, 161
NTC's Dictionary of American Slang (Spears), 47
Number 9, x, 39
Nunberg, Geoffrey, 11, 51, 67, 107
nuts, 89

Oakland, California, 142
Oakland, California, Board of Education, 76

O'Donnell, Rosie, 142
O-face, 150
Office (television show), 58, 60, 106
Office Space (Judge), 134, 150, 160
officey, 168–169
Official Dictionary of Unofficial English (Barrett), 4–5, 50
Official Preppie Handbook (Birnbach), 55, 106
off message much, 171
"Of Modern Poetry" (Stevens), 144, 161
ofrigginkay, 131
Oh as usual dear, 141–142
Oh frickin' dear, 141
-ok- (Prokem), 177
okay, 86–87
okelly dokelly, 138
"Old Gumbie Cat" (*Old Possum's Book of Practical Cats*), 50
Old Possum's Book of Practical Cats (Eliot), 1, 49
Old Wok, 28
Old Wykehamist, 28
Oliver Twist (Dickens), 35, 52
ollie, 23–24
om, 39, 44, 46
on, 184
on a wait, 18–19
Onion, Rebecca, 142, 161
"On Language: Izzle" (Miller), 159
"On Not Teaching English Usage" (Sledd), 52, 73, 158
onomatopoeia, 124–125
on the d.l., 186
on the down low, 186
on the fly, vii, 19
on the slang, 7
oolerfer, 38
Opie, Iona and Peter, 115, 158–159
Organization Man (Whyte), 26, 51
Origin and Diversification of Language (Jablonski and Aiello), 210
"Out of Sight, Out of Mind" (*Buffy the Vampire Slayer*), 110
Out of the Mouths of Slaves (Baugh), 75, 108
over-, 120
overidentify much, 171
overprotective much, 170
Oxford Companion to the English Language (McArthur), 51

Oxford Dictionary of Nursery Rhymes (Opie), 159
Oxford Dictionary of Rhyming Slang (Ayto), 52
Oxford Dictionary of Slang (Ayto), 4, 34, 47, 52
Oxford English Dictionary (OED), 9, 35, 45, 48, 53, 66, 71, 106–107, 115, 158, 167, 208

pachuchos (Mexican Spanish), 73
paddle the pickle, 118
Page, Ellen, 209
paired off, 97
-palooza, 3
pantomamime, 122–123
Paradise Lost (Milton), 43
para-fucking-chute, 128
Parco, Wong Tat Man, 85, 108
parler á l'envers (French), 177
parma violet, 39
partially erect, 148
Partick Thistle, 39, 42
Partridge, Eric, viii–ix, 47, 49, 52, 158
part timer, 39, 42
pass, 82–83
"Passions" (*Buffy the Vampire Slayer*), 109
Passions of the Soul (Descartes), 192, 210
pathetic much, 169, 171, 187, 195
Pattie, Michelle, xiv
peace, 56
peach, 113
Peacham, Henry, 139
peachy fucking keen, 137
peachy fuddy keen, 137
peachy fungi keen, 137
peachy funky keen, 137
peachy funny keen, 137
peachy fussy keen, 137
peachy fuzzy keen, 137–138
peachy keen, 137
pee, 91
pegging, 79
Penn, Sean, 107, 143, 161
pepper, 113
Peppermint Pat-Eye, 130–131, 160
perception, 55–63, 77–78, 85, 87, 94, 111
Perez, Emilia, 170
perf, 20, 24
perma-laid, 82
Perry, Eleanor, 159
Perry, Frank, 118, 159
Perry, Theresa, 76, 108

personal check, 30
Personal Influence (Katz and Larzarsfeld), 110
Peters, Mark, xiv, 121, 125, 159, 179–180, 210
Pete Tong, 39, 42
Petrie, Doug, 209
phase 4, 39
phat, 6
Phillips, Todd, 161
Phoenix, River, 179
-phor-, 143
phrasal verbs, 95–103
pibe (Spanish), 176
Pickett, Joseph P. 50, 158
pick up, 97
"Pickups and Patchouli" (Larsen), 51
picky, 124
picot loop, 31
pie hole, 148, 157
pig, 34
pill, 39
pimped out, 64
pineal gland, 192, 199, 210
Pinker, Steven, 174–175, 196–197, 199, 201, 209–210
Pink Panther, 39, 41–42
pins, 35
Pinsky, Robert, 161
piss, 44
pissed, 97
pissed off, 97
pit bull, 39
Pitts, Greg, 162
pizzicati, 31
plague out, 79, 97
"Plain Morphology and Expressive Morphology" (Zwicky and Pullum), 160, 178, 209
plastered, 89
Plato, xiii, 194
playa, 62
Playboy, 39
Please don't pout, my sauerkraut, 116
plenty, 92
plummy and slam, 35
plunder, 5
Poet (Emerson), 45
poetics, 203–208
poetry, xii–xiii, 43–46, 111–113, 117–120, 123–127, 130, 139, 142, 144–145, 148–149, 155–157, 165, 183, 190, 192, 196, 204–206

Pokaski, Joe, 209
police, 118
polish the pearl, 118
pollutant, 39
polluted, xi, 14
pongo, 1–2
pop her cherry, 113
pops, 79
pork chop, 113
Posey, Stephen, 109
posse, 25
postage, 79
pot, 38
pound your pork, 118
poverty of stimulus, 174
powder, 21
power pill, 39
pragmatics, 121, 126, 128–131, 133–136, 139, 178, 180, 193, 195
Prague School, 204–205, 212
pre-, 120
preman, 177
Preminger, Alex, 161
Pressions et Impressions sur les Sacres, au Québec (Vincent), 108
Pressman, Ellen S., 108
pretentious much, 170
pretty, 79
Prichard, Peter, 160
Princeton Encyclopedia of Poetry and Poetics (Preminger and others), 139, 161
Principles of Linguistic Change (Labov), 108, 110
printit, 104
Proceedings of the Royal Society of London, 211
Proceedings of the Thirteenth Annual Meeting of the Berkeley Linguistics Society (Aske and others), 160, 209
productivity, 167–169
Prokem, 177–179, 209
prokem, 177
props, 186
prosody, 121–125, 139
Prucher, Jeff, 127, 159
prune, 115
"Prune Song," 115
psycho, 89
pull, 92, 150
pulling root, 147

pull it out of your ass like anal beads, 147
Pullum, Geoffrey, 136, 160, 178, 209
pull your pud, 118
punish Percy in the palm, 118–119
punish the pope, 118
punning, 136
"Puppet Show" (*Buffy the Vampire Slayer*), 81, 108

Q (magazine), 159
Québec profanity, 85
Queen Bees and Wannabes (Wiseman), 93, 95, 98, 109
quidds, 34
q.t., 186

Racine, Jean, 122
rad, 25
ragamuffin, 123, 159
rain, 167
rainy, 167
Raising Their Voices (Brown), 109
ralph, 15
RAM, 26
rappin, 75
Raunch, xii, 145–151, 153, 155, 157
razzle dazzle, 123, 126, 206
razzmatazz, 123, 126, 206
razz-tazz, 123
re-, 120
Read, Allen Walker, 67, 106
Reagan, Gillian, 92, 109
Real Ebonics Debate (Perry and Delpit), 108
realism, 194
"Realism" (Dummett), 211
Realism and Anti-Realism (French, Uehling, and Wettstein), 211
Reardon, Jim, 160
Reaser, Jeff, xiv
Rebel without a Cause, 178
recursion, 198–199
red hot, 39
reduplication, 123, 138, 206
"Red Wheelbarrow" (Williams), 117
reefer, 63
Reeve's Tale (Chaucer), 71, 107
Regina (*Mean Girls*), 95, 109, 138, 153, 160
Reitman, Ivan, 208
relax, 10
"Reptile Boy" (*Buffy the Vampire Slayer*), 109

resetamabob, 123
respect the narrative flow much, 171
restaurant jargon, 16–19
restrictive labels, 2–4
retarded, 25
Rhimes, Shonda, 208
rhubarb, 44
rhubarb and custard, 39, 44
rhyme, xii, 46, 111, 114–119, 195
rhyming slang, 36–38, 44
Riach, Alan, 161
rib, 39
Rickford, John Russell, 67–68, 107, 152, 162
Rickford, Russell John, 67–68, 107, 152, 162
rider, 21–22, 25
ridiculous, 82–83, 186
right, 87
righto, 2
rigoddamndiculous, 120, 128
ripped, 14–15
rip off, 63
ritual spirit, 39
Riverside Chaucer (Benson), 107
road cunny, 147, 149–150
road head, 147, 149–150
Road Trip (Phillips and Armstrong), 145, 161
Rob, 123
Robert, 123
Roberts, Chris, 103, 110
Roberts, Neil, 163
Robinson, Craig, 58
roca, 39
rock-a-bye, 127
"Rock-a-bye, baby," 123
roll, 39
roller, 39
rolling, 39, 41, 154
Rollins, Hyder Edward, 162
ROM, 26
Roman Jakobson Centennial
    Symposium, 212
Roman Jakobson: Echoes of His Scholarship
    (Armstrong and van Schoonvald), 212
Roman Jakobson Selected Writings (Rudy), 212
Rooney, Kathy, 50
Rosenberg, Willow (*Buffy the Vampire
    Slayer*), 96, 98, 100–102, 110, 141
Rota-Kiwan, 115
Rotary, 115
ROTFLMAO, 172, 187

"Roxanne, Roxanne" (UTFO), 126
RSVP, 172
Rubin, Theodore Isaac, 159
rub your radish, 118
Rudy, Stephen, 212
rulesy, 168
Rumpleteazer (*Old Possum's Book of
    Practical Cats*), 4
runner, 19
running, 39
Ruse, Michael, 201, 211
Ryder, Winona, 133

S, 132
-s, 120
sack, 82
Sacks, Oliver, 211
Salvator (Latin), 132
Sancho, 79
Sapir, Edward, 206
Sarandon, Susan, 142
Sass, Eric, 91, 109
Saturday Night Fever, 179
Saturday Night Live (television show), 169
saucer, 39, 43
Saussure, Ferdinand de, 204
saviory, 168–169
Sawyer, Diane, 142
saxamaphone, 122–123
"Scales" (Eisner), 211
schlep, 68
schmuck, 130–131, 133, 143
-schmucking-, 130–132
schmucking, 130
Science (journal), 197, 211
Scientific American, 4
scob, xi, 28–29
Scooby Gang (*Buffy the Vampire Slayer*),
    96–103, 166
Scooby snacks, 39
score, 6
Scott Catalogue, 20, 41
Scott, Lesley, xiv
scram, 89
screw, 82–83
Scrubs (television show), 73, 107
Seabrook, John, 6, 50
Sebeok, Thomas A., 107, 212
section, 18
Seeds of Speech (Aitchison), 210

See you later, alligator, 114–115, 117, 119
seize, 154
Selected Poems (Williams), *159*
Semel, David, *110*
semitumescent, 148
senders, 26
Seneca College (Toronto), 104
serious as a heart attack, 74
"Server's Lexicon" (Adams), *51*
setup, 18
Seven Dwarves, 180
sewage, 166
sextasy, 39
"Shadow" (*Buffy the Vampire Slayer*), 128, 160
shag, 10
Shakespeare's Bawdy (Partridge), 47
Shakespeare, William, 122, 163–164, 208
shamey, 168
shamrock, 39, 42
Shearer, Harry, *160*
Sheidlower, Jesse, xiv, 130, *160*
sherm, 42
Sherzer, Joel, 176–177, 206–207, 209, 212
shibitchinit, 181
shift, 17
shipper, 3
shishittinit, 181
shit, 111, 126, 180, 187
shit-faced, 14–15
shiznit, 94, 126, 180, 187
"Shiznit" (Snoop Dogg), 126
shizzy, 82
show, xii, 97–98, 100
Showalter, Elaine, *159*
show up, xii, 97, 101
shut the fuck up, 134, 166
sick, 186
"Sidewalks of New York" (song), 82
sidework, 18
Simes, Gary, 47
Simpson, Abe (*Simpsons*), 93, *109*
Simpson, Homer (*Simpsons*), 122, 177
Simpson, J. A., *106*
Simpsons (television show), 121, 125, 138, 159–160, 177, 179
"Simpsons: Embiggening Our Language with Cromulent Words" (Peters), 121, *159*
Singer, Bryan, 81
Singleton, Arthur James, 64
"Sisters of No Mercy" (Onion), *161*

sitcomy, 168
Six Feet Under (television show), 167, 208
sixty-nine, 10
Sixty-Ninth Street Bridge, 10
skinnin' and grinnin', 154
Skov, Martin, *212*
Skywalker, Luke, *179*
slackery, 168
slam, bam, thank you ma'am, 114
slammin', 39, 154
slang, viii–ix, 7–8, 32, 48–49, 50, 136, 191
"Slang" (Eble), *51*
"Slang" (Lighter), ix, 46, 52–53, 112, 158, 162, 211
Slang and Its Analogues (Farmer and Henley), 47
Slang and Sociability (Eble), ix, 4, 11, 46, 50, 63, 106, 108, 112, 158
"Slang as Poetry" (Eble), 46, 52
Slang Dictionary (Cotton), 36, 52
slanget, 7
Slang Flashcards (Knock Knock), 55, 59, 93, 106
"Slang Gang" (*Mad TV*), 57–58, 106
"Slang in America" (Whitman), 45, 119, 183
Slang of Sin (Dalzell), ix, 10, 32, 51–52, 159
SlangSite.com, 69, 104, 107, 110, 126, 129, 143–144, 159
"Slang: The Poetry of Group Dynamics" (Gaston), 46
Slang To-Day and Yesterday (Partridge), viii, 52, 158
Slang U. (Munro and others), 4, 27, 50, 106
slangy, 120
slap five on her, 147
Slap my femur, little lemur, 117
slayage, 166
Slayage Conference on the Whedonverses, 110
Slayer Slang (Adams), vii, 95, 108–110, 140, 161, 166–167, 208
"Slay the Critics" (Dark Horse Comics) 140, *161*
Sledd, James, 33–34, 45, 48, 52, 59, 70, 73–74, 78, 81, 114, 158
slengja (Norse), 7
slip, 22
slip out, 97
slit, 39
sloshed, 89
Sly Records, 146–150, 162

smashed, 14–15, 68
smelt, 34
smile like a donut, xii, 147, 150
smiley, 39
Smiley, Tavis, 70
Smith, Charles Martin, 109
Smith, Roger, 132, 160
Smitherman, Geneva, 72, 74, 76–77, 93, 107, 151–152, 154, 162, 178, 210
snack, 34
sneak up, 97
snockered, 14–15
Snoop Dogg, 126
snow, 167
snowball, 39
Snowboarder (magazine), 51
SnowboarderGirl (magazine), 25, 51
snowboarding jargon, 21–25
Snowboarding Know-How (Weiss), 51
Snowboarding Life (magazine), 51
Snowboarding to the Extreme (Gutman), 51
snowheart, 39
snowy, 167
so, 86
"Social and Language Boundaries among Adolescents" (Labov, T.), 107
social negotiation, vii, 93–104, 189–192
social networks, 95–103, 105, 189–192
Sociolinguistic Patterns (Labov), 110
Sociolinguistic Study of Youth Slanguage of Hong Kong Adolescents (Parco), 108
so friggin what, 131
solo style, 25
Soloman, David, 209
some, uh, some, 58
sort of, 86
Soukhanov, Anne H., 50
sound on, 64
Sound Shape of Language (Jakobson and Waugh), 205, 212
Southall, John, 66
"So Weird; So Cool" (Tagliamonte and Roberts), 110
spaced out, 82
space pill, 39
spandrels, xiii, 201–204, 208
"Spandrels of San Marco" (Gould and Lewontin), 201–202, 211
Spark, Muriel, 116, 158

sparkage, 79
Spears, Arthur, 108
Spears, Richard A., 47
speech acts, 121, 187–188
speech communities, 105
Speech Play and Verbal Art (Sherzer), 176–177, 206, 209, 212
Spender, Dale, 78
Spicoli, Jeff (*Fast Times at Ridgemont High*), 73, 107
Spike (*Buffy the Vampire Slayer*), 135–136, 160–161
spin, 22
spliced a hollis, 28
spliff, 84
split, 89, 98
splits, 26
Spoken Soul (Rickford and Rickford), 67, 107, 152, 162
spoon cancellation, 20, 26
Sporting Magazine, 48
sprezzatura, 156–157
sprung like a slinky, 147–148
squeeze, 89
Stacy, 39
stalefish, 24
stall out, 23
stamp collecting jargon, 20–21
Standard Theory, 174
Staples, Brent, 76
Star Trek: The Next Generation, 60
station, 18
stay iny, 167, 187
steady, 75, 108
Stein, Darren, 136, 160
Stenström, Anna-Brita, 85–86, 108
Stevens, Charles, 28–29, 51
Stevens, Wallace, 144–145, 161
stiffie, 24
stiff upper lip, 167
stiff upper lippy, 167
stir your stew, 118
Stjernfelt, Frederik, 212
stone cold fox, 111
stoned, xii, 14–15
stoner, 15
Storr, Will, 159
Stray, Christopher, 28, 51
Strength (magazine), 51
stridin', 154

strung, 102
strung up on, 102
Stuart: A Life Backwards (Masters), 142, 161
stubby, 3–4
stuff, 86
stump, 35
stunt words, 143–144, 157
style, xi–xii, 81–104, 144–158
Style in Language (Sebeok), 212
suck, 11, 42, 51
suck eggs, 11
suck off, 111
suck rope, 11
suck wind, 11
suf-, 120
suffixing, 166–169, 173
sugary, 166
Sullivan, Arthur, 37
Summers, Buffy (*Buffy the Vampire Slayer*), 95–103, 110, 135, 141, 166, 169, 171, 209
Summers, Dawn (*Buffy the Vampire Slayer*), 171, 209
Summers, Joyce (*Buffy the Vampire Slayer*), 98, 110
Superficial (celebrity-focused blog), 170, 209
superman, 39
Super Mario, 39
super-protecty, 168
surface, 164
Surfing (magazine), 51
Sutherland, Kristine, 110
Sweeney, 37
Sweeney Todd, x, 36–7, 118
swig, 91
Swyden, Thomas A., 109–110
Synonymic Fallacy, 93–94
synonymy, 15–16, 114, 165, 173, 186, 195
syntax, 165–166, 169–173, 193, 198

tablet of MDMA, 41
Tagalog, 178
Tagliamonte, Sali, 103, 110
tail grab, x, 23, 25
tail shovel, 22
tail wheelie, 23
taint/t'aint, 147–150
taintalingus, 147–148, 150
taintmeat, 150

Talkin and Testifyin (Smitherman), 74, 107, 152, 162, 210
Talkin That Talk (Smitherman), 77, 107
Tamasi, Susan, vii
tangerine dream, 39
tan much, 170
-tap-dancing-, 133
Tavis Smiley Show (National Public Radio), 70, 107
tease, 154
techKNOWLEDGEy, 142
Ted (*Buffy the Vampire Slayer*), 103
"Ted" (*Buffy the Vampire Slayer*), 109
tent, xi, 150
tent check, 30
tenter, 30
tent shift, 30
Terence, 212
text, 164
på slänget (Swedish), 7
Thatcher, 39
"That Sucks" (Chadwick and Bates), 51
The Man, 70
"They Aren't Sluts" (Reagan), 109
"Theory Theory as an Alternative to the Innateness Hypothesis" (Gopnik), 209
Thierry, Guillaume, 163
thingamajig, 123
thingy, 86
Third Pot, 28
"This Week's Hip New Slang Word or Phrase" (Sly Records), 146–150
"Those Who Speak Prokem" (Chambert-Loir), 209
Thrasher (magazine), 51
thunderdome, 39
tick frickin' tock, 129
tickle the pickle, 119
Tigrinya, 178
tindy, 25
tip, 22
tip out, 17
tips, 17
tittoo, 148
tizzy, 186
tmesis, 129, 132–133, 139, 142, 148
to, 165
toasted, 113
Tod, Andrew, 108
Toldervy, William, 48

-toma-, 122
tomato, 113
too cool for school, 114
top o' reeb, 37
top shelf, 17
Toronto Star, 4
totally, xii
Tower of Power, 156
Trachtenberg, Michelle, 209
track down, 97
traf, xii, 148–150
tramp stamp, 148–149
Transworld Snowboarding (magazine), 25, 51, 160
trash, 5
trashed, 14–15
trash talking, 25
Travolta, John, 179
Treatise of Buggs (Southall), 66
Treatise on Man (Descartes), 210
Trends in Teenage Talk (Stenström and others), 108
trick, 21–23
triple crown, 11
triple play, 11
triple-sat, 18–19
trippin' the light fantastic, 82
Troilus and Cressida (Shakespeare), 139
trouble and strife, 37
truck, 63
trumpets, 39
Truth and Other Enigmas (Dummett), 211
tshinji (Bantu), 66
tuna much, 169, 187
Tupperware party, 56
turd, 148
Turkey-Lurkey, 206
Turr, Elyse, xiv
tutu, 39
Twain, Mark, 132, 160
tweak, 25
tweaking, 21

uber-, 120
ubershit, 126
ultimate exphoria, 39
unbelievable, 187
uncool, 187
under-, 120
underdeveloped much, 169

underling, 120, 178
unfuckingbelievable, 128, 142, 187
United Parcel Service (UPS), 25–27
Universal Grammar, 174, 207
universe, 140
University of Liverpool, 163
University of Michigan, 142–143
University of Wales, Bangor, 163
unload, 150
unload the groceries, 148–149
unstable the stallion, 118
uppity, 63
upsell, 17–18
UPS (United Parcel Service) jargon, 25–27
UPS Stylebook, 25, 51
up yours! 186
Urban Dictionary, 95
USA Network, 137
USA Today, 133–134, 136, 160
US-fuckin-A Today, 133–134, 137, 157, 164
USP, 39
U.S. Senate, 77
Usual Suspects (Singer), 81
UTFO, 126

V & E, 39
Vadnais, Janelle, xiv
vagueness, 185
van Schoonveld, C. H., 211
Vargas, Rosalyn, 106
Vaughn, Charlotte, xiv
Verbatim: The Language Quarterly, 159
very, 121
vicarage, 166
Victor, Terry, 40, 47, 49, 114
Vincent, Diane, 85, 108
Virginia Quarterly Review, 200–201, 211
virusy, 168
vitamin E, 39
vittle, 92
vrijman (Indonesian Dutch), 177
vu ja de, 186
VW, 39, 42

wafer, 39, 41–42
Wagner, David, 162
walk much? 169–170
Wall Street Journal, 133
Walters, Barbara, 142
wanker, 86

wanksta, 55
wanna, 82
Warnke, Frank J., *161*
Washington, George, 66
wasted, xii, 14
Watcha doin' pruin, stewin'? 115
Waters, Daniel, *160*
Waters, Mark, *109, 160*
Waugh, Linda R., *205, 212*
wave the wand, 118
way, 186
Way We Talk Now (Nunberg), *51, 107*
WBUR (National Public Radio, Boston), *51*
"'We didn't realize that lite beer was supposed to suck': The Putative Vulgarity of 'X Sucks'" (Butters), *51*
weed, 15, 38, 44, 113
weeded, x, 19
Weiner, E. S. C., *106*
Weinrich, Harald, 185–186, *210*
Weiss, Christof, *51*
Welby, Earle, 45, *52*
"Welcome to the Hellmouth" (*Buffy the Vampire Slayer*), 110
well lined, 35
well liquor, 17
Wentworth, Harold, 47
Wernicke's area, 192–193
West—by God—Virginia, 139
West, Cornel, 70, *107*
Wettstein, Howard K., *211*
whacked, 14
whacked out, 14
whadiddlyat, 180
whafuckinat, 180
whafuckingat, 180
whale road, 148
what, 180
whatever, 154, 200
whatever floats your boat, 114
whatever turns you on, 114
"What Is Hip?" (Tower of Power), 156
what it is, 154
What's shakin'? 114
What's shakin', bacon? 114
What's your story, morning glory? 114–115, 117–118
What the fuck? 187
Whedon, Joss, 109–110, *160*
wheelie, 24

wheeze, 154
"When Nouns Surface as Verbs" (Clark and Clark), 164, *208*
"When She Was Bad" (*Buffy the Vampire Slayer*), 109
where in the effin hell, 131
Whistler (*Buffy the Vampire Slayer*), 103
white bloody knights, 134
white robin, x, 39, 42
white trash, 63
Whitman, Walt, xii, 45–46, 49, 52, 119, 128, 151, *159*, 183, 196, 205, 207, *210*
Who's There, Inc., 55
Why Darwin Is Still Right, 200
Why so glum, sugar plum? 115
Whyte, William H., 26, *51*
Why We Talk (Dessalles), 190–191, *210*
wicked, xii
wig, 95, 97
wiggage, 166
wigged, 103
wigit, 39
wig out, 95, 97
wild flower, 39
Williams, William Carlos, 117–118, *158*
Wilson, Debra, 57
Wilson, Margaret D., *210*
Winchester jargon (or slang), 27–30
Winchester Notions (Stevens), 28, *51*
wind, 167
wind-lilylocks-laced, 129
windy, 167
wipe, 35
Wiseman, Rosalind, 93, 98, *109*
with, x
Wolfram, Walt, xiv, 75, *108*
Woody Woodpecker, 39, 42
Wordell, Charles B., *51*
word hoard, 148
Word of Valios, 141
Word Origins (Liberman), *159*
work, 120
Works Progress Administration, 4
World in So Many Words (Metcalf), *50*
"Wouldn't It Be Lovely?" (*My Fair Lady*), *160*
wrap up, 97
wrecked, xi, 14–15
wrongo, 2

WTF, 187
Wykhamist, 28

x, 39, 41, 186
X-Files E, 39
x-ing, 39
XTC, 39

-y, 65, 120, 166–169, 172–173,
    187, 208
-y-, 180
Yaitanes, Greg, 209
yank the plank, 119
yeah, 82–84, 87, 200
yee diddly fucking ha, 125
yee-diddly-fuckin'-haw, 128, 206
yee diddly haw, xii
yee fucking diddly haw, 155
yeefuckin'haw, 125, 128

yo, 91, 111, 186
Yo, dawg, check it, 70
yoke, 39–40
you go, girl! 60
you know, 86
youth, xi, 85–93
Yo, wassup? 114
Yu, Alan C. L., 122, 159, 177–179, 209

-z-, 126
zebraey, 168
Zeki, Semir, 185, 210
Zimmer, Ben, xiv
zit, 186
zoot-suiters, 73
zooty, xii, 62, 64
Zutty, 64
Zwicky, Arnold, 136, 160, 178, 209
Zwinky, 65